S...

Spokeso...
Nightshade, Pratt's Fall

Spokesong: 'The best stage debut I have seen for years . . . *Spokesong* is not only a quirky, freewheeling music-hall extravaganza about a piece of history but also a cunning symbolic creation. It takes an oblique and deeply human look at the way we live now and glances back, with affection but entirely without sentimentality, at the things we have lost. The writing is both tough and poetic.' *Sunday Times*

'A most funny and piercingly intelligent play . . . Stewart Parker has made an out of history in a tradition that goes back through Tolstoy and Stendhal.' *New York Times*

Catchpenny Twist: 'The most appealing thing about Parker's work is the ease with which he blends lunatic humour with a gritty sense of reality. He's done it before in *Spokesong* and he does it again in this hard, ribald and hilarious little play. His characters are quickwitted innocents who are taking a surrealistic stroll across a minefield, cracking jokes in the dark; but they are also real people with a real past in an all-too-real city.' *Sunday Times*

...shade: 'Probably Stewart Parker's best play. Certainly his most complex. It a comedy in which the jokes, both verbal and visual, bubble merrily from a potion whose essence is the deepest gloom: champagne fermented from hemlock . . . it also offers answers to questions much more profound about the relationship between living and dying . . . And it is complex, too, its structure – a surrealistic amalgam of parable and reality, of the prosaic and the scarcely imaginable, of the comic and of the profoundly sad . . . it is as original and as diverting a serious play as has been seen in Dublin for years.' *Irish Times*

...att's Fall: 'A delicate, unusual and rather beautiful vehicle . . . a fascinating and delightful entertainment . . . Parker's chosen approach is to tackle serious themes – often related to the experience of his native Northern Ireland – through a kind of lyrical comedy, deceptively lightweight, fast-moving, and slightly surreal.' *Sunday Standard*

The volume is introduced by Lynne Parker, artistic director of Rough Magic Theatre Company.

Stewart Parker was born in Belfast in 1941. During the early sixties at Queen's University he was active in a group of young writers which included Seamus Heaney and Bernard Mac Laverty. His first stage play *Spokesong* (1975) won him the 1976 *Evening Standard* Most Promising Playwright Award and his TV drama *I'm a Dreamer, Montreal* (1979) won the Ewart-Biggs Memorial Prize. His stage plays include *Catchpenny Twist* (1977), *Nightshade* (1980), *Pratt's Fall* (1983), *Northern Star* (1984), *Heavenly Bodies* (1986) and *Pentecost* (1987), which won the Harvey's Irish Theatre Award. He died in London in 1988.

by the same author

STEWART PARKER PLAYS: 2
(Northern Star, Heavenly Bodies, Pentecost)

STEWART PARKER

Plays: 1

Spokesong
Catchpenny Twist
Nightshade
Pratt's Fall

introduced by Lynne Parker

Methuen Drama

METHUEN CONTEMPORARY DRAMATISTS

1 3 5 7 9 10 8 6 4 2

This collection first published in the United Kingdom in 2000 by
Methuen Publishing Limited
215 Vauxhall Bridge Road, London SW1V 1EJ

Peribo Pty Ltd, 58 Beaumont Road, Mount Kuring-Gai,
NSW 2080, Australia, ACN 002 273 761
(for Australia and New Zealand)

Spokesong first published in 1980 in the United States by Samuel French Inc.
First published in the United Kingdom in this edition
Copyright © 1980 by The Estate of Stewart Parker
Lyrics copyright © 1975 by Irish Evergreen Ltd
Catchpenny Twist first published in 1980 in the Republic of Ireland by
The Gallery Press
First published in the United Kingdom in this edition
Copyright © 1980 by The Estate of Stewart Parker
Nightshade first published in 1980 in the Republic of Ireland by
Co-op Books (Publishing) Ltd
First published in the United Kingdom in this edition
Copyright © 1980 by The Estate of Stewart Parker
Pratt's Fall first published in the United Kingdom in this edition
Copyright © 2000 by The Estate of Stewart Parker

Collection copyright © 2000 by The Estate of Stewart Parker
Introduction copyright © 2000 by Lynne Parker

The right of the author to be identified as the author of these works
has been asserted by him in accordance with the
Copyright, Designs and Patents Act, 1988

Methuen Publishing Limited Reg. No. 3543167

A CIP catalogue record for this book
is available from the British Library

ISBN 0 413 74340 3

Typeset by Deltatype Ltd, Birkenhead, Merseyside
Printed and bound in Great Britain by
Cox & Wyman Ltd, Reading, Berks

Caution

Contents

Stewart Parker
Chronology

1975   *The Iceberg*, BBC Radio Ulster
        Spokesong, John Player Theatre, Dublin Theatre
        Festival

1976   *Spokesong*, King's Head Theatre, Islington, London
        The Actress and the Bishop (one act), King's Head
        Theatre, Islington

1977   *Spokesong*, Vaudeville Theatre, London; wins
        Evening Standard Most Promising Playwright Award
        I'm a Dreamer, Montreal, BBC Radio 4
        Catchpenny Twist, Peacock (Abbey) Theatre,
        Dublin, and BBC Play for Today

1978   *Spokesong*, Long Wharf Theatre, New Haven,
        Connecticut
        Kingdom Come (musical), King's Head Theatre,
        Islington

1979   *Spokesong*, Circle in the Square Theatre, New
        York
        I'm a Dreamer, Montreal, Thames Television; wins
        Ewart-Biggs Prize
        Kamikaze Ground Staff Reunion Dinner, BBC Radio 3

1980   *Nightshade*, Peacock (Abbey) Theatre, Dublin
        Kamikaze Ground Staff Reunion Dinner wins Giles
        Cooper Award

1981   *Kamikaze Ground Staff Reunion Dinner*, BBC TV
        Iris in the Traffic, Ruby in the Rain, BBC TV

1982   *Joyce in June*, BBC TV

1983   *Pratt's Fall*, Tron Theatre, Glasgow

1984   *Northern Star*, Lyric Players Theatre, Belfast
        Blue Money, London Weekend Television film (US
        video)

1985   *The Traveller*, BBC Radio 3
        Radio Pictures, BBC TV

1986   *Heavenly Bodies*, Birmingham Repertory Theatre

Introduction

> You burst upon the world, expecting to astound it
> with your astounding self, and you don't so much as
> ruffle the water that your name's written on.

This is Delia, speaking in *Nightshade*. The line has a
strong resonance for someone who works in theatre.
Plays can have an ephemeral existence: one hot blaze in
a glaring spotlight, then back on to the shelves waiting
for the next production, which is why it is crucial to get
them printed and into the public domain. It is
particularly good that Stewart's stage plays, which had
an unusually nomadic history, are now published as a
major body of work. I am acquainted with Stewart's
writing partly through being his niece, more importantly
through having directed his plays. In order to write this
introduction I read, for the first time, all of the early
plays as a continuous line. What comes through is an
extraordinarily cogent philosophy expressed through a
vast, humane intelligence. Stewart wrote variously in
prose, poetry and journalism, forms where he had a
certain degree of control over the impact of his thinking.
He chose ultimately to articulate his ideas through
drama, where control is handed over at the cloakroom
on entrance. Was he out of his mind?

Spokesong is the beginning of the story. It was an
extraordinary debut, which would never have happened
if Michael Heffernan and some good friends had
decided to take no for an answer. They believed in the
play, got some money together to put it on and ended
up with the hit of the Dublin Festival of 1975. The rest
is history. *Spokesong* became an international success and
continues to be produced today.

It also contains the nucleus of what followed. You can
see the fascination with Christian imagery, the
multiplying dualities, the battle of the mind and spirit
with the banana skins of the brute world. Also, crucially,

the struggle to deal with the inner self, the idea that order can be imposed on chaos through personal discipline, humour and an acknowledgement of what he called 'ancestral wraiths'. Wrestling with the past is a constant thread. The plays in this volume can be read with pleasure as complete entities but the bigger picture really comes through in the body of work as a whole. *Spokesong* began a cycle that was completed with *Pentecost*.

Stewart Parker had a poetic sensibility, an academic training and a historian's mind. He also came from a family of engineers and craftsmen and his instincts were those both of an artist and an artisan, so that complicated ideas are harnessed to practical skills. As directors and actors, we gnash our teeth frequently at the technical demands of his work but he knew all along that those very complexities are what turn us on. You can't be a shrinking violet for this stuff. And it works. One might think the notion of seven or so bicycles hurtling around a ten by twelve foot stage pretty ludicrous. It happened, though, when *Spokesong* was done at the King's Head. To some extent the work benefits from this kind of claustrophobic energy, where the scalding soup of ideas threatens to lift the lid off the pot. Joyce was Stewart's passion, but another hero was Ibsen. He once spoke admiringly of 'the oily mechanics beneath the pristine fuselage' in Ibsen's plays; this could easily be applied to his own work.

Ideas are the co-ordinates of the plays but the stories consist of action and journey, whether it takes the form of a struggle towards self-knowledge, as with Frank Stock in *Spokesong* and Quinn in *Nightshade*, or flight from danger and a quest for optimism as in *Catchpenny Twist*. Navigation triggers the story of *Pratt's Fall*; the play is really about faith. Its style reminds me of the Hollywood screwball comedies, tough and cynical, although occasionally poetic vision breaks the surface.

Mahoney Think of it fourteen hundred years ago. Those monks were living on the final precipice. The

west coast of Ireland, the absolute edge of the known
world. Every day lifting their eyes across a great grey,
heaving desert of a sea, stretching to the very rim of
the earth itself. An unknown cosmic turbulence.
Imagine what it meant to cast yourself into that. No
map, no compass, in a shell of stretched cowhide.
The boat you can maybe reconstruct ... but not the
state of being. Not the unconditional surrender to
God's will. Not the wild surge of faith. Or the
rapture of it, the blind leap into the dark. That class
of a voyage is no longer in the sea's gift.

As we grapple with millennial notions of belief and
spiritual dimension in a secular, mercantile world, the
time for another look at *Pratt's Fall* may well have come.

Originally commissioned by the Hampstead Theatre,
Pratt's Fall came close to a West End production.
Stewart wanted to seduce audiences with an entertaining
brew of complex questions and, along with Stoppard
and Frayn, he had the ability to combine difficult
intellectual ideas with a good night out. Commercial
theatre had considerable appeal for him. He was never
really welcomed into the great super-subsidised houses,
mostly because they were too slow to track him. A good
deal of his success came about through small, radical,
maverick companies, and through television. Ironically
this meant that he was about twenty years ahead of his
time. Here is someone massively informed by cinematic
techniques and rock music, whose career is a blueprint
for some of the most successful contemporary
playwrights, but whose practice of theatre was truly
traditional, who adored the physical machinery of the
buildings and felt most at home in the dilapidated
grandeur of the old Victorian houses. I think that is why
he loved the theatre. It is because out of the most
unlikely, crude elements – bits of wood and hemp, plugs
and wiring, *actors* – you create, through an act of
collective will, a kind of magic. And if that isn't a
metaphor for human aspiration, I don't know what is.

Stewart once told me that some time after *Nightshade* was completed, he made an interesting discovery, namely that in ancient Greek the words for undertaker and magician were identical. He loved this. It was as if he had received some kind of confirmation that he was on the right track. Given the magnitude of the task he set himself, any assurance from the ancients must have been welcome. If there is a model for *Nightshade* it could be *The Tempest* – the Magician and his daughter, the attempt to control natural order, the coming to terms with loss etc. But if Quinn echoes Prospero he has to make the journey of a Lear, with Delia as his wise Fool. Quinn is no crazed monarch, just a small businessman who hasn't cottoned on to the psychological dangers of his bizarre profession. It is this very ordinariness that makes him an ideal, if unlikely, Everyman.

Nightshade tackles huge, elemental questions in a characteristically playful way. Please note that Stewart's playfulness generally involves a degree of difficulty which seems to border on insanity. An actor playing Prospero can generally sit back, do the lines and let stage management and the design team take on storm effects, quaint devices and so on. Quinn has to do magic tricks all by himself, naked, exposed, except for a chorus of malevolent props, eager to confound the fumbler on press night and sniggeringly aware of the *Guardian* critic three rows from the front. So you have to get yourself an actor of substantial charisma and technical virtuosity who is confident enough not to give a tinker's curse because he knows he can get away with it. Simple, really.

Orson Welles thought of the movies as the biggest train set in the world. Stewart had a similar attitude to the theatre.

And then there's the hidden agenda. Much of Stewart's work reads like very clever naturalism. He has a superb ear for casual speech and a breezy use of vernacular. What you don't realise, until you try to speak it, is that the dialogue is *scored*. *Catchpenny Twist* isn't just about the music business, the text itself is musical.

Martyn What's another word for 'nation'?

Roy Country.

Martyn No good.

Roy Land.

Martyn Longer.

Roy Mausoleum.

Pause.

Look at the time.

Martyn Don't fluster me.

Roy Is that her?

They listen intently for a moment. Silence.

Martyn I do the words, you stick to the music.

Roy What music? They're only after the usual traditional whinge.

Martyn 'Then sing with me the ballad of the death of Sean McVeigh, He will not be forgotten' . . . Not for a day or two anyway.

Roy Are you looking shot?

Martyn She's lost her sense of humour, Marie. (*Pause.*) What rhymes with McVeigh?

Roy Slay.

Martyn Pray? . . . Obey?

Roy Decay.

Martyn Great. Thanks. That's terrific. 'He gave his life for Ireland, On account of tooth decay.'

Now this apparently simple little exchange *will not work* unless the rhythm is obeyed, you won't get the sense and you most certainly won't get the laughs. Everything is built into the scoring, the tension, the relationship, the comedy, even to the extent that 'Not for a day or two anyway' doesn't scan. The terse one-liners are the pulse of the dialogue, a bit like they are in Mamet, while the build towards the main punchline is as carefully structured as in Wilde. Geilgud, talking about the technique of playing Wilde, describes holding off the audience's laugh until the moment of maximum payoff. Exactly the same applies here; if the dialogue is delivered lazily the laugh comes too early, tension is dissipated and the climax is blown. Positively sexual.

You are dealing with a Big Brain here, and just as you think you have grasped the method, the key, the *doing* of the plays you find that it's all part of a much more complicated mosaic. The intellectual breadth is staggering, as is the audacity. Let us remember that this writer was not above the contrived and gleefully cheap gag.

Daisy How's Frank?

Julian Missing in action.

Daisy You don't think he was out there?

Julian I saw him helping some old lady into an ambulance, he was all right.

Daisy Who in the name of Jesus would want to blow up a pet shop?

Julian For one magic moment . . . it was raining real cats and dogs.

Now I ask you . . .

Then there's That Woman. She appears in nearly all the plays, from Daisy Bell in *Spokesong* to Marian in *Pentecost*. She bears a striking resemblance to Frances Tomelty in appearance and tone, just like there's this

bloke who looks and sounds just like Stephen Rea. In
fact she is a particularly acerbic strand of the author's
personality which, thankfully, he kept in reserve for
much of the time. Say what you like about her though,
she knows how to give an audience a good time.

Tomelty and Rea were two of the actors Stewart
worked with and wrote for. They were, in his head,
members of the Stewart Parker permanent company. A
relationship with such a company in reality was the
great missing link in his career as a playwright. Although
his work was produced by various organisations, from
the Birmingham Rep to Field Day, and although he was
writer-in-residence at the King's Head Theatre Club, he
lived mostly outside the rooted theatre institutions and in
several locations. In practical terms this may have
contributed to a certain confusion about his context as a
dramatist. On the other hand he would be the first to
point out that a confused, or at least multi-layered, sense
of identity was part of his psychological heritage, and
that silence, exile and cunning is no bad starting-point
for a writer.

But there is no mistaking where he came from. The
Belfast idiom, in all its dry bleakness, is his mother
tongue, and the tangled relationship between the two
islands of Ireland and Britain his artistic terrain. Even in
Nightshade, the setting of which he keeps deliberately
vague, the lingo is Northern and urban. Belfast. The city
appalled and obsessed him. In the characters of Julian in
Spokesong, Roy and Martin in *Catchpenny Twist*, right up to
Peter in *Pentecost*, you see the element of Stewart that
was constantly raging against the place of his birth.
Equally present, and represented more sympathetically, is
the part that sought to come to terms with it.

Frank Have you not learned anything at all? You
are your own past, kid. You're the sum total of its
parts. Hate it and you hate yourself. No matter how
calamitous it may have been, either you master it or
you die.

The violent history of Northern Ireland is a major
subject of Stewart's work; it could hardly have been
otherwise. Yet he constantly seeks to enlarge the frame.
The grotesque politics of Ulster are read as symptoms of
a dark distortion of the human condition. It is a
universal state, as is the angry spirit that kicks against it.

Nightshade is the most abstract of the plays in this
volume, and the one he felt most satisfaction at having
written. Ironically it appears to have little to do with
politics, the Troubles or Ireland. Death is the great
terror for most of us and it was a particular obsession of
his. He chooses, of course, to deal with it in a very un-
solemn manner, employing magic, wrestling, Jacob and
the Angel, and the Sleeping Beauty to tell the story of a
bereaved undertaker.

> **Delia**   Once upon a time the damsel and the
> christening. The spell and the spindle and the castle
> in the forest. Which brings us nearly to the end.
> What is she, lying there, with her damaged thumb, in
> a pure dreamless sleep? The prince jangles in, trailing
> mud, smelling of horse. He has come from a world of
> furious transactions. His body is all itches and
> sniffing, ready to kiss. Who is she? A stateless person.
> An unresolved chord in the waltz of time. He shuffles
> round the catafalque and peers at her. One kiss
> would crack this nimbus open for time to flood her
> veins again. He bends over the pale, perfect lips
> ready to kiss. He looks. He ponders. He hesitates.
> And of course, is lost.

I suppose we are all a bit like the prince. The mystery
of death eludes us because we can't make the
connection between the physical and the spiritual world.
The state of profound embarrassment this leaves us in is
a recurring note of the play, most wonderfully illustrated
in a creakingly awful funeral service, as funny as it is
desperate. Stewart seizes upon this surreal comedy. In its

chaotic hinterland lurks the demon he spent his life wrestling to the ground.

Delia Looks. Ponders. Hesitates. Is lost. Tries a tentative kiss. Nothing happens. The prince cleared his throat and shuffled his feet a bit. Did I get the year wrong? he thought. Is this the right address? And he thought, it's more like a dungeon, this, than a stately mansion. And he thought, it'll certainly take a lot of redecorating. And he thought, no point trying to sneak back through that cursed wood. And he thought, what the hell − I suppose after a hundred years of suspended animation you can't expect miracles. And he said, people really amuse me though. It's so typical. It's disgusting. It's no joke. It's the living end.

Lynne Parker
June 1999

Spokesong

or The Common Wheel

For Kate

Spokesong was first performed at the John Player Theatre at the Dublin Theatre Festival in 1975, with the following cast:

The Trick Cyclist	Pitt Wilkinson
Frank	Raymond Hardie
Daisy	Ruth Hegarty
Francis, *Frank's grandfather*	Allan McClelland
Kitty, *Francis's wife*	Maire Ni Ghrainne
Julian, *Frank's brother*	Barry McGovern

Directed by Michael Heffernan
Music by Jimmy Kennedy
Lyrics by Stewart Parker
'Daisy Bell', words and music by Harry Dacre
'Spinning Song', words by Madelyne Bridges

Spokesong was performed at the King's Head Theatre, Islington, on 7 September 1976, with the following cast:

The Trick Cyclist	Robert Bridges
Frank	Niall Buggy
Daisy	Annabel Leventon
Francis	Patrick Waldron
Kitty	Valerie Hermanni
Julian	Don MacIver

Directed by Robert Gillespie

Setting

The action takes place in Belfast, Northern Ireland, during the early 1970s and the eighty years preceding them.

Above the stage, down front, hangs a large, ornate shop-front sign:

FRANK STOCK   THE 'SPOKES' MAN

CYCLES AND ACCESSORIES

There are essentially three acting areas. The shop area, which is entered through a solid old wooden door with glass panels, has a counter, cash register, noticeboard, and a forest of bicycles and components hanging from the ceiling. As a downstage appendage of it there is a work space with a stool and a tool box in the centre of it. Adjoining the shop is the living-room area which has a plain wooden table and chairs and a Victorian sideboard. Finally, there is a stretch of street along which bicycles can be ridden.

Realism is only one mode among several adopted during the action. The setting should consist only of bare essentials, but the essentials should all be real.

The **Trick Cyclist** *wears a typical variety-act outfit of bowler hat, shabby tailcoat, black tight-fitting trousers, dirty white socks and pumps. His make-up is also typically garish.*

Act One

A honkey-tonk piano plays 'Daisy Bell'. The **Trick Cyclist** *rides across the stage on a unicycle, singing.*

Trick Cyclist
  Daisy, Daisy . . .

Rest of the Cast (*offstage. Sings*)
  Give me your answer do . . .

Trick Cyclist (*re-crosses, singing*)
  I'm half crazy . . .

Rest of the Cast (*offstage*)
  All for the love of you . . .

Trick Cyclist (*now enters on foot, singing*)
  It won't be a stylish marriage . . .
(*And cocks his ear as the* **Rest of the Cast** *sings.*)

Rest of the Cast
  I can't afford a carriage . . .

Trick Cyclist
  But you'll look sweet . . .

Rest of the Cast
  Upon the seat . . .

Trick Cyclist
  Of a bicycle built for two.

He throws his hat into the wings, and sits down at the table.

I'll just say a word or two to those of you who have come here for the first time. We're all present for the purpose of an inquiry into matters of great importance affecting every one of us. Now I don't want anybody to feel intimidated or inhibited by these proceedings. This is not a court of law or a tribunal or anything of that kind. The learned gentlemen and technical experts assisting me are public servants and so am I. I am up here in fact to represent you, and to see that all of your interests are fully taken into account in my final recommendations. Now, if Mr Stock is present, I'll be happy to hear his submission.

Frank *comes out and addresses the inquiry.*

Frank It's just like this – internal combustion has gone too far.

Trick Cyclist Could I have your full name, please?

Frank What, all of it?

Trick Cyclist If you would.

Frank Francis John Boyd Dunlop Stock.

Trick Cyclist Thank you.

Frank Not at all. You see, all these terms you're using – traffic flow, communications infrastructure, grade-separated systems . . .

Trick Cyclist You mention in your letter that you're a shopkeeper, Mr Stock.

Frank Right.

Trick Cyclist And your premises are presumably affected by the plan?

Frank That isn't what concerns me. A single shop's neither here nor there. I haven't come to haggle, I'm here to talk values.

Trick Cyclist Quite, quite.

Frank Imagine the city as a giant body . . . That's what it really is. Diagnosis – not good. Circulation sluggish. Lungs, badly congested. Severe constipation. So what does this plan propose as a cure? Great Scott – a heart transplant!

Trick Cyclist Sorry to butt in again, Mr Stock . . . Just to say, if you could be as concise as possible, for the sake of the other objectors...

Frank Two words, that's all. It's brutal. It's demented. Ripping out the houses and shops and people – whole communities – so that you can truss up the city centre with enormous roads, coiling thirty feet up in the air, ramming themselves across the river and through parks and into every resident's nervous condition. Sit back and think about it – just for a minute. (*The* **Trick Cyclist** *begins to read a newspaper.*) You can look out from my shop straight up a hill that's a main route into the city centre. Every morning, down they come, roaring and tumbling headlong – the commuters – the gaberdine swine. They get to the intersection at the bottom – and immediately turn into a snarling, writhing, ravelled-up knot of ulcerous vindictiveness. We shouldn't be promoting that. We ought to be outlawing it. The time has come to rediscover the faithful bicycle.

Trick Cyclist Thank you, Mr Stock. (*He remounts his unicycle.*) You have saved mankind at a single stroke!

The piano plays the last line of 'Daisy Bell' fast, as he cycles off.

Frank Because it's been around so long, we overlook the miracle of it. Fastest form of urban transportation. Carries you a thousand miles on the food-energy equivalent of a gallon of petrol. Sixteen of them can fit into the space required to park one car. (**Daisy** *comes through the door into the shop, pushing a ten-year-old, rusty-looking lady's bicycle.*) And so on and so forth. They've no common sense, but statistics always impress them. (*He goes upstage to behind the counter.*) Hello and welcome.

Daisy Do you repair bikes here?

Frank At every opportunity, kid.

Daisy This specimen here has been lying out in our back yard for years now.

Frank It's time you recycled it.

Daisy   It's rotten with rust.

Frank   I'll take a look over it for you, if you like.

Daisy   I'm afraid it needs a lot more than looking over.

Frank   A look, a smile, a lingering caress. It's crying out for a bit of loving attention, like the rest of us.

Daisy   So long as I can afford it.

Frank   It'll be the best of value . . .

Daisy   (*walking to the door*)   When should I call back, then?

Frank   . . . especially for a teacher.

Daisy   (*stopping*)   You don't say.

Frank   Not only well within your budget – but getting you to your work in a manner which compensates for its sedentary nature.

Daisy   There's nothing sedentary about the school I work in.

Frank   In brief – a transport of delight.

Daisy   How did you guess my job?

Frank   A certain chalk dust between index finger and thumb.

Daisy   So I've started looking like a teacher.

Frank   A certain authority of manner.

Daisy   Elementary, no doubt.

Frank   But yes . . . Holmes was shaking his head. A bicycle, certainly, but not THE bicycle, said he. I am familiar with forty-two different impressions left by tyres. This, as you perceive, is a Dunlop, with a patch upon the outer cover. Heidigger's were Palmer's, leaving longitudinal stripes . . . It is of course possible that a cunning man might change the tyres of his bicycle in order to leave unfamiliar tracks. A criminal who is capable of such a thought is a man whom I should be proud to do business with.

Daisy Thanks, we'll let you know.

Frank This bike's a good model.

Daisy My grandparents bought me it. As a prize for conning my way into university.

Frank You couldn't have had it that many years, then.

Daisy Ten. So that must make me about twenty-eight. Okay? (*She goes through the door. He follows her as far as the door.*)

Frank Call in tomorrow same time. I can tell you then what needs doing.

Daisy If there's a lot of work involved I might just buy a new one. I need it pretty quickly, my car died on me yesterday.

Frank One of a dying species – headed for extinction.

Daisy Is that so? I suppose the bicycle is immortal.

Frank Bicycles are human, kid.

Daisy (*studies him*) I'll leave you with my friend, then. (*Exit.*)

Frank Till tomorrow.

The piano bursts into 'Daisy Bell'. **Frank** *vaults back into the shop, picks up the bicycle by the frame, and waltzes round with it, then staggers and collapses to the floor with it on top of him.* **Daisy** *re-enters the shop. Silence.*

Daisy I never left you a name and address.

Frank Good thinking.

Daisy   I'll write it down here. (*She goes to the counter, produces pen and paper, and writes.*) Just in case I forget to call back. (*She finishes, walks back to the door, turns and looks at him.*) I take it this is the outcome of the look, the smile and the lingering caress.

Exit. **Frank** *goes to the counter and picks up the piece of paper.*

Frank (*reading*)   Margaret Bell ... Great Scott ... Oh, rapture ... Oh bliss ... an actual Daisy Bell!

Music. He sweeps up the bicycle and sings to it, as he carries it down to the work area, puts it up on its stand, and removes the saddle.

(*Sings.*)
  There is a flower within my heart, Daisy, Daisy,
  Planted one day by a glancing dart
  Planted by Daisy Bell.
  Whether she loves me or loves me not
  Sometimes it's hard to tell
  Yet I am longing to share the lot
  Of beautiful Daisy Bell ...

(*He holds the saddle up and apostrophises it.*) Would that I had been where thou hast been, kid. (*He replaces the saddle, sets the bicycle upside down, and seats himself beside it. Lights dim on the shop area, and intensify on the work space.*) With trembling fingers he removed the spring clip from her chain – (*Does so with pliers.*) and unhooked the connecting link – (*Does so and removes chain.*) he gazed at last upon the ravishing yet strangely vulnerable symmetry of her crank assembly. A sense of wonder mingled with the swelling drumbeat of his desire, his hands sweeping across the firm young spokes, up, up to their nipple-heads, until the soft pliant tyres yielded to his touch and sent his senses spinning.

He spins the front wheel. Simultaneously, the lights on the work space dim, and those on the shop area come up, revealing **Francis** *behind the counter, and the* **Trick Cyclist** *in front* *of it wearing a dog collar. During this scene,* **Frank** *works quietly on at dismantling* **Daisy***'s bike.*

Trick Cyclist Dangerous excitation of the senses ... overheating of the blood ... derangement of the internal organs.

Francis You must believe me, Dr Peacock.

Trick Cyclist Medical facts, Mr Stock. I am sorry to have to say it – you are a man of industry and thrift. I lament to see you suborned by this instrument of the devil.

Francis But even gentlemen of the cloth are riding bicycles now.

Trick Cyclist Not of my cloth, sir.

Francis Of course, everything in moderation, I quite agree.

Trick Cyclist But everything is not by any means in moderation. Young men are hurling themselves recklessly about the streets on these contraptions.

Francis Scorchers, yes, I quite agree, there are occasional scorchers. Deplorable. But furious riding is now in breach of the law.

Trick Cyclist Unnatural movement of the legs ... flaunting of the human form ... it's unseemly, moreover, it's subversive. You notice how the materialists and the Socialists have taken it to their hearts.

Francis Dr Peacock, I am a loyal servant of the Empire, and a fully subscribed member of the Conservative and Unionist Association.

Trick Cyclist All the more regrettable, Mr Stock, if I may say so, all the more regrettable that you have chosen to trade in such an ungodly commodity.

Francis Queen Victoria rides a tricycle!

Trick Cyclist   I cannot answer for the foreign
influences at work upon the behaviour of my monarch. I
do know that the spectacle of a woman on a bicycle is
an abomination before the Lord. In this very town,
unchaperoned women are blithely riding along lonely
lanes . . . (**Kitty** *rides along the street on an 1895 safety
bicycle, long red hair streaming behind her. She is wearing
bloomers.* **Francis**, *seeing her, is captivated and rushes to the
door. The* **Trick Cyclist** *continues, oblivious.*) a prey to any
passing tramp, desperate with hunger and naturally
vicious.

Francis   Did you see that?

Trick Cyclist   Their limbs are on display for the
world to leer at.

Francis   Magnificent!

Trick Cyclist   Petticoats fluttering brazenly . . . sleeves
drawn back, bosoms unlaced. (**Kitty** *rides back across. The*
Trick Cyclist *turns and sees her.*) Aaargh!

Francis   A perfect vision!

Trick Cyclist   Did you see what she was wearing?

Francis   Ravishing!

Trick Cyclist   Bifurcated garments!

Francis   Who is she?

Trick Cyclist   Divided skirts! Never did I believe I
would see it in my own street. The shape of a woman's
legs in trousers . . .

Francis   Was she wearing bloomers? I didn't notice.

Trick Cyclist   Now you see what your bicycles have
brought us to – licentiousness and depravity. (**Kitty** *rides
across again. The* **Trick Cyclist** *turns away,* **Francis** *is
drawn after her.*) Get thee behind me, Satan!

Francis   Her hair!

Trick Cyclist   Her legs!

Francis   Her eyes!

Trick Cyclist   Her flesh!

Francis   Her road-handling! It's superb! (*He rushes out in pursuit of her along the street.*)

Trick Cyclist   I'm going straight to my study. The papers will hear about this!

Exit through the door and off. Lights up on work space. **Frank** *is still working on the bike.*

Frank   Francis was too late. By the time he had reached the end of the street the magnificent red-haired creature had vanished. Who was she? Where did she live? Above all ... was she as yet unwed? He had to find out, but how? As luck would have it, he had but a little time to wait. The very next morning, as he browsed through catalogues of cyclist-corsets and saddle-bags, half-dreaming of tossing red hair and radiant eyes, in walked the very subject and object of his dreams. (**Daisy** *enters the shop.* **Frank** *stands up.*) At least that's the way he always told it to me. (*He goes up to behind the counter.*)

Daisy   How's my bike?

Frank   Naked and unashamed.

Daisy   Does it need much done?

Frank   Come on through and see for yourself. (*He leads her down to the work space as he talks.*) What did you learn in school today?

Daisy   Plenty – such as how to booby-trap a car. Is this place all yours?

Frank   The premises aren't mine, but the business is. It was left me by the old man.

Daisy   It's a beautiful old shop.

Frank   Established 1895.

Daisy   By your father? You couldn't be that old, surely.

Frank   I love you more with every sentence, Margaret.

Daisy   Daisy.

Frank   Oh? Frank ... How're you doing? (*He shakes her hand.*) It was my grandfather, in fact.

Daisy   What?

Frank   Opened the shop. I was reared by him and my granny.

Daisy   (*looking at her bicycle*)   A sorry sight.

Frank   Your problems are few. Your crank-lever's a bit loose there – it needs a new cotter-pin. New gear cable ... I haven't looked into your wheels yet, but I would say the rim-tapes would be rotted away. A few new spokes are called for, too, and brakeblocks ... beyond that it's just cleaning off rust, retouching, and a general lubrication. There'll be change out of ten pounds. Marry me and I'll do it for nothing.

Daisy   So you're only interested in me for my bicycle?

Frank   Vice-versa. As a matter of fact, I'm jealous of your bicycle.

Daisy   That was the year of Oscar Wilde's libel suit.

Frank   What's this?

Daisy   1895.

Frank   So – a history teacher.

Daisy   Elementary. But yes.

Frank   Let me see ... 1895 ... the ladies' safety model achieves a mass market. Basic design unchanged from that day to this – there it is right in front of us.

Daisy How did you get like this, Frank?

Frank I was born and reared right in there. (*He gestures.*) The old man had me on a trike before I could walk.

Daisy It's not just a business to you though – it's more like a religion.

Frank Put it like this, kid – to you this machine is nothing more than a sorry sight. But look at it again – what you've got here is the realisation of a dream as old as mankind.

Daisy You astonish me.

Frank The power of superhuman speed right there in your own two shanks. Like Mercury – like the Centaurs – it took a whole lot of civilisation to bring it to the point of perfection you see here.

Daisy No offence, Frank, but it hardly looms large in the history of the world. I couldn't even tell you who invented it.

Frank (*springing up*) The Evolution Of The Bicycle: An Illustrated Lecture! (*He illustrates the following by dashing around the shop, improvising the various set-ups with two chairs, two wheels, a plank and so on.*) 3500 BC. Wheeled vehicles originate in Lower Mesopotamia. Your basic cart. No extras. Pause, pause, pause. Nothing much happens during the next 5,000 years.

Daisy So much for the Greeks, the Romans, Jesus Christ, Mohammad and Shakespeare.

Frank Bikeless every one.

Daisy Think of the difference it would have made . . . the Vikings on bikes.

Frank And then . . . 1791 AD. A couple of young French bloods line up two wheels, join them with a beam, throw their legs over it and scoot themselves along with their feet. The barricades are going up, the guillotines are whistling down – the king's taking a powder for his headache – Jean-Paul Marat's soaking in his bath-tub – and these maniac comrades are running velocipede races up and down the Champs-Elysées.

Daisy   Your spiritual forebears.

Frank   Next – 100 years of evolution. German forester develops steerable front wheel. Scottish blacksmith attaches cranks and treadles to rear wheel hub, and invents pedalling. 1860s, first commercially produced model, the Boneshaker. 1870s – hunger for speed enlarges the front wheel to five or six feet tall – the penny-farthing era. 1880s – invention of the diamond-shaped frame combines speed with safety and comfort. By the turn of the century, the vision has been realised in every perfect detail. Tubular metal. Lightweight spoked wheels running on ball-bearings. Chain-driven rear wheel, air-filled rubber tyres, the lot. And then came the internal combustion engine.

Daisy   You sound displeased.

Frank   It's a question of control over your own life, kid. So far as personal transport goes – the bicycle was the last advance in technology that everybody understands. Anybody who can ride one can understand how it works. That's crucial.

Daisy   I couldn't care less how a machine works so long as it goes on working.

Frank   It never does, that's the trouble.

Daisy   So you pay a rude mechanic to fix it.

Frank   Why do you think we're all unhinged – our lives are at the mercy of alien machines, mysteries for other people to solve.

Daisy   You get wet on a bicycle, Frank. Soaked through to the pelt, if memory serves.

Frank Have you ever looked around you at the faces in a plane preparing for takeoff? They're all thinking the same thought as you – how the hell does a plane fly? All bunched up together wondering what makes it go up in the air. They can see for themselves how ungainly it is, lumbering down the runway like a sort of big tubular lorry. Secretly they all believe it deserves to crash. Clenched jaws and sweaty palms all round. Helplessness. Estrangement. If it doesn't crash, they congratulate technology for having put one over on nature yet again. (*Pause.*) Who told you how to make a booby-trap?

Daisy I'd forgotten that. You and your sermonising. I've got a hooligan class of fourteen-year-olds. I was trying like a conscientious fool to get them talking about their own interests. Before I know where I am, this pathetic pixillated child is halfway through a description of how to boobytrap a car. Some of the others were correcting him on points of detail. It was educationally very high-grade ... plenty of pupil involvement, spontaneity of ideas, combined with an orderly discussion, scope for follow-up activities. They're the same on guns and explosives as you are on boneshakers and ball-bearings.

Frank Come on out and I'll stand you a drink.

Daisy I'm not sure you should be allowed out in public – anyway you've got a shop to tend.

Frank Not for much longer. They're knocking it down.

Daisy Who is?

Frank The city planners.

Daisy They can't. Why?

Frank Re-development. We're in the middle of a massive motorway intersection here.

Daisy This is a beautiful old Victorian shop, they

can't just knock it down.

Frank A single shop's neither here nor there. It's all these wasteful useless roads.

Daisy There's a public inquiry, isn't there? You'll have to go to the public inquiry and defend yourself.

Frank I'm already on their agenda . . .

Daisy Good. There must be some conservation group that would help.

Frank I'm not going to argue about the shop, love. I'm going to put forward my master plan. For 50,000 free bicycles distributed around the city centre. (*He starts to go off and then pauses.*) That put a spoke in your wheel, kid.

Exit. **Daisy** *follows as the piano strikes up. The sound of* **Francis** *singing is heard from offstage.*

The Parlour Song.

Francis
    I can hear the soft hum of the spokes
    When I'm pedalling down a green hill
    It's the song I first learned from my folks
    And the melody follows me still –
    Song of the spokes, spokesong,
    Music of the spheres
    How happily it evokes song
    Spinning along through the gears
    How easily it provokes song
    Each cyclist's favourite folk-song,
    Song of the spokes, Spokesong,
    Whisp'ring through the years
    Music that's good for the ears
    Song of the spokes, Spokesong,
    Spinning along through the gears.

Kitty *enters and inspects some books on the sideboard.* **Francis** *follows her. As he continues to sing,* **Julian** *appears outside the*

*shop door, carrying an overnight bag and a camera. He knocks
tentatively, peers in and then goes off. The song ends, and*
Francis *strides about nervously.*

Francis   Miss Carberry ... I cannot tell you of the joy
and delight which our cycle club outings have conferred
upon me. You have done me the honour ... of gracing
with your presence my humble shop ... I find that I
can hold back no longer ... the words that have been
burning on my tongue these many weeks now ... Oh,
Miss Carberry, Kitty, I was yours from the moment you
swept by that window like a princess from legend, proud
and radiant ... (**Kitty** *lights a cigar.*) Forgive me, I forgot
myself. Miss Carberry – I beg your permission – to call
upon your father – and request your hand in marriage.

Kitty (*sets down the book and wanders into the shop*)   Where
do you stand on the franchise, Francis?

Francis   Excuse me?

Kitty   I have resolved never to give the world a child
until it gives me a vote.

Francis   But my dear Kitty ... that might never be.

Kitty   Then I shall never fructify.

Francis   Now, now, now. Tracts and theories.

Kitty (*picking up a magazine from the counter*)   Oh, look – a
bell that rings when you twist your handlebar grip.

Francis   Yes, the twist-grip bell. I have some in stock.

Kitty   You can ring without taking your hand off the
bars. How very convenient.

Francis   I shall fit one to your bicycle this evening if
you wish.

Kitty (*wanders back to the room still holding the magazine*)   I
trust you don't approve what they're doing to Oscar
Wilde.

Francis My dear Miss Carberry, surely you must agree ... such a name ... it's scarcely fitting ... such a subject ...

Kitty On social issues he has nothing to offer. But a great writer none the less.

Francis Are you familiar with the works of Conan Doyle?

Kitty In my opinion there are two casualties in that kind of writing: one is truth; the other is fiction. (*She has been flicking through the magazine.*) How curious – a pneumatic saddle ... The Henson anatomic. Why does it have that odd kidney shape?

Francis It's filled with compressed air. It's made up of two air pads, with a depression in each. They're meant to give support to the rider's ... (*Clears throat.*) ischial tuberosities. (*Slight pause.*) Kitty – can I – may I – return to the subject of my proposal.

Kitty Which proposal? Oh yes – you were proposing to call upon my father. You may certainly visit my father any time you like, Francis.

Francis My dearest!

Kitty Personally I shall find nothing that he might say of any interest. It certainly won't have the slightest influence over me.

Francis You mean ... you won't marry me?

Kitty You haven't yet asked me.

Francis Asked you? ... But I ... Miss Carberry: will you marry me?

Kitty No.

Francis Why not?

Kitty For one thing, you'll have to reorganise your business practices. I've been looking through your

accounts here – if you can call them accounts. So far as
I can gather from the muddle, you're running something
closer to a philanthropic foundation than a commercial
enterprise.

Francis   Of course, the shop has only been opened for
eight months.

Kitty   It will be lucky to achieve a full year as things
stand at the moment.

Francis   It's true that I have no head for figures. And
no patience with them either. In fact, what I need,
Kitty, is someone like you to introduce method and
order into my affairs . . .

Kitty   I shall take these accounts home with me and
attempt to wrest some sense out of them.

Francis   I am most deeply grateful.

Kitty   There are a number of questions arising from
them for which I shall need your answers.

Francis   I will do my very utmost to provide them.
(*Slight pause.*) Forgive me if I venture to say, Kitty . . .
that were we man and wife . . .

Kitty   There are other matters. For one thing, I could
never bring myself to marry an anti-Parnellite.

Francis   But I'm not an anti-Parnellite – I'm not even
a Nationalist.

Kitty   That at least is to your credit. Better an honest
self-avowed Unionist than a Pharisaical patriot.

Francis   Naturally, I can only abhor the man's
behaviour but he has paid dearly for it.

Kitty   One day, Francis, Ireland will be a sovereign
nation, and womanhood will be a sovereign estate. Not
until that day will the ghosts of Parnell and Mrs O'Shea
be laid to rest. (*Pause.*)

Francis (*producing a package from his pocket*) I hope you'll accept this small token from me, Kitty.

Kitty May I open it?

Francis Of course. (*As she does so.*) It's the Cyclists' Touring Club Irish Road Book.

Kitty They've published it at last, then.

Francis I had it sent to me direct from the printers. Also, I took the liberty of asking them to inscribe a certain message on the fly-leaf.

Kitty (*reading it*) You are an incorrigible sentimentalist, Francis. Thank you for your gift ... It will be invaluable to both of us. (*She shakes his hand.*) I must go now. I will leave my bicycle here so that you can fit the twist-grip bell. I shall pay for it, of course.

Francis Good gracious, I wouldn't dream of such a thing.

Kitty (*holding aloft the account books*) Precisely. (*On her way out.*) I would be interested to hear, Francis, how you ever conceived the idea of opening a bicycle shop. (*Exit.*)

Francis It all started the day I met Dunlop! (*Exit.*)

Frank *is heard singing the chorus of 'Daisy Bell' from offstage.* **Julian** *enters and knocks on the door.* **Frank** *now appears along the street singing and doing a softshoe routine. He stops, brought up short.*

Frank Are you looking for me?

Julian Who else?

Frank Where's your key?

Julian Sacrificed to the waves, in a ritual of abnegation aboard the Liverpool boat fifteen years ago.

Frank (*opens the door, they enter the shop*) It's bad for my nerves, this. You should have rung me.

Julian (*surveying the shop*) You haven't changed a thing. There's just more of it all. Stock has increased. You've put on weight.

Frank What brings you over, Julian?

Julian (*holding up a camera*) This.

Frank You're still on the magazine?

Julian I'm recording the demise of Western society.

Frank Is that a part-time or a full-time job?

Julian (*smiles*) Great to be home, Frank.

Frank Listen, don't let me interrupt you, but I have this bike to work on. (*He goes down to the work space and resumes work on the bike.*)

Julian Surely you don't still have customers.

Frank Business is booming.

Julian So I hear. (*He observes.*) A lady's model, I notice.

Frank Elementary.

Julian A fairly recent one ... not ridden a lot ... left out in the rain ... a mark of youthful carelessness, most likely ... This is a youngish lady. How'm I doing?

Frank You're the champ. You always were.

Julian What's her name?

Frank A. Customer.

Julian You know, this is really moving, Frank. You in this dear old shop wooing your beloved just as Francis wooed Kitty all those years ago, fiddling with her bike.

Frank Bugger off, Julian.

Julian As bashful a rogue as ever. (*He wanders around the shop.*) Why have you not been bombed yet?

Frank You forget that I'm irrelevant.

Julian They've long since abandoned those piddling restrictions, surely; the papers claim that targets last week included a ladies' lavatory and a War on Want shop.

Frank Major bastions of British imperialism. Give them time – they'll get to me.

Julian I'm a disappointed man. I can't conceal it. Here I stand, having made the perilous journey, against all advice, against the tide, against doctor's orders, back to the old home town. Because I wanted to be here at the end, Frank. In at the kill. I wanted to take my place amidst the falling masonry. What do I find? Most of the buildings are still standing, most of the people are still alive. It's most vexatious. They'll have to do better than this.

Frank They mean well.

Julian It's not enough.

Frank You're worse than ever, Julian.

Julian My anger's more refined.

Frank Your heart's full of pus.

Julian Let's drink to that.

Frank I have a meeting to go to.

Julian I've been reluctant to say it, Frank, but your welcome has been less than fulsome. One is supposed to slay the fatted calf on these occasions.

Frank There's a packet of mince in the meat-safe.

Julian Meat-safe! ... God Almighty ... how long is it since I heard those words used in living speech. MEAT-SAFE ... with one bound he was back in the nineteenth century.

Frank Don't complain to me, kid. You're the absentee landlord, after all.

Julian (*perusing the noticeboard*) What's your meeting –
the Junior Chamber of Commerce?

Frank This is just a flying visit, I hope?

Julian Ah, here we are ... Public Inquiry Into The
Urban Area Redevelopment Plan. So. You're still trying
to make the world safe for small shopkeepers.

Frank Naive liberalism.

Julian Don't think I'm sneering, Frank. But surely
even you find it – quaint – arguing about urban
planning just at the moment.

Frank I think you're sneering.

Julian There's so much freelance redevelopment going
on, I mean.

Frank I have good reasons, kid. They never convinced
you on previous occasions, there's no point in another
argument at this stage.

Julian Are you sleeping in their room now?

Frank Yeah.

Julian I'll take ours, then.

Frank I hope you haven't been preaching
Armageddon round the streets.

Julian The only conversation I've had so far was with
two British Army gunmen. They insisted on frisking me
– it was tantamount to a sexual assault.

Frank Is that what you said to them?

Julian I urged them to shoot their officers, desert, and
join the forces of liberation.

Frank You're damn lucky they didn't take you
seriously.

Julian They might have if I'd told them my real

name. How long will it take you to be politely ignored at this Public Inquiry?

Frank I could be away for several weeks. It depends.

Julian I'll take a bath in that case. (*He moves towards the right.*) I seem to have indigestion. But perhaps it's nostalgia. (*Exit.*)

Frank (*puts down his tools and stands up*) What it all comes down to – is personal mobility in an area of maybe five square miles. At the moment there's just five square miles of anger and internal combustion. But supposing all the cars could be banished . . . What would be left? Buses. Taxis. Feet. Buses travel on fixed routes at fixed intervals. Taxis are expensive, wasteful and luxurious. Feet take too long and get too tired. Something more is needed . . . Imagine a fleet of civic bikes . . . gleaming with the city's coat of arms . . . stacked on covered racks on the corner of every street . . . which anybody can ride anywhere, free of charge, inside the city centre. The air clean. The people healthy. The time saved. The energy conserved. Earth would not have anything to show more fair. (*He picks up the detached wheels of* **Daisy***'s bike, carries them upstage into the shop, and stows them behind the counter.*) Take the cost of the roads scheme alone – for one per cent of that figure, the city could buy a bicycle for every able-bodied adult who travels during peak hours. (*He wheels his own bike through the door.*) Minimum upkeep. Parking attendants. Screws with left-handed threads. (*He gets on his bike.*) They can even have this one to start them off.

He cycles off. Simultaneously the **Trick Cyclist** *rides on, wearing a top hat and white tie, standing on the downstage pedal of an elegant black roadster, and sporting an enormously long cigarette holder. Music. He comes through the door downstage and sings.*

Cocktail Song.

Trick Cyclist
What takes you where you want to go –
Yes, energy.
What makes the lights go way down low –
No energy.
There's not a lot of it to spare
So let's celebrate –
A conveyance that reduces
The uses
Of juices –
What drives the wheels within the wheels –
High energy.
What happens when you miss your meals –
Low energy.
The rich and famous all agree
We must undertake
A resolute pursual of
Fuel
Renewal –
When voltage levels plummet
And you're down to your last ohm
You've got to overcome it
The time has come to slum it.
When cylinders stop firing
And you can't afford the fares
Don't sit about enquiring
It's time to start perspiring.
What shakes you in the dawning light . . .
It's what makes gelignite ignite . . .
So here's to a full-four-score-and-twenty of
That which Casanova had got plenty of
And what Dante warned the cognoscenti
Of –
En – er – gy!

He remounts and rides off. **Julian** *enters wearing a dressing-gown and towelling his hair. Simultaneously,* **Daisy** *comes through the front door into the shop.*

Daisy Frank, what's the verdict . . . Oh. Pardon me.

Julian The name's Julian.

Daisy Where's Frank?

Julian You must be his customer. I saw you leaving the shop earlier.

Daisy Oh . . . Did I see you?

Julian Evidently not.

Daisy Yes I did. I saw you buying a newspaper.

Julian Morning or evening?

Daisy It was at three in the afternoon. (*Pause. They scrutinise one another.*)

Julian Frank is off somewhere, applying cosmetics to a corpse.

Daisy You were in front of the bus station.

Julian I buy all the papers, they're so exhilaratingly short-lived.

Daisy It was just after three. You were looking round you with great interest.

Julian Impossible, else I'd have noticed you.

Daisy I was on a bus.

Julian Ah. (*He smiles, enjoying himself.*) I only arrived in town this morning from across the water.

Daisy How do you find it?

Julian Distressingly intact.

Daisy That must be a bore. (*Slight pause.*) I was driving my car down the road towards that bus station when it was blown up the first time. There wasn't any warning. Just a sudden flash. The first thing I saw was a bundle of old rags, just about on the spot on the footpath

where you were buying the paper. A pile of old torn
clothes, smouldering slightly. Then I realised it was
actually an old woman. (*Pause.*) The second time they
did it was when six or seven people were killed. I don't
know if they ever established the right number. It was a
question of counting fingers. Or fingernails. Bit of a
conundrum.

Julian Yes, I remember reading something about it.

Daisy Was that in the morning or evening paper?

Julian But I also find the people here so very friendly
and warmhearted. (*Slight pause.*)

Daisy You've been having me on.

Julian Have I?

Daisy What brings you over?

Julian I'm a freelance photo-journalist.

Daisy I see. I suppose you've just popped over to
cover the Lord Mayor's Show?

Julian Is there still a Lord Mayor? How vexatious.
What's your name?

Daisy M. Bell. Where did you say Frank was?

Julian Some kind of inquiry into something.

Daisy The motorway plans. You should have gone
with him, you could have done an amusing story on it.
A crowd of grown men earnestly discussing the pros and
cons of a road system . . . in a city that's being blasted
asunder all round them.

Julian Yes, he appears to believe that the
redevelopment plans are somehow important.

Daisy He thinks bicycles are important.

Julian You don't?

Daisy How did you two meet?

Julian Quite by accident. A very long time ago.

Daisy How long are you staying for?

Julian My plans are fluid.

Enter **Frank** *cycling. He dismounts, and shoulders his bike, and comes through the door.*

Frank Well, well, well. Fraternisation. Hello and welcome. (*To* **Daisy**.) Marry me, kid.

Daisy Your front tyre's soft.

Frank You see how much she cares? Solicitous to a fault for the well-being of my pneumatics. You've met, I take it?

Julian We just ran into each other.

Frank I see (*To* **Daisy**.) Sorry I'm forced to do this to you. Daisy Bell. Meet my kid brother Julian.

Daisy Brother?

Julian I'm the black sheep to his sacred cow. How do you do, Miss Bell? (*He shakes her hand.*) I love the way he says that – 'kid brother'. It gives me a kind of tremor in my oesophagus.

Frank Maybe it's indigestion.

Julian (*to* **Daisy**) I've been admiring your bicycle.

Daisy I think I'd better go away and start over again.

Frank Ignore him. He's just a mouth. With a poisoned tongue in its cheek.

Julian Always the bitter word, Frank.

Frank Kindly leave the stage, kid.

Julian You're right, I must take care of things. The plumbing calls me. Please excuse. (*As he goes.*) It used to cost him half a crown to get rid of me. I've grown cheaper over the years. (*Exit.*)

Daisy What in the name of God do you two live on – blood pudding?

Frank There's not much love lost.

Daisy You never said you had a brother.

Frank He's the last person I ever expected to see.

Daisy How long has it been?

Frank A good five years. For a long weekend. He left town that time with my cheque-book, my personal diary and the week's takings from the till. I haven't heard a peep since, till he walked in today.

Daisy You're so unlike each other. Has he always been the same?

Frank This is the truth – when our parents were killed I was six and he was two. And on the day of the funeral he pushed my tricycle under a bus. That's the only thing I remember about it.

Daisy You've never told me what happened to them, Frank.

Frank The blitz. Their whole house was demolished. Julian and I were with Francis and Kitty in an air-raid shelter. They were stuck with the pair of us forever after, God help them. (*Pause.*)

Daisy So what about the inquiry?

Frank The Inquiry. A melodrama. Act One. A half-coiled spring goes slowly limp. Rows of worried men push their glasses up on their foreheads, pinch the bridges of their noses, and yawn with their mouths shut tight. From secret nozzles the stultifying odour of mental decrepitude creeps through the room.

Daisy This one will run and run.

Frank The inspector sits on his throne. He feels the weight of his authority. At all costs he mustn't make a fool of himself. As a precaution, he has admitted his imagination into the morgue. Act Two. Enter a happy idiot advocating the bicycle solution. Nobody smiles. Nobody dances. Nobody rides a bike. Riding a bike would be making a fool of yourself, adopting the bicycle solution would be making a colossal fool of yourself. It's common sense – it's cheap – it's healthy – it's practical – but it's funny! They stare at me in fear. This man is propounding a solution that's funny! He's asking us to entertain a scheme that's funny! The room pullulates with corporate anxiety. Behind a mass of bifocals pupils dilate with terror. The inspector thanks me with a smile of rigor mortis. I step down. He reaches for his hanky with a trembling hand and blows a sticky clot of fear down his nose. Safe again! Now where were we? Ah, yes – the spokesman for the Automobile Association. Wheel him on in.

Enter **Julian**, *hair combed and wearing shirt and jeans, applauding.*

Julian This is close to actual subversion, Frank.

Frank (*to* **Daisy**) He's an anarchist.

Julian I'm off to the bank.

Daisy Are you going to rob it?

Julian Photograph it.

Frank What's the point, it's still standing.

Julian How long, oh Lord, how long? Let's all have tea together. There's a packet of mince in the meat-safe. (*He exits through the door.*)

Daisy Is he really a journalist?

Frank He works for a couple of magazines. There's one called *The Wart*.

Daisy You made that up.

Frank Invite me home for tea, kid.

Daisy All these buzzards flocking in with their
cameras and tape recorders. I walked by a street with a
suspect car in it this morning. They were stretched right
across the road in a horseshoe, mike-booms and
notebooks and cine-cameras at the ready, dozens of
them, as if it was a film premiere.

Frank People love catastrophes.

Daisy They were longing for it to blow sky-high.
We've even had them up at school, provoking the kids.
As if it wasn't hard enough to cope. It's beginning to get
rather foolish, me standing up there, saying, 'Now, class,
open your books at the Wars of the Roses . . .' and them
fresh in from stoning soldiers, and setting fire to shops.
They've already got more history than they can cope
with out in the streets.

Frank That's not history, that's depraved folklore . . .
bogeyman stories.

Daisy It's got more appeal than the truth, Frank;
whatever that is.

Frank I don't see the truth in battles or the lives of
the celebrated megalomaniacs. That's not the important
history either. I see it in all the things that ordinary
people do with their time.

Daisy Like riding bicycles, maybe.

Frank For example. The old man was a whole-
hearted Imperialist. But as far as he was concerned,
there was only one really important date in Irish history.

Daisy What was it?

Frank 1887. John Boyd Dunlop invents the pneumatic
tyre.

Daisy What's that got to do with Ireland?

Frank He invented it just round the corner from here.

Daisy I never knew that.

Frank The Story Of The Pneumatic Tyre! An average hard-working Scottish veterinary surgeon is pottering round his Belfast home one day. His name – John Boyd Dunlop. His little son has a tricycle, and keeps whimpering about the discomfort of wheels covered in solid rubber on a cobbled street. Dunlop's eye falls on his garden hose. He picks it up thoughtfully. He loops it tentatively round the wheel of the tricycle. Promising. He picks up the garden shears, cuts a length of hose off, and lashes it round the rim of the wheel, and then ditto with the other two wheels. The son tries it – no longer a boneshaker, but still pretty bumpy. Not enough of a cushion. And then – great Gordon Highlanders! – Dunlop sees it in a flash – air, the tube needs to be filled with air! That's the sort of history you should teach.

Daisy So you want to come home and meet the family?

Frank Any time.

Daisy Let's go.

Frank What about clothes?

Daisy You're close enough to urban guerrilla scruff to be presentable. My father's one of the neighbourhood gangsters. He even wears his sunglasses now at the dinner-table.

Frank Do you think he'll give his blessing to our union?

Daisy Are you kidding? He'd give me away with a pound of tea. You lead a sheltered life, Frank. This'll be a salutary experience for you. (*They go out through the door.*)

There's a war on, you know. It doesn't leave room for enthralling stories of human enterprise.

They exit. The piano plays the Wedding March. Enter the
Trick Cyclist *wearing the uniform cap and jacket of an Irish Guards major of 1899, followed by* **Kitty** *in a wedding veil.*

Trick Cyclist   Do not mistake my presence here for a change of mind, miss.

Kitty   Missis, if you please.

Trick Cyclist   Marry your bicycle tradesman and be hanged.

Kitty   I have just done so, Father.

Trick Cyclist   But don't expect a settlement from me.

Kitty   I never have, consequently its absence in no way upsets the calculations of my economy.

Trick Cyclist   Doubtless you would refuse it if it were offered.

Kitty   Certainly not, I would invest it in Irish-owned industry.

Trick Cyclist   Irish-owned twaddle. At least your gallant mother was spared this unedifying spectacle.

Kitty   It's a great pity that you did not spare yourself the unpleasantness, Major.

Trick Cyclist   I am here, madam, because I will not have scandal in my family – to compound the ridicule which you have already brought upon it.

Kitty   In other words, you lack the courage of your convictions.

Enter **Francis** *in his best suit.*

Francis   Major Carberry – I am delighted and honoured by your presence here today.

Trick Cyclist I hope I know my familial obligations, sir.

Francis May I say that I consider myself the happiest and most fortunate man alive to have won the hand of your daughter.

Kitty The Major considers himself more fortunate again, Francis, in having got rid of me. (*She exits.*)

Trick Cyclist As you well know, Mr Stock, I was not in favour of this match; frankly I consider it calamitous. Since my daughter has seen fit to disregard my wishes in the matter, she comes to you without a penny. None of this, naturally, reflects upon your personal integrity. It's simply that my family has a proud military tradition . . .

Francis I believe, Major, that you were active in the Matabele campaign.

Trick Cyclist In the latter part of it, yes.

Francis You didn't by any chance observe the use of military bicycles in the campaign?

Trick Cyclist I heard something of it, yes.

Francis It appears that one chap cycled several miles carrying one and a quarter hundredweight of ammunition, whilst sustaining a running fight with the natives.

Trick Cyclist The poor devils were probably frightened out of their wits.

Francis It's my belief that the bicycle has considerable potential as a military machine, Major. The British Small Arms Company has just produced a folding bicycle for use against the Boers. In fact, I have a few ideas of my own, I would be very pleased to have your comments on them. Oh – there's the Reverend Peacock. Please excuse me, Major, for one moment. (*He exits.*)

Trick Cyclist   It will never replace the horse!

Music. He takes off his cap and jacket and throws them into the wings and sings.

Cowboy Song.

Trick Cyclist
Oh I can't forget the past
And the days that went too fast
When Old Bob and me were buddies day
And night.
Now his oats are in the stall
And his saddle's on the wall
But Old Bob is in the knacker's yard
Tonight.
My guit-ar is unstrung
And my final yippee sung
And my silver spurs are hidden out of
Sight
For Old Bob ain't by my side
He has taken his last ride
And he's down there in the knacker's yard
Tonight.
There's a bicycle outside
But it don't excite my pride
Even though it's got a saddle-bag and
Light
It don't nuzzle, it don't bite
It don't whinny with delight
It don't hang its head and shiver in the
Night.
Now I'm feeling sore and sad
For the best pal that I had
Looked so lonesome as they led him out
Of sight.
He was faithful, he was true, now he's
Dog food or he's glue
And he's down there in the knacker's yard
Tonight.

(*He sits down at the table.*) Turning now to the question of pedal cycles: as the consultants have pointed out, cycle travel has been decreasing in the city at a rate of eight per cent per annum. Although this may in part be due to present traffic conditions – as several objectors have urged – I feel that the plan is justified in not providing specifically for pedal cycles – but considering them together with pedestrians and non-motorised forms of transport. Surveys did not demonstrate any particular problems in this regard which warranted special provision. Since the plan is, after all, sufficiently flexible to allow for specific routes if the need becomes apparent, I see no grounds here for not implementing the plan as it stands. (*He stands up and begins to move offstage, then pauses.*) One objector did put forward a rather ingenious plan for a free pedal cycle scheme. However, such a scheme would be entirely unresponsive to public demand ... although it would be funny and sunny and simply appealing and prettily witty and zippy and peppy and gay!

He throws his papers into the air. Music. As in the opening, he sings alternate lines with the rest of the **Cast** *offstage.*

We will go tandem as man and wife,
Daisy, Daisy,
Pedalling away down the road of life
I and my Daisy Bell.
When the road's dark we can both despise
P'leecemen and lamps as well,
There are bright lights in the dazzling eyes
Of beautiful Daisy Bell . . .

Exit **Trick Cyclist**. *As the piano plays the chorus, the houselights come up for the end of Act One.*

Act Two

Music. The **Trick Cyclist** *rides in and sings:*

Music-hall Song.

Trick Cyclist
    Salome danced for Herod, the chroniclers report,
    She hated John the Baptist for spoiling all her sport.
    When the music stopped King Herod said
    Choose any gift you like.
    Salome cried with passion
    'Bring me John the Baptist's bike!'

Frank *comes on and joins in, harmonising the chorus.*

Frank *and* **Trick Cyclist**
    It wasn't nothing personal,
    It wasn't mere dislike.
    She simply longed to pedal all around
    On John the Baptist's bike.

Frank *now takes the song over, while the* **Trick Cyclist** *does appropriate tricks on various machines.*

Frank
    When Jesus entered Jerusalem, Hosannas rang aloud,
    The leafy palms were waved at him by
    Wildly-cheering crowds.
    He sat upon a donkey, as the gospels claim alike,
    But the Dead Sea Scrolls insinuate he rode in on his
      bike.

    It's not that donkey-riding
    Excited his dislike,
    He just preferred to enter there
    Upon his old push-bike.

    Cycling is a pastime that tyrants can't abide,
    They see us all in uniform marching side by side,

So the next time that a Führer tries to build another
   Reich,
Just tell him that you'd rather
Go out riding on your bike.

It isn't something personal,
Speak into the mike,
The one thing that's beneath you
Is your trusty old push-bike.

Exit the **Trick Cyclist**.

Frank   Christ on a bicycle. You can see that. You
can't see him driving a Jaguar. Or an Avenger. Or a
Sting-ray. A car is just a hard shell of aggression, for the
soft urban mollusc to secrete itself in. It's a form of
disguise. All its parts are hidden. No wonder they're
using them as bombs. It's a logical development. A
bicycle hides nothing and threatens nothing. It is what it
does, its form is its function. An automobile is a weapon
of war.

Francis *enters along the street, riding a military bicycle with rifle
attached to crossbar, and dressed in a Great War Army Cyclists
Corps uniform.* **Kitty** *comes through the room in hat and coat.
They meet in the shop.*

Kitty   For a minute I thought you were my father.

Francis   You must try and understand, Kitty.

Kitty   I will not have a British Imperial uniform worn
in my house, take it off.

Francis   I have enlisted . . .

Kitty   West Briton!

Francis   I have enlisted, my dear, because my country
has been good to me in her hour of plenty. She has a
right to call on me in her hour of need.

Kitty   Ireland is your country. Now take that John Bull
fancy dress off this minute.

Francis You'll want to see the machine we're using
. . . (*Gestures towards bike.*)

Kitty Francis, when I married you, this business was
disintegrating. You were renting this shop from one of
your Presbyterian Unionist tycoons. It has taken me a
very long time to turn your accounts to profit and to
buy this shop for ourselves. And you are now proposing
– at the behest of their royal English whoremasters – to
cycle off to Flanders and leave me to cope with this
entire enterprise alone?

Francis You must try and be brave, Kitty.

Kitty (*surveys him for a moment*) Right. (*She starts removing
her hat and coat.*) When do you leave?

Francis My dearest – I knew you'd see where duty
lay.

Kitty Stuff. You can tell Kaiser Bill that I wish him
every success.

Francis You don't mean that, Kitty. That's childish
talk. (*She is now tugging at his tunic.*) What are you doing,
dear?

Kitty How much time is there?

Francis I'm leaving tomorrow.

Kitty Come with me.

Francis Don't send me to the battlefield with a bitter
word, Kitty.

Kitty There won't be time for that. I've decided to
have a child. (*Pause. He looks at her astonished.*)

Francis You mean – right away?

Kitty With luck.

Francis But the vote?

Kitty The War will no doubt bring us the vote, along

with all its other blessings. At any rate, by the time you return from it, I may be past the age of child-bearing. Alternatively, you may never return from it. I would prefer to avoid the inconvenience of another marriage. Come along, Francis. (*Exit.*)

Francis For God and the Empire! (*He follows.*)

Frank A war child. Aren't we all.

Explosion offstage. **Frank** *is thrown slightly forward, knocking over* **Daisy***'s bicycle frame. The shop sign lurches crooked, as does the noticeboard. Some bits of bicycles fall from the roof.* **Frank** *dusts himself off and dashes out through the door and off left.* **Julian** *appears from the street right, taking photographs of the damage. He enters the shop and looks around.* **Daisy** *appears at the door.*

Daisy How's Frank?

Julian Missing in action.

Daisy You don't think he was out there?

Julian I saw him helping some old lady into an ambulance, he was quite all right.

Daisy Who in the name of Jesus would want to blow up a pet shop?

Julian (*fetching drinks*) For one magic moment . . . it was raining real cats and dogs.

Daisy Is that all you've got to say about it?

Julian (*looks at her, gives her a drink*) Austin Beattie owned that pet shop. He preaches in the missions. He's got a perpetual line of brown scum on his lips, his breath has a kind of sickly fetid sweetness to it. I know this because every time I went into his shop he'd bend over me and put a hell-fire tract into my trouser pocket. He'd enjoy a furtive little feel while he was at it. (*He raises his glass.*) One last round for Austin Beattie. (*He drinks.*)

Daisy Why did you not tell me you were Frank's brother right at the start?

Julian Why didn't you guess it?

Daisy You don't look like brothers.

Julian We aren't. I was adopted.

Daisy Oh.

Julian One last round for my blood parents – the mother, I understand, was an unmarried Catholic skivvy, who'd been taught that abortion was a greater sin than giving birth. Whereas in fact it would have been a lesser crime, but then crime merely causes human suffering, whilst sin gives Goddy a pain. And not forgetting Dad, Protestant person unknown: then there's my adoptive parents – Frank's folks – let's have a round for them – and finally one for the foster-parents, the ones who had the actual rearing of me, to revert to the native idiom, dear old Francis and funny old Kitty. You'll have heard about those two. One thing I never lacked was parents.

Daisy It's easily seen where you come from, Julian. You're gifted in hatred.

Julian Please. Spare the blushes.

Daisy What did you really come back here for?

Julian I'm taking care of business. (*Pause.*) You're not exactly lacking in spleen yourself.

Daisy (*stands up and walks around a little, inspecting the damage*) It's a wonder this is still standing. Do you think he might move out?

Julian Out of the shop, possibly. Out of the city, never. You might as well ask a parrot to move out of its plumage.

Daisy Who's asking? (*Short pause.*)

Julian What about you?

Daisy What about me?

Julian Leaving town.

Daisy It's crossed my mind.

Julian Destination?

Daisy Unknown.

Julian What are your views on London?

Daisy Shows promise. Should do very well for itself in all subjects.

Julian I can put you up in my flat if you like.

Daisy I didn't know you cared.

Julian It has a ghost who coughs in the attic. That's unusual in a flat. I'll be going back soon. Two months of this town is enough to see me through the decade. We can travel together.

Daisy One last round for Frank. Do you hate him as well as all the rest?

Julian Frank is a saint. A saint on a bicycle. Even I can't hate that.

Daisy You envy him.

Julian Don't vulgarise me with your staffroom psychology.

Daisy Well – an actual human reflex. There may yet prove to be life on this bleak planet.

Julian Further exploration alone will tell. (*Pause. They survey each other.*)

Daisy I'm off.

Julian Think it over.

Daisy I'll let you know.

She exits via the street. **Julian** *cogitates for a moment, finishes his* *drink, and goes off. Music. The* **Trick Cyclist** *rides on in the helmet and jacket of a First World War sergeant-major and sings:*

Trick Cyclist
　　Song of the spokes, Spokesong,
　　Music of the spheres,
　　Song of the spokes, Spokesong,
　　Spinning along through the gears,
　　How easily it evokes song,
　　Each cyclist's favourite folk-song,
　　Song of the spokes, Spokesong,
　　Whisp'ring through the years,
　　Music that's good for the ears,
　　Song of the spokes, Spokesong,
　　Spinning along through the gears.

(*He dismounts and directs his voice towards the wings.*) Are we standing by our bicycles? (*Slight pause.*) Henceforth, when I say cyclist, I refer to a soldier using a cycle as a means of locomotion. From now on, gents, your cycle is your legs, your cycle is your sixth sense, your best friend – your weapon. Therefore I say first to you: Know Your Cycle. Upon it may depend your life and your country's victory. Right. I need a volunteer, you'll do. Come over here. (**Francis** *enters in full First World War Army Cyclists Corps uniform, pushing his military bike.*) Name?

Francis　Stock, Sergeant.

Trick Cyclist　What age are you?

Francis　Thirty-five, Sergeant.

Trick Cyclist　I thought you looked like a man of experience. Right, Private Stock. I'm going to put you through the rudiments of cycle drill. In this company – we go by the book. You learn by the book, and you go by the book. If you don't like it – get a horse. Now then. I deal first with the question of coming to attention. The position of the cyclist at attention is the same as that of any other soldier except that he will grasp the left steering handle with his left hand and place the right hand at the point of the saddle, elbow to the rear, is that clear?

Francis   Yes, Sergeant.

Trick Cyclist   'Ten ... SHUN! (**Francis** *comes to attention.*) At ease. (**Francis** *stands at ease.*) I deal second with the question of saluting, which is done with the right hand, the cyclist returning it to the point of the saddle on the completion of his salute. A party of cyclists on the march will salute to the command Eyes Right, which will be followed by Eyes Front from the officer or NCO in charge, is that clear?

Francis   Yes, sir.

Trick Cyclist   I deal now with inspection of cycles. At the command Inspection, grasp the left grip with the left hand, and the upper bar of the frame at the balance with the right hand. At the command Cycles, run the cycle forward on the rear wheel, at the same time raising the front wheel in the air, take one step to the right, bring the saddle against the legs, and grasp the right hand grip with the right hand, is that clear?

Francis (*hesitantly*)   Yes, sir.

Trick Cyclist   As the inspector approaches, draw the handlebar towards the body, lifting the rear wheel from the ground. After the cycle is inspected, lower the rear wheel to the ground, grasp the upper bar at the balance with the right hand, take one step to the left, run the cycle backwards, bringing the front wheel to the ground, and resume the position of standing by cycles, is that clear?

Francis (*dubiously*)   I think so, Sergeant.

Trick Cyclist   I ask again, is that clear?

Francis   Yes, sir.

Trick Cyclist   Inspect … shun! … Cycles! (**Francis** *upends the bicycle with too much violence; he staggers, it topples over, and he gets hopelessly tangled up in it.*) You don't quite have the hang of that one, do you, Private Stock …

Francis   I think I could acquire the knack if I just had a few goes at it.

Trick Cyclist   That's nothing to the knacks you'll lose if it isn't right for me tomorrow, is that quite understood, is that entirely clear?

Francis   Yes, sir.

Trick Cyclist   I deal now with the question of mounting and dismounting. The cyclist mounts or dismounts in the manner to which he is accustomed, the quickest method to do so being from the pedal, are there any questions? (*Pause.*)

Francis   Ah … Sergeant.

Trick Cyclist   Private Stock.

Francis   I wonder whether you might offer us some guidance … on the actual firing of our weapons whilst cycling.

Trick Cyclist   The use of the cyclist's rifle and pistol is left to his own initiative; however, instructions in the care and handling of his firearms will follow in due course, any other questions? (*Silence.*) I deal with one other matter today then we fall out. That is the question of capture by the enemy. In the eventuality of capture it is imperative that the cyclist should not allow his machine to fall intact into the enemy's hands. It is his duty to disable it by smashing the spokes with his rifle, buckling the frame by jumping up and down on it, and slashing the tyres. Right. Company … 'Ten … SHUN! Fall out!

Exit **Francis**. *Music. The* **Trick Cyclist** *remounts his bicycle and sings.*

Army Song.

Trick Cyclist
  I've washed behind my ears, Ma
  I've washed away the stains
  I've washed away the skin, Ma
  I've washed away the brains

  The dew is on the tulips, Ma
  The colonel's on his spouse
  The company's on its hands and knees
  And the blood is on the house

  One day while greasing my nipples
  I heard the sergeant say
  You can always rely on a bicycle pump
  To blow your blues away

  One night I heard a loud report
  Who's there? called out the guard –
  Oh pardon me, the sergeant said
  I pumped a bit too hard

  I haven't lost your letter, Ma
  I haven't lost my knife
  I haven't lost my rifle, Ma –
  I've only lost my life

Frank *appears along the street and enters the shop, surveying the damage. He fetches the ladder from offstage and climbs up it to straighten the shop sign.* **Julian** *appears in the room, eating a piece of cheese.*

Julian   Business as usual.

Frank   How are the living quarters?

Julian   Lamentably undamaged. The dust has merely been redistributed.

Frank   There's bits of animals all over the street.

Julian   Any recognisable portions of Austin Beattie?

Frank He was able to escape out the back. I met him on my way home from the hospital. He was heading for the City Hall to lodge his claim for damages. (*He's climbing down the ladder and putting it away.*)

Julian Shit. I'm the one who deserves damages. Why couldn't they have blown up this dump of mine?

Frank Maybe you'd like me to move out so you can do a deal with them?

Julian Why not? You're a disappointing tenant, Frank.

Frank Who's been in?

Julian Just the usual ceaseless flow of customers. Who's expected?

Frank There's a Community Association Meeting.

Julian So there is, so there is. What's this week's agenda? Solving the litter problem? Flower tubs on the footpaths?

Frank Listen, Julian, do us a favour – go away and photograph some old winos bleeding to death in a gutter somewhere.

The **Trick Cyclist** *appears on the street dressed in a leather jacket and wearing dark glasses. He knocks on the door.*

Julian Too late. The community has arrived. (*He opens the door. Pause.*)

Frank Duncan.

Trick Cyclist Frankie.

Frank How're you doing?

Trick Cyclist Bravely.

Frank This is Julian ... Duncan Bell. Daisy's father.

Trick Cyclist (*shaking hands*) The brother, is it?

Julian How do you do?

Trick Cyclist   Rightly. (*Slight pause.*)

Frank   What brings you in here, Duncan? Don't tell me you're after a bike.

Trick Cyclist   You're joking. I'm running a station wagon now.

Frank   Nifty enough. (*Slight pause.*)

Trick Cyclist   The street's half destroyed.

Frank   I got off lightly.

Trick Cyclist   It's atrocious. (*To* **Julian**.) Isn't it?

Julian   Appalling.

Trick Cyclist   It's got to be stopped, that's all there is to it. What's more, it's going to be. You'll be wanting to pull your weight, Frankie.

Frank   What do you have in mind?

Trick Cyclist   A wee contribution, just. To cover the men's expenses.

Frank   Sorry, Duncan, count me out.

Trick Cyclist   What's the matter, have you no belief in law and order?

Frank   Not when you phrase it in the abstract like that, no.

Trick Cyclist (*to* **Julian**)   A car bomb blows up across the street, and he doesn't believe in law and order.

Frank   One army and one police force, that's already more than enough.

Trick Cyclist   The army and the police? You must be joking. It's urban guerrilla warfare, friend, against the likes of you and me. It's a job we've got to do ourselves. (*Slight pause.*) I'm disappointed in you, Frankie. I thought you had more community spirit.

Frank   Funny you should use that phrase, Duncan.
I've been running the Community Association here for
the last year and a half. In fact, there's a meeting due
to start any minute.

Trick Cyclist   That's what I called in to tell you. The
meeting's been shifted.

Frank   Where?

Trick Cyclist   Up to our club. It's safer up there. The
rest of them are up there already.

Pause. The **Trick Cyclist** *takes out a packet of small cigars,
strips the cellophane off one, and puts it into his mouth.*

Frank   I'm puzzled, Duncan, by your sudden interest
in redevelopment. You don't even live in the
neighbourhood.

Trick Cyclist   It's a part of my command. (*To*
Julian.) Cigar?

Julian   No, thanks.

Trick Cyclist   I hope you change your mind, Frankie
– about the donation, I mean. Don't misunderstand me,
we're forcing nobody to do nothing. It's just there's a
terrible lot of young hotheads roaming the streets these
nights. We keep them in check as best we can. But it
only takes one tearaway with a petrol bomb and your
whole business is gone for a burton. (*He's been searching his
pockets for matches.* **Julian** *produces a box, strikes one and lights
the cigar.*) Thanking you.

Julian   Keep the box. (*He puts it in the top pocket of the
leather jacket.*)

Trick Cyclist   There's your home to think of as well.
You live here, don't you?

Frank   That's right, Duncan. I live here. (*Slight pause.*)

Trick Cyclist   How's Daisy this weather?

Julian She was in a little earlier.

Trick Cyclist Tell her that her da says hello. (*He turns to go.*) I'll be seeing you, Frankie. (*To* **Julian**.) You try and talk a bit of sense into him. (*Exit.*)

Julian What a charming man.

Frank You didn't tell me Daisy was in.

Julian He'll make a wonderful father-in-law.

Frank Tinker Bell. He goes in every Friday to collect his dole money with an armed bodyguard.

Julian He's the future of this town, big brother.

Frank He's the king of the rackets. King for a day, most like, there's been a high turnover in political hoodlums here.

Julian Cultivate him. I'm going out. See you later.

Exit via the street. **Frank** *removes the ladder, then seats himself again at* **Daisy**'s *bike.* **Kitty** *appears in the room, dressed as an old woman, her hair white and in a bun. She is carrying a tray containing three plates of sausage and mash, cutlery and salt. She lays the table with these.*

Kitty Food's on the table, young man.

Frank Coming. (*But he stays put.*)

Kitty (*calling off*) Eating has commenced, Francis.

Francis (*off*) I'm on my way down.

Kitty (*sitting down*) Your grandfather's writing his memoirs.

Frank Again?

Kitty His memory keeps improving, he says. So he fills in more and more details.

Frank Was my father like him?

Kitty Maybe to look at, but not so far as character went. A wild and wayward young man was our Bobby. If I didn't know better, I'd swear that Julian took after him.

Frank If my parents adopted Julian ... why couldn't you give him back?

Kitty Frank! Never let me hear another remark the like of that. Julian is your only brother.

Frank He's no brother of mine.

Kitty He's your brother and your equal in the eyes of God. And when your grandfather and I are gone, this building and business will be shared between the two of you and you'll be held responsible to each other. Do you hear me? (*Enter* **Francis**.)

Francis It was Flossie's eczema! (*Pause.*) The cat. Flossie.

Frank What about my mother?

Kitty Your mother was a beautiful child, as innocent as the day is long. Whose cat?

Francis Our family cat.

Frank She didn't have much of a life, then.

Francis God sometimes loves the young and fair so much, Frank, that he takes them unto himself.

Kitty Sentimental twaddle. They were killed by a German bomb. If Ireland had been a united country it wouldn't have been dropped. (*Short pause.*) There was never a cat called Flossie in this house.

Francis No, no, she was my mother's cat. I'd been trying to remember. Then it suddenly came to me – just a few moments ago – Flossie's eczema.

Kitty What about it?

Frank That was how he came to meet Dunlop!

Francis I remember the day vividly now. I arrived back from a spin to Comber, I walked in flushed and famished – Francis, says Mother, you're taking Flossie straight to that animal doctor in Gloucester Street. I want to hear no more excuses. Ten minutes later I was sitting in the surgery, most disgruntled, with Flossie creating inside the basket, in the full Belfast Cruisers' Club regalia.

Kitty Brown Norfolk jacket.

Frank And the green cap with the yellow tassel. Hello – you're a wheel man, I see. Those were the first words he spoke.

Francis He was a very reserved softspoken man – Scottish, you see. Thoughtful. But even at that age I could sense right away the reserves of wisdom. Foresight. Something told me even then as I watched him examining Flossie's flank that here was a great man.

Frank Why great? He was just another small-time capitalist with a bright idea.

Kitty That'll do.

Frank Well – that's what you always say too.

Kitty Expressions such as 'small-time' form no part of my vocabulary.

Francis You see, it's hard for you to realise, Frank – but the wonderful things we take for granted today didn't always exist. The pneumatic tyre changed the course of human history.

Frank The name of that obscure Caledonian animal doctor is today a household word throughout the length and breadth of the land.

Francis What's your mount? he said. What do you ride?

Kitty   You were still on your Rudge-Whitworth
Ordinary then.

Francis   No – I'd only just bought my Beeston-
Humber Safety. For racing on. Fast enough machine? he
asked. Not bad – could never be fast enough for me, I
said. I'd never come in higher than fifth in a race, and
even that was because the two leaders collided and took
imperial crowners. Supposing you could ride on air, he
said suddenly. Just like that. His eyes on me.
Penetrating. Supposing you could ride on air. (*Pause.*)

Frank   It wasn't even as if he made a fortune out of
it.

Francis   He sold the patent to Harvey DuCros, moved
to Dublin, opened a drapery shop in a Dublin suburb.

Kitty *and* **Frank**   Ballsbridge.

Francis (*standing up*)   Before Dunlop, the bicycle was a
lusty fledgling. After him, it was a strong-pinioned bird.
I had the extraordinary good fortune to be the man
who proved him right. And all because of Flossie's
eczema! (*Exit.*)

Frank   Did he make it all up?

Kitty   Are you asking me whether your grandfather is
a liar?

Frank   It's just that he made it all sound like the
pictures.

Kitty (*clearing dishes onto tray*)   He has a gift for telling
the truth with a certain flair. (*Exit with tray.*)

Frank   Love, war and the bicycle ... the gist of their
lives ... mine too. My love, my war, my bicycle.

Daisy *comes into the shop. He goes through to meet her.*

Daisy   Well, slacker?

Frank   Well, princess?

Daisy   Resplendent amidst the ruins.

Frank   They call me the Phoenix Kid.

Daisy   You've been talking to yourself again.

Frank   Thinking out loud. What'll it be tonight? The pictures or the pub? Sex or violence?

Daisy   I've made a decision. (*Short pause.*)

Frank   Come with me to the whiskey bottle. (*He leads the way to the table in the room and sets out drinks.*) I know it won't be favourable because it hasn't been my day this year.

Daisy   I'm clearing out, that's all.

Frank   I was right. (*Short pause.*) Don't go, Daisy.

Daisy   I've handed in my notice. I'm leaving at the end of next week.

Frank   How about taking me with you?

Daisy   Not a chance. You live here.

Frank   Would you marry me if I went?

Daisy   No comment. We're just good friends.

Frank   I'd like to know, kid.

Daisy   Don't expect to hear it from me, well. I don't believe in emotional blackmail. Especially when it's invited. This is your natural habitat.

Frank   Yours too.

Daisy   Not any more.

Frank   I'm still sold on you, Daisy. More than ever. Smitten for life.

Daisy   You know, I'll swear you learned to talk in the front stalls of the Regal cinema.

Frank   It was the Alhambra, actually . . . (*Pause.*)

Daisy What do you think'll happen to the shop?

Frank If the bombers don't get it, the planners will.
Between the devil and the deep. Two kinds of madness.

Daisy What'll you do if it goes?

Frank Future conditional – I'm not too fluent in that.
Re-open somewhere else, I suppose. *You* could make a
go of this business, you know. Introduce some order and
method into it. All this nervous energy of yours.

Daisy Nobody could make a go of this business. Good
God, in a building scheduled for demolition. Bombs
going off all round you. Selling a product that went out
of fashion twenty years ago.

Frank You can't have everything.

Daisy I believe my da was round to see you.

Frank He sends his regards.

Daisy If he shows up again, let me know. I don't
mind blackmailing him. (*Pause.*)

Frank I don't get it, Daisy. You were so full of
concern. The peace meetings, the marches – you've
been hammering away at me for not doing enough to
stop the fighting. What's happened?

Daisy I found out the truth about this country at last.
It's all granite, all the way through – a great flat thick
slab of granite. Oh, there's a rich vein of humanity in it,
no doubt. But it's not worth quarrying, Frank. It's too
narrow and too damned shallow.

Frank Good words, kid. By God, they're needed.
You're needed.

Daisy You think so . . . just what Ireland needs most,
another stirring speech. (*She stands up and turns away a
moment.*) I was coming home from school today and I
met a child from the backward class, the hopeless ones.

He had a mongrel dog that used to follow him
backwards and forwards to school. He'd been attacked
by a gang of the other crowd. They'd hung the dog to
a lamp-post and set fire to it. (*She sits down again.*) It
won't make the newscasts or the press bulletins – it can
scarcely compete with the latest hooded corpse or pub
massacre. But that child's soul has been butchered. As
surely as if they'd taken a meat cleaver to him. This is
the day he'll remember. When he's putting a bullet into
somebody else. There are thousands like him. Too
many, Frank. (*He pours her a drink and hands it to her.*)

Frank   Here. (*She drinks.*) God knows it's a brutal hole,
kid.

Daisy   I hadn't any plans to say all this. It tends to
blurt itself out.

Frank   Every word's true. The place is poison. It's
been building up in the system for generations, and now
the boil has burst. You can't stop it, it's everywhere,
even in your own veins. Bad blood. But that's just the
snag. You can't get away from it. You just carry it
round with you. It *is* you.

Daisy   At least you can get away from having to eat it
and drink it every day.

Frank   It's a plague. It'll work itself through like every
other plague.

Daisy   Never in an age, and you know it. It'll simmer
down again for a few years. Then there'll be another
eruption. Somebody else can dignify it with the name of
history and ram it down children's throats. I'm out.

Frank   For good?

Daisy   Once I make the move, I won't go back on it.

Frank   Where to?

Daisy   London. Julian has offered me a room

in his flat.

Frank (*after a moment*)   This is the blow that brings a man to his knees, kid.

Daisy   It's convenient. (*She looks at him.*) Maybe it isn't fair to you, Frank, it probably isn't fair to him. Doubtless it isn't fair to me either. To hell with all three of us. (*She drinks.*)

Frank   You're doing the wrong thing, Daisy. You're doing violence to yourself.

Daisy   Don't preach to me. I do not want to hear any more bicycle philosophy. I do not want another piece of cranky wisdom or dogmatic idealism. You're a lovable man, Frank. But try being muddled and normal for a while. Try riding your damn bike out into the real world. I'm going, I'll be in again to say goodbye.

Frank   You can't just leave me floundering, kid.

Daisy   I'll see you.

Exit. He stands dumbstruck for a moment, then walks downstage to the work space with the bottle. He sits down, makes as if to work, swigs from the bottle, and begins to sing an unaccompanied lament:

Frank
    The maiden with her wheel of old
    Sat by the fire to spin
    While lightly through her careful hold
    The flax slid out and in . . .

(*Speaks.*) Fighting Kitty Carberry. The scourge of the British Empire. A queen amongst Republicans.

(*Sings.*)
    Today her distaff flax and reel
    Far out of sight are hurled
    And now the maiden with her wheel
    Goes spinning round the world . . .

Julian *has entered the shop quietly; he comes downstage and stands over* **Frank** *during the next lines.*

Frank (*speaks*)   She was seventy-nine when she died. She still rode her tricycle up to three months before the end.

Julian   You still miss them.

Frank   Deeply.

Julian   You're a liar to yourself, Frank. They weren't in the smallest degree like that. Your memory's an entire school of romantic fiction.

Frank   It's not a question of remembering. They are me. A big part of me. You too.

Julian   He was a vain and obsequious little Ulster tradesman, a crank and a bore, going over and over the same dog-eared tales of his youth and his war experiences.

Frank   Let's drop it.

Julian   She was a spoiled daughter of the regiment, slumming it in the quaint back-streets and in her ridiculous lace-curtain nationalism.

Frank   Don't try to reduce them to your own withered clichés.

Julian   You can't go on escaping, Frank. The world and his ugly wife are beating on the door.

Frank   What did I ever do to deserve you, Julian.

Julian   Look at yourself. Hunkered down in this . . . blocked-up latrine of your own memories. That's what memories are, big brother, that's what the past is, history, the accumulated turds of human endeavour. I don't like it, I'm a cleanly fellow. It has to come down, the whole edifice, brick by brick. Wiped. Flushed.

Frank   Have you not learned anything at all? You *are*

your own past, kid. You're the sum total of its parts.
Hate it and you hate yourself. No matter how
calamitous it may have been, either you master it or you
die.

Julian   One last round for humanistic aphorisms.

Frank   Why the hell did you bother coming back at
all?

Julian   To sell the shop. (*Pause.*)

Frank   What?

Julian   I've sold the shop.

Frank   You can't do that.

Julian   Your lease has run out, Frank.

Frank   I'm not tolerating this.

Julian   It was their will, chew on that. Frankie gets the
bikes and Julie gets the bed and board, a house divided
against itself. They were heart-scared I'd fall into a life
of crime. So long as he has a place to come back to
and a bob in his pocket . . .

Frank   It's one thing for it to fall in the path of a
bomb or a bulldozer. One of them's bound to strike it
sooner or later. That's like an act of God. But I won't
allow you to sell out their shop.

Julian   They're over twenty years dead, Frank, it's
mine to sell.

Frank   If it's a bigger rent you want, I'll pay it.

Julian   Money's no object.

Frank   It's market value is next to nothing.

Julian   It went for a song. Which was the asking price.
(*Slight pause.*)

Frank   Who to?

Julian   Duncan Bell. He wants it for a headquarters.

Pause. **Frank** *picks up the frame of* **Daisy***'s bike and pitches it into the middle of the shop.*

Julian (*edging to the door*)   That's my boy.

Frank   You're next.

Julian   Remember your code. Non-violence.

Frank   I only mean to chastise you.

Julian   Rejoice, Frank, say thank you. I've launched you on a great new trip, you're cycling out of the past into the future.

Frank   In his womb he took his brother by the heel, and in his manhood he strove with God. Who crippled him.

He moves toward **Julian***, who makes a sudden dash through the door and along the street. He runs headlong into the* **Trick Cyclist***, who has appeared in an overcoat and soft hat.*

Trick Cyclist   Steady, son.

Julian   Excuse me.

Trick Cyclist   Hold fast, I want a wee word with you. (*Slight pause.*)

Julian   Who are you?

Frank (*in doorway*)   What's up, Gus?

Trick Cyclist   Is it yourself, Frankie?

Frank   That's my kid brother, Julian.

Trick Cyclist   I know he is, indeed.

Frank   He's been over staying with me.

Trick Cyclist   We just want to talk to him about a wee matter.

Julian   What the hell do you mean?

Trick Cyclist Go you over to the jeep there and identify yourself to the sergeant.

Julian Not before I hear from you . . .

Frank Do what he says. Go on. (*Exit* **Julian**.) Come in, Gus. (*They enter the shop*.)

Trick Cyclist The thing is – I'm sorry, Frankie, but we had a wee look over your premises last night. (*Slight pause . . .*)

Frank You didn't ask me, Gus.

Trick Cyclist Now when I say we, I'm not meaning the lads down in the station and me. The Army. Nothing missing, I hope.

Frank I haven't looked. I didn't know.

Trick Cyclist Now just you lodge a complaint if there is. They get away with blue murder, them squaddies.

Frank That's been my impression, too.

Trick Cyclist The thing is – they found something.

Frank They what?

Trick Cyclist Incriminating documents.

Frank Holy Christ.

Trick Cyclist They were going to lift you, but I told them – it's the brother, isn't it?

Frank What documents?

Trick Cyclist He's a bad boy, Frankie. He's prone to mischief.

Frank Our Julian? He's harmless. A bit wild and wayward, maybe, but nothing more.

Trick Cyclist Would you vouch for him?

Frank   Certainly. (*Slight pause.*) His holiday's nearly over, anyway. He's going back to London soon.

Trick Cyclist   He keeps odd company.

Frank   That's not in breach of any law, Gus.

Trick Cyclist   It's not the law he's up against. The thing is – it's really out of my hands.

Frank   What'll happen?

Trick Cyclist   They might slap an interim custody order on him. I'll do what I can, Frankie, have no fear.

Frank   I'll stay in touch.

Trick Cyclist   Do indeed. It'll maybe come to nothing.

Exit. **Frank** *goes back into the shop, puts the frame of* **Daisy**'s *bike back on its stand and begins distractedly to reassemble the other bits and pieces as he speaks.*

Frank   If everybody who could ride one ... had access to one ... the city might be secure. It's just a suggestion. It's not a solution. It's just an idea. You can't despair for the human race ... when you see somebody riding a bicycle. (*He sits on the stool.*) Ah, forget it, kid.

As he starts to work, the 'Army Song' music strikes up. The **Trick Cyclist** *rides on in his own gear, ushering* **Francis** *on behind him with a flourish.* **Francis** *is wearing his Cruisers' Club jacket and badge, and is pushing an 1889 racing model.*

Trick Cyclist (*sings to tune of 'Army Song'*)
We're up to here in mud, Ma,
Like piggies in a sty,
The mud is in the tea, Ma,
So here's mud in your eye –

We're muddling through the mud, Ma,
We're mucking through the rain,
The mud's gone down the hatch, Ma,

The mud is on the brain.

He settles down to observe.

Frank   I'm deep in it myself, Francis, up over the knees. There's no riding on air now. I'm straddling a somewhat tougher frame of reference.

Francis   It was the rain that did for us. It turned the roads directly to mud, you see. You just bogged down or else your machine seized up and you were forced to carry it, an easy target. The craters were worst. They'd fill up with mud so you couldn't see them. Several chaps in our company rode headlong into them and drowned. You were sucked down, there was no way to get them out.

Frank   It's not just the same as it was for you. There's no simple enemy. There's no Back Home. No Boche. And no Blighty.

Francis   I remember once seeing – in 1917 – a case of forty brand new bicycles – unridden. They'd only been delivered that week. The town was being evacuated. They were lying out in the open, in the rain and the mud, slowly turning into a mass of rusted metal. I found myself crying . . .

Frank   I don't see any future for an advocate of cycling in this town.

Francis   It's healthier not to remember those things – best to blot them from your mind. Concentrate on life's forward march . . . supposing you could ride on air . . . those were his words . . .

Frank   I don't know what to do, Granda. I'm lost for something to do. I'm lost for words. I'm lost.

Francis   He took me through to the garden and showed me his son's tricycle. I was transfixed. Thunderstruck. How would you like to be my guinea-pig, he said. I'll have pneumatic tyres fitted to your

steed, and you try them at the next race. There was a
trophy race coming up at the end of the month. Can
you do it? I asked. Yes, he could.

Frank   You've told me this before, kid. I've heard it.

Francis   It was a major event. Bentley came from
Liverpool, he was the favourite. Randolph from
Harrogate. Several Dublin riders.

Frank   Nobody noticed you at first.

Francis   Nobody noticed me at first, until they saw the
tyres. They were very fat and held on with wire. Arthur
DuCros was the first to spot them, his father was
already a big business power in the land. What's this, he
says, I don't think German sausage is allowed in this
race. Well, of course, it was a huge joke. Our Club
Captain was infuriated and tried to order me off the
course. I stood firm, though. Then we lined up. The
race started. I pedalled a few times – and then the
machine seemed to gain a life of its own. It soared
forward, it sang like an arrow, my breath left me, I was
out in front on my own, my ears were roaring, still it
went faster, I was hurtling towards the finish soundlessly
– and then I had won!

The **Trick Cyclist** *ushers on* **Kitty**, *dressed in the militant
garb of an 1890s bicycle-poster heroine, and striking the
appropriate pose with her machine.*

Kitty   Let us salute the instrument of our potential
freedom – Ireland's freedom and Woman's freedom!
The day is not far off when the tyrant on horseback will
vanish from the face of rural Ireland.

Frank   In the name of Jesus . . .

Kitty   This is the steed upon which the dispossessed
will come into their inheritance at last. The housewife
going to market – the priest attending his flock – the
young man riding to meet his beloved!

Frank (*as he lurches to his feet, he overturns the bicycle frame and tools*)   May the God of strong drink deliver me! (*He rushes out, followed stealthily by the* **Trick Cyclist**.)

Francis   There was a dinner that evening in the club rooms, they called on me to speak.

Kitty   A woman who has tasted the intoxicating freedom of the bicycle will never again torment her body with corseting, or suffocate it with skirts. She will hold at last her destiny in her own two hands!

Francis   Gentlemen, I said – I give you Mr John B. Dunlop, for his momentous contribution to our sportsmen, our industry, our armed forces, and so to the greater glory of our Queen, our Empire and our God!

Music.

The Anthem.

Kitty *and* **Francis** (*sing*)
    Hark, the bells are proudly ringing
    All the people rise as one
    And their shining chains are singing
    To the rising of the sun . . .

Daisy *has entered and is knocking at the door, calling 'Frank!' and peering in. She considers for a moment, then leans against the door and lights a cigarette.*

Kitty *and* **Francis**
    . . . for we share a common wheel
    Made of brightly tempered steel,
    Riding side by side
    In an ever-swelling tide,
    Companions, good companions,
    Companions of the common wheel!

The music ends. They have frozen into emblematic figures.

Daisy (*sings quietly to herself*)
    Hushabye, my fallen angel,

Dry your eyes and raise your face,
We are all just running level
In the losing of the race.
For we share a common weal,
A hidden wound that will not heal,
Wings bereft of flight,
Children crying in the night . . .

Julian *appears.*

Julian   I was just about to look for you. We'll have to leave tonight.

Daisy   What do you mean 'we'? You and your other face, is it?

Julian *(studies her for a moment)*   I've got a feeling we're on the verge of a big scene. *(He strikes a mock-dramatic pose.)* 'The Wronged Woman.'

Daisy   Where's Frank?

Julian   Isn't he at home?

Daisy   Not unless he's gassed himself.

Julian *(searching his pockets)*   Damn. The key's gone. I mustn't have picked it up after the search.

Daisy   What search?

Julian   The Army lifted me.

Daisy   That was unusually intelligent of them, did they offer any reason?

Julian   Reading people's pamphlets. It's a crime here, it seems. I should be inside by now.

Daisy   Why aren't you?

Julian   The captain in the barracks turned out to be old Shorty Frizzell. We went to school together.

Daisy   So he let you go, just like that?

Julian We have a gentleman's agreement that I transport myself back across the water at the first opportunity.

Daisy That suits you down to the ground, doesn't it. No doubt you carefully set it up, along with everything else.

Julian I *was* expecting it, sooner or later.

Daisy How obliging of it to fulfil your expectations.

Julian How's your father?

Daisy We're coming to that.

Julian I thought we might be.

Daisy You're standing out in the light now, Julian. I can see clean through you. (*Pause.*)

Julian Well, I'm waiting. Aren't you supposed to say next, 'You've just been using me for your own selfish ends'?

Daisy Hold on, lover. Maybe there's a twist you didn't expect. Maybe you can't set everything up.

Julian Save it for the girls in the lower fourth – Miss Bell. If you're coming with me, let's go. If not – cheers.

Daisy No, it won't be that easy for you. I know you hate smudging your clean jacket and getting dirt in your fingernails, but too bad, Julian. You should have learnt in that case to stay out of other people's lives.

Julian Anything but another moralising lecture . . .

Daisy You can quit the condescension now, it's threadbare. We're talking straight. You're a worse casualty than your brother, you know. Bang goes the country, bang goes Frank, and you sail triumphantly home to Hampstead with the girl . . . it doesn't work that way, Julian. The world's not that methodical. Selling the shop to my da is just not a blow for the revolution, I'm afraid.

Julian I'm sure there's a reason for all this – maybe you're having your period? (*Pause.*)

Daisy That's what you'd like, isn't it – wind-up people. Everything explained away. So if somebody doesn't work the way you want, you can just sweep them into the bin with all the other broken toys.

Julian This stuff must go down well with the girls in your Social Studies class . . .

Daisy Shut your face. (*She turns away.*) God only knows how this hell-hole will ever redeem itself. But we'll start by dealing with the people the way they really are. In all their sweet reason as well as their depravity. It's time for you and your brother both to look around you and act wise. There'll be no fresh start with a nice clean sheet – not for this city and not for you either. You're coming with me.

Julian Where to, the headmaster's study?

Daisy First to find Frank and then to see my dear old dad. (*She starts off.*) What's keeping you?

He shrugs and follows her off. Pause. From offstage, **Frank** *is heard approaching, drunkenly singing 'Daisy, Daisy'. He appears at the door, drunkenly supported by the* **Trick Cyclist**.

Frank Sssh! Kitty and Franny don't know we're here. First we surprise them. Then we extinguish them. (*He flings open the door and leaps in.*) Boo! I give you Speedo, the magician and exterminator extraordinary who will now demonstrate the amazing and impossible feat of putting the dead to bed. (*The* **Trick Cyclist** *approaches* **Kitty**, *holds up his hands before her, and makes a quick gesture.*) Presto shazam! Before your very eyes and nose. (*The light has faded and* **Kitty** *recedes into the darkness.*) And yet again . . . (*The* **Trick Cyclist** *repeats the act on* **Francis**, *who similarly fades away.*) Bazoom! Goodnight, Francis, you

needn't have waited up for me. I have been taken into
the protection of a gentleman beyond price, mute of
tongue and deaf of ear ... who for his next trick will
produce from his very own person ... spirituous liquors
... glug, glug. (*He mimes drinking to the* **Trick Cyclist**,
*who shows comprehension, and produces bottles of beer from his
coat pockets.*) ... How does he do it, you tell me, kid ...
listen, listen ... pull up a lump of shrapnel and sit down
... (*The* **Trick Cyclist** *has opened the beers and given him
one.*) ... (He hears not, neither does he speak.) ...
(Twice blessed.) ... (But he always stands his round.) ...
herewith, An Ode! Intimations of Negativity in Late
Childhood. (*The* **Trick Cyclist** *strikes a poetic pose, and
during the rest of the speech he performs a running commentary in
mime.*) ... I am Frank Stock, Spokesman and Jokesman
... (late late childhood, I'll be thirty-nine next month)
... a man of great moral fibrositis. You see around you
here, my friend, the nub and hub of my former
existence. Say what you like ... the bicycle has a great
past ahead of it ... Listen to this, when I was a small
kid ... this is where all the parents used to come, to
buy their kids bikes ... for Christmas and passing
exams, mostly. So I always knew who was getting a bike
in my class at school ... and the colour and the make
and everything else ... and I used to tell them for
sixpence. (*He chortles.*) The Elementary School Oracle ...
short of living in a sweetie factory, they could not
conceive of any place closer to paradise than a bicycle
shop. But the ones I told hated me because I'd robbed
them of the pleasure of surprise ... and the ones I
didn't tell hated me even more ... because they knew I
knew anyway. What none of them ever realised was ...
that I didn't give a curse about bikes. I could take my
pick of dozens of them ... it was no treat to me. (*Pause.*)
So that's how I came to be a pacifist, a philosopher and
a lone wolf by the age of seven. (*His eye falls on the frame
of* **Daisy**'s *bike lying on the ground.*) Aha! Why look'st thou
so? ... with my crossbow ... I shot the albatross. (*He*

picks the frame up and drapes it round his neck.) It's like this, kid ... there's breakers and there's bouncers. Daisy breaks, I bounce. Except I think I've lost my elasticity. Bounce, bounce, bounce, crack. How's your elasticity? (*He drinks. The* **Trick Cyclist** *bounces and cracks.* **Julian** *and* **Daisy** *appear on the street and* **Julian** *knocks at the door. Unhearing,* **Frank** *continues.*) But it's all past tense now. Blood under the bridge. This property is condemned. What I want to know is ... your past ... the past, I'm talking about ... the air's full of it ... you have to breathe it ... but you can't grab hold of it ... you see what I'm saying ... it's everywhere but you can't locate it ... you see where I'm driving ... how can something that's fundamental ... be irrecoverable ... and uncontrollable ... answer me that ... you take the point ... how are you supposed to live? (**Daisy** *knocks at the door.*)

Daisy   Do you think he's in the land of the living?

Julian (*calls softly*)   Frank.

Frank (*still unhearing, speaking very close to the* **Trick Cyclist**)   Answer me that. How. Tell me that one. (*The* **Trick Cyclist** *draws back and makes incomprehensible sign language.*) What? (*More sign language.*) I can't hear you. (*Still more.*) You're too drunk. You're incoherent. Your hands are slurred. (*The* **Trick Cyclist** *puts his hands in his pockets, smiles, holds a shrug and recedes towards the door.*) Ach, what's the odds ... the heart's nothing but a pump ... the world's only a wheel bearing ... God's a bad trick cycling act.

Silence. **Daisy** *knocks again. The* **Trick Cyclist** *whips open the door.* **Daisy** *enters the shop, followed by* **Julian**.

Daisy   Frank – why did you not answer the door?

Frank   I've gone out and I don't think I'm expected back.

Julian   He's polluted.

Daisy Are you all right?

Frank You won't believe it, Daisy . . . but underneath this burly unkempt frame there's a wasted heartbroken sniveller. How did he get here?

Daisy The Army let him go. On condition that he clear out of the country.

Frank Bon voyage then, Daisy.

Daisy I'm afraid I'm staying, Frank. I've decided to buy the shop. (*Pause.* **Julian** *moves off to collect his belongings.*) Some credit's due to him. He reduced the price to my kind of level.

Julian It's what they call a knockdown price. (*Exit.*)

Frank Your father . . .

Daisy No problem. I've threatened to turn him in if he doesn't let me have it. I know enough about him to put him away for the rest of his life. (*Pause.*) There'll have to be changes, Frank.

Frank There's been some already, kid.

Daisy I'm intending to live on the premises. This place is an utter disgrace, look at it.

Frank I can think of a few ideas for improving business.

Daisy I've thought of more than a few myself. (*Slight pause.*)

Frank You haven't . . . by any chance . . . reconsidered . . .

Daisy No wedding bells, Frank. I'm not being responsible for another child growing up in this town. Without kids there's no point. All that's on offer is me and my shop. You look all in.

Frank I know I badly need something, but it can't be

a drink.

Daisy Is that *my* bicycle frame you're wearing?

Frank I believe it is.

Daisy There'll definitely have to be changes round here, Frank. It's near time that job was finished.

Frank What would you say to a new model?

Daisy So long as we can afford it.

Frank It'll be the best of value. (*He starts off.*) Wait right there. (*Off.*) I have it all ready. (*He re-emerges minus the frame and pushing a tandem.*)

Daisy You great clown.

Frank Would this be satisfactory?

Daisy I'll give it a whirl. (*Music. She climbs on to the front seat, and he takes the rear.*) Let's go.

They cycle off. The piano continues. The **Trick Cyclist**, *who has remained beside the door all this time, watching the scene with interest, moves to behind the counter.* **Julian** *re-enters with his baggage and heads for the door. The* **Trick Cyclist** *rings open the till.* **Julian** *goes to it, takes the money out of it and pockets it. The* **Trick Cyclist** *moves round the counter.*

Trick Cyclist (*sings*)
   I will stand by you in wheel or woe,
   Daisy, Daisy . . .

Julian (*sings*)
   You'll be the belle which I'll ring, you know,
   Sweet little Daisy Bell . . .

Trick Cyclist
   You'll take the lead in each trip we take . . .

Julian
   Then if I don't do well . . .

Trick Cyclist

I will permit you to use the brake . . .

Both

My beautiful Daisy Bell . . .

Exit **Julian**.

Trick Cyclist

Daisy, Daisy,
Give me your answer do,
I'm half crazy
All for the love of you,
It won't be a stylish marriage,
I can't afford a carriage,
But you'll look sweet
Upon the seat
Of a bicycle built for two.

Catchpenny Twist

A charade in two acts

For Kate

Catchpenny Twist was first performed at the Peacock Theatre, Dublin, on 25 August 1977, with the following cast:

Martyn Semple	Desmond Cave
Roy Fletcher	Raymond Hardie
Monagh Cahoon	Deirdre Donnelly
Marie Kyle	Ingrid Craigie
Man *who between them*	Des Keogh
Woman *play all the other*	Billie Morton
Girl *parts*	Fiona MacAnna

Directed by Patrick Laffan
Designed by Wendy Shea
Lighting by Tony Wakefield
Music by Shaun Davey
Lyrics by Stewart Parker

Act One

School Hall. Music. **Roy**, **Martyn** *and* **Monagh** *stride on in a follow spot, holding each others' waists, dressed in gowns and mortar-boards.*

Roy, **Martyn** *and* **Monagh** (*sing*)
  Pack up your bags, pack up your books
  Get off to where the sunshine really cooks
  The dream boat's leaving
  The magic carpet's weaving
  Over the Assembly Hall
  Round the boundary wall.

  Pick up your fags, pick up your feet
  We'll soon be on our way to Easy Street
  The steamboat's puffing
  The gravy train is chuffing
  So go wherever Destiny awaits thee –
  And you can't go soon enough
  No you can't go soon enough
  You can't go soon enough for me!

They take a bow. The **Man** *– as a Headmaster – sweeps on, arm extended towards them.*

Man Our fiddlers three, the masters and mistress of terpischore and rhyme, give them a bit of a hand now! (*He leads the clapping.*) Come on, show grateful, hands out of pockets for once in the year! (*Gestures abruptly for applause to cease.*) It's in that proper spirit of appreciation and indeed gratitude for where would we be in these dark days of strife without an occasional quip and a jolly snatch of song on our lips to lift the heart and quicken the step ... that's the spirit as I say in which as always on these end-of-term occasions of frolic that I extend an emphatic thank-you in all our behalf from the whole school, to Miss Cahoon, Mr Semple and Mr Fletcher, for their mirthful mouthfuls and their witty ditties! Now

it only remains for me to wish you all a happy holiday
– an industrious holiday – and above all a well-
conducted holiday, for I don't want to be reading any of
your names in the headlines this summer, I have no
wish to see the good name of the school being dragged
through the courts of law yet again and especially not in
connection with guns and explosives! Right. Dismiss.

Blackout.

Classroom. Raucous laughter from **Monagh** *and* **Martyn** *is
heard in the darkness. They are seen, as the fluorescent lighting
flickers on, removing their gowns and mortar-boards.* **Roy** *is
opening a bottle of champagne.*

Roy   It didn't turn out the way I thought it would.

Monagh   No post-mortems, please, we got through it.

Roy   Fell through it, more like.

Martyn   You could sing that, you know. If you had a
tune to it. Falling Through . . . a song for horny
window-cleaners.

Roy *pops the cork and pours the champagne into glasses.*

Monagh   A fine young sparkling cider, I suppose?

Roy   Do you mind – it's the genuine article.

Martyn   'The true, the blushful Hippocrene, winking
at the brim.'

Roy   You both owe me for it.

Monagh (*to* **Martyn**)   So young and yet so profligate!

Roy   It's scandalously over-priced.

Martyn   What the hell – Happy Anniversary. (*He
drinks.*)

Monagh   Mud in your eye. (*Drinks.*)

Roy Absent friend. (*Drinks.*)

Monagh Thanks, that's real cheery. Enter the ghost at the banquet. (*To* **Martyn**.) Have you seen her recently?

Martyn She's been up in court. Possession of a dangerous weapon. With intent to endanger life. Why do they say that? You would hardly have it to hammer in nails with.

Monagh You've got to hand it to Marie Kyle, raving mad as she is. At least she has the courage of her convictions.

Martyn She hasn't had a conviction yet, the judge let her go.

Roy (*to* **Martyn**) You're a tonic, you know that?

Monagh All we ever shoot off is our mouths.

Roy We?

Monagh Yes. We . . . you and him and me. We're still here, aren't we? After seven years? Still stuck in the same hole? Enjoying our seventh annual end-of-term frolic? Christ, just look at this school. It's a clapped-out shell. It's a jerry-built seven-year-old ruin. You could punch your way out through the walls.

Martyn Most of the third-year kids already have.

Monagh Right, they're out in the streets fighting a war, and what am I doing? Teaching the rest of them to sing 'The Skye Boat Song'.

Roy I know what you're saying, it's age. I saw a girl in the playground this afternoon. She wasn't in her school uniform. She was in a suede skirt. Talk about lubricious . . . I'd never clapped eyes on the like of it. And then I suddenly realised – it wasn't a girl at all. It was a girl's mother. (*He reflects.*) I never would have believed that it would come to that. Fancying the mothers.

Monagh Is this the best you can manage? Middle-aged lechery?

Roy We should have done the strip number.

Monagh Oh certainly – with me flying kamikaze and you two on the ground crew.

Roy By God that would have put ould Cochrane's nose out of joint, all the same.

Martyn More than his nose. (*Imitating the headmaster.*) Come on come on hands out of pockets for once in the year! (*He has a hand thrust in his trouser pocket to suggest an erection.*)

Monagh You've been repeating this every year for seven years now. My God, think of it. Seven of them. Think of what's been happening to this country. It's clean passed us by. We're not even relevant.

Roy Who needs it? All I want is out.

Martyn None of us ever intended to be teachers, remember?

Monagh I can't even say I've been unhappy. There's nothing as definite as that. Whenever I think it over, when I weigh it up moment by moment – it all seems as good as you can expect. But if I look back on a week or a month – it always turns out to be as bad as you can get. Like as if the best you can say about anything is – it could be worse. It could be worse. What kind of an epitaph is that?

Martyn 'It could have *been* worse.'

Monagh What?

Martyn For an epitaph you would need to say 'It could have *been* worse.'

Monagh Wanker!

Roy Take it easy.

Monagh I'm trying to express despair and he gives me English grammar!

Roy This summer – Fletcher and Semple make the big break.

Monagh . . . and only at the seventh attempt, listeners.

Roy We've got experience behind us now. Three songs in professional circulation.

Monagh Don't forget to call in and show me your Oscar.

Roy At least we've got plans. What are your plans?

Monagh I'm still making plans for my twenty-first birthday party. You might not remember, but I came down with shingles two days before it.

Martyn I remember that. I sent you Polaroid photographs of Marie and me singing Happy Birthday.

Monagh I still haven't decided what to wear. Perhaps the Lurex halter top and the green silk harem pants . . . set off by a polished emerald in the navel . . .

Roy *begins to vocalise some strip-tease music, clapping his hands.* **Martyn** *joins in.* **Monagh** *goes into a half-parodied strip routine. As the tempo increases, the drums join in.* **Martyn** *and* **Roy** *are on their knees. When* **Monagh** *is down to her underclothes, the headmaster suddenly enters wearing an appalled expression. They freeze. Silence. Blackout.*

Street. **Marie Kyle** *and the* **Woman**, *in raincoats, are standing studying a copy of the* Irish News.

Marie There you are. Deaths. Three columns all to himself. It's a credit to you to have borne a son like that.

Woman It would have made him very proud. He was a good Catholic boy and never did a wrong thing to nobody.

Marie He died a patriot's death and it'll never be forgotten.

Woman God bless you, Marie. I'll take this home and clip it out to keep.

Martyn *has appeared, walking towards them, holding up an open umbrella.*

Martyn Hello, Marie.

Woman I'm away, love, I'll be seeing you.

Marie Yes indeed, bye-bye.

The **Woman** *goes off.*

Marie What are you doing out of school at this hour?

Martyn I got the sack.

Marie You never did.

Martyn Roy and Monagh as well. All three of us. We were just horsing around after the end-of-term revue. When in walks Cochrane. And that was it. Curtains.

Marie You were never that serious about teaching, were you?

Martyn It was a job.

Marie You were never too serious about anything.

Martyn One or two things, Marie. You and the night and the music.

The **Man** *and* **Girl**, *as a military police patrol, have appeared and are approaching them.*

Marie Kiss me.

Martyn What?

She pulls his free arm round her shoulders, embraces him tightly and kisses him. The **Man** *and* **Girl** *pass by them, smiling, the*

Man *whistling softly at them, and stroll off.*

Marie (*disengaging abruptly*)   Sorry about that.

Martyn   Don't be sorry.

Marie   Those English bastards have photographs of me now.

Martyn   Is that why you've dyed your hair?

Marie   It's easier if you're a man, you can grow a beard.

Martyn   It looks nice that way.

Slight pause.

Marie   What will you do now?

Martyn   We're living on the dole. Trying to write songs.

Marie   Any luck?

Martyn   In this town? You're joking.

Marie   I might be able to put some work your way.

Martyn   You?

Marie   Ever try writing ballads?

Martyn   You mean street ballads? Come-all-ye's? Sure they're traditional, nobody writes those.

Marie   Traditions need to be maintained. (*She starts to walk off.*) It's worth thirty pounds a throw, if you're interested at all.

Martyn   Tell me more.

He follows her. They go off together. Music.

Stage. A spot appears on the **Woman** *standing at a microphone as a folk-singer, in a mantilla and green peasant-style dress.*

Behind her is a large Sacred Heart portrait of Jesus.

Woman (*sings*)
  He came forth in some poor hovel
  With the livestock close at hand
  But his mother smiles upon him
  He was born for Ireland

  In his father's holy temple
  He was forced to make a stand
  He drove out the money-changers
  For the sake of Ireland

  Forty days he was forsaken
  Foul temptation did withstand
  Then to the foe he was delivered
  By a traitor's cruel hand

  So he died in brave defiance
  Crucified by their command
  But on Easter Monday morning
  He rose again for Ireland.

Blackout.

Bedsitter. **Martyn** *is seated at a typewriter.* **Roy** *is standing about aimlessly.*

Martyn   What's another word for 'nation'?

Roy   Country.

Martyn   No good.

Roy   Land.

Martyn   Longer.

Roy   Mausoleum. (*Pause.*) Look at the time.

Martyn   Don't fluster me.

Roy   Is that her?

They listen intently for a moment. Silence.

Martyn I do the words, you stick to the music.

Roy What music? They're only after the usual traditional whinge.

Martyn 'Then sing with me this ballad Of the death of Sean McVeigh, He will not be forgotten' ... Not for a day or two, anyway.

Roy Are you looking shot?

Martyn She's lost her sense of humour, Marie. (*Pause.*) What rhymes with McVeigh?

Roy Slay.

Martyn Pray? ... Obey?

Roy Decay.

Martyn Great. Thanks. That's terrific. 'He gave his life for Ireland, On account of tooth decay.'

Roy She'll be here any minute, you know.

Martyn We were mad to take this on, Roy.

Roy It's work. It's money.

Martyn It's not real. I'm a pacifist.

Roy Fine, if you want to hunt for another teaching job, go ahead.

Martyn What's the use? You can imagine asking Cochrane for a reference. (*Imitating.*) 'Pure filth.' He really had us nailed to the wall. Lewd and indecent behaviour in the very classroom.

Roy My only regret is, it didn't happen sooner.

Martyn The drink he might have overlooked – what with being an alcoholic – but Monagh in her undies, that was the three of us blacklisted for keeps.

Roy Listen, you know as well as I do – those schools are just child labour camps. You're not hired as a teacher at all, you're hired as a commandant.

Martyn He was beside himself with glee, of course, the old fart. He'd been waiting seven years for a chance like that.

Roy It was our good luck, not his. We were in the wrong business, Sempo. At least we're on our way now. (*Slight pause.*)

Martyn What about Monagh?

Roy Have you heard anything?

Martyn Not since she went down to Dublin.

Roy She's a bit old to start a singing career.

Martyn Aren't we all.

Roy Although she could pass for twenty-five.

Martyn On a good night. If the lighting was right. (*Slight pause.*) What happened to her distinguished lover in television?

Roy Still plugged in, as far as I hear.

Martyn Playfair ... it's an odd name.

Roy Doesn't quite suit in his case, he's married with four brats.

Martyn It rhymes with Mayfair, though.

Roy So?

Martyn McVeigh ... McVeigh ...

Roy What about 'array' ... 'affray' ... 'say nay' ...

Martyn What do you think this is, Alexander Pope?

Roy What about 'weigh' ... (*He mimes scales.*) ... or 'way' (*He indicates direction.*) ...

Martyn   Wait a minute, it's coming. (*He starts scribbling.*)

Roy   'Old and grey.'

Martyn   Shut up. I'm getting it. (*The doorbell rings.*)
Don't answer it. (*He gets up.*) You type. (**Roy** *sits at the
typewriter.*) Are you ready?

Roy   Chrissake get on with it!

Martyn (*dictating*)   'A British soldier cursed at him' . . .
(**Roy** *types.*) . . . 'A British soldier cursed at him' . . . 'As
his life-blood flowed away', no, 'ebbed away' . . . (*The
doorbell rings.*)

Roy   We'll have to let her in.

Martyn   . . . 'as his life-blood ebbed away' . . . (**Roy**
types.) . . . 'But Ireland's sons will not forget' . . .

Roy   Will not what?

Martyn   Will not forget, 'But Ireland's sons will not
forget . . . (**Roy** *types; the door is knocked.*) . . . the name of
Sean McVeigh.' Read it over.

Roy (*reading it*)   'A British soldier cursed at him As his
life-blood ebbed away But Ireland's sons will not forget
The name of Sean McVeigh.'

Martyn   Not bad, sure it isn't?

Roy   Open the bloody door!

Martyn *rushes out to hall door.* **Roy** *staples the lyric sheet to
the music hastily, then crams it into an envelope.* **Martyn** *returns
with* **Marie**.

Martyn (*re-entering*)   How are things with you, Marie?

Marie   I was just on the point of giving up.

Martyn   We were putting the bins out.

Roy   Here's the stuff.

He hands her the envelope. She takes the song out and starts to read it.

Martyn   I'll put the kettle on.

Marie   Not for me.

Martyn   You've time for a coffee.

Marie   They're waiting for this, down in the studio.

Roy   You people certainly work fast.

Marie   It's urgent business we're on. (*She pockets the song.*) That's quite satisfactory. (*She pulls out three crumpled ten-pound notes and throws them carelessly on to the desk.*)

Roy   Is that your thirty-pieces-of-silver gesture?

Marie (*to* **Martyn**)   We lost a volunteer called Quigley last night.

Martyn   Yeah, the van driver, I heard it on the news. (*Slight pause.*) You want a ballad.

Marie   I'll call on Friday. Right?

Martyn (*glancing at* **Roy**)   Friday. Sure. Okay.

Marie   Here's the clipping about it. (*She gives him a newspaper cutting.*) His widow has specially requested 'Four Green Fields' as the air.

Martyn   Fine. Right. So. How've you been keeping, Marie?

Marie   My health's excellent, thank you.

Roy   How's the tightness round your arse?

Marie (*going*)   See you.

Roy   Shot anyone interesting lately?

Martyn (*to* **Marie**)   He hasn't changed, same old joker. (*To* **Roy**.)   Easy on.

Roy   She's not going to walk in here and act as if we were some unpleasant form of plant life!

Marie (*going*) You can sort this out between you.

Roy We want no part of your doings.

Marie (*holding up the envelope*) What do you call this?

Roy Gunk.

Marie (*pointing to the money*) I have a similar name for that.

She goes. **Martyn** *follows.*

Martyn Friday at the same time then, Marie.

Roy, *left alone, thumps the furniture. The door is heard closing, off.* **Martyn** *re-enters.*

Roy The smug stuck-up piece of scrag!

Martyn (*sniffing*) Smell that perfume?

Roy Typical Irish bitch . . .

Martyn Odour of sanctity, it's called.

Roy You couldn't prise her knees apart with one of her own bombs. (*He follows her off.*) I hope the Special Branch gets you!

Martyn (*looking at clipping*) What rhymes with 'Quigley'?

Roy (*re-entering*) Here, we've got some letters. (*He's been opening one.*) Look at this – from the agency. (*Reads it.*) They're offering us a jingle.

Martyn Seriously?

Roy Yeah.

Martyn Sensational! What's it for?

Roy Brady's Frozen Chickens.

Martyn That's great. (*He considers.*) Putting the freeze on . . . there's a lot of possibilities . . . getting the bird!

Roy We're on our way.

Martyn If this one hits, it'll break us into the market!

Roy Make your mark with commercials and you're a gilt-edged songwriter, no looking back.

Martyn It's a real opening.

Roy We're going to make it big, Sempo. Stick with your Uncle Roy. (*He's been opening the other letter. He shakes two objects out of it into his hand.*)

Martyn What's that?

Roy Two bullets.

Blackout. Music.

Lounge bar. **Monagh** *on stage, at mike, glamorous.*

Monagh (*sings*)
  Though I can't explain
  All the anger and the pain
  Still I think you will agree with me
  What's going on's insane
  Houses open to the rain
  Only misery and hate remain
  But I for one, you and me for two
  Need to move on to something new . . .

During this, lights also come up on:

Street. **Martyn** *and* **Roy** *stand by a wall, with suitcases, confronting the* **Man** *and* **Woman** *as a military police patrol.*

Man Hands on the wall. Feet apart.

They lean face-forward against the wall, as ordered. While the **Man** *frisks them, the* **Woman** *searches their cases.*

Meanwhile the song continues.

Monagh (*singing*)
    All the world agrees
    There's a cure for our disease
    Just by helping one another
    To get off our hands and knees

    You know love can be the answer
    You know love can show the way
    Once we get ourselves together
    There can be a brand new day

    I for one, baby you and me for two
    Need to move, need to move to something new
    And I for one hope that you for one
    Will travel that way too
    'Cos I for one, baby you and me for two . . .

*By now, the lights have faded out on the street search. During the
ensuing bridge,* **Roy** *and* **Martyn** *are seen entering the lounge
bar and sitting down at a table. The* **Girl***, as a waitress, serves
them drinks.*

    . . . How we long to travel home
    But home is something deep inside
    We've lost our way
    Home is just a place where we can hide away

    I for one, baby you and me for two
    Need to move, need to move to something new
    So I for one hope that you for one
    Will travel that way too
    Yes, I for one, baby you and me for two
    I for one, baby you and me for two
    I for one, baby you and me for two
    And I for one hope that you for one
    Will travel that way too.

Monagh *bows and exits,* **Martyn** *and* **Roy** *applauding.*

The **Man** *enters, as a comedian, and takes the mike. He is
dressed in scuba goggles and baggy shorts. Round his waist is a
gunbelt, with an old revolver in a holster and bottles of Guinness
stuck in loops all the way round.*

Man   Monagh Lisa, ladies and gents, Miss Monagh
Lisa, a lovely lady from the black North, with a great
future ahead of her and a great behind as well, good
evening! (*Fixes on* **Martyn** *and* **Roy**.) Hey lads, tell us
this, tell us the truth now – speaking as outsiders, what
do you think of the human race? Eh? Did you ever
consider surgery? You know, I met a fellow like you the
other day, a Belfast lad. And he tells me he threw a
grenade at an English soldier. My God, says I – what
happened? Well, says your man – he just pulled out the
pin from it and threw it straight back again. I'm a navy
man myself, of course. You may laugh – it's been
known to happen – but what you see standing here
before you is the Irish Naval Services Anti-Submarine
Patrol. That's me. Hang on, there's a message coming
through from the interior. (*He flips the cap off a Guinness
bottle and removes it from his belt.*) I don't have to do this,
you know, I could work for a living. (*He takes a swig.*)
You should try this underwater, lads, a different story
altogether. Terrible trouble keeping your weapon dry,
you'd know all about that of course. Anyway. The
backroom boys came up with a great solution, look at
this. (*He pulls out the revolver and squirts water at them.*) Isn't
it rich? Isn't it good? Youse can sleep safe in your beds
from now on, the two of youse. Snuggled up together.
I'm away back to the frigate. I said frigate. Listen, I
know there's somebody out there, I can hear breathing.
Tomorrow you can hear me singing that evergreen
favourite, 'I'll Be Seizing You In All The Old Familiar
Places' – till then good night and good luck.

*The band plays him off. The fluorescent pub lighting comes on, the
band exits, chatting.*

Martyn (*looking around*)   They're not doing very good
business.

Roy   You can see why.

Martyn   Monagh wasn't bad, though.

Roy   She was singing our song.

Short pause.

Martyn   She mightn't have seen us.

Roy   Couldn't have missed us.

Martyn   Maybe we should ask . . .

Roy   Relax. She'll be changing.

Martyn (*sings*)   There's been a change in the weather
and a change in me . . . (*Speaks.*) How's the money?

Roy   About thirty quid left.

Martyn   We'll have to go home, Roy.

Roy   How can we go home? You want to get shot?

Martyn   We can't sign on the dole down here, we're
not citizens.

Roy   We're going to sell songs. We're going to write
hits.

Martyn   How long will thirty quid keep us alive?

Roy   Isn't there a month's rent paid on the bedsitter?
(*Slight pause.*) You always have qualms. Could we just –
once – enter into something – qualmlessly?

Martyn   You're the one with the ulcer.

Roy   You're the one ordered the drinks.

Martyn   You're the one with the cousin in the
Protestant gestapo.

Roy   Give it a rest, will you? He plays the drums,
that's all.

Martyn   Just to keep in practice. (*Pause.*) We must have
been mental to write that stuff for him.

Roy   Will you quit grumping? It was a couple of
parodies, a corny cabaret act they take round the

drinking clubs. Nobody cares who writes the numbers so long as they go over well.

Martyn By God, that stuff should have gone over well. It curdled the ink in my ball-point.

Monagh *rushes on in jeans and sweater.*

Monagh My public!

Martyn The star herself.

Monagh (*as she hugs them*) God, this is marvellous. You both look great.

Martyn We've been slimming.

Roy You look pretty picturesque yourself.

Monagh Sure – with a name like Monagh Lisa.

Martyn Whose idea was that?

Monagh You'll meet her. Did you like the act?

Martyn It's a killer.

Monagh It's killing me, anyway.

Roy So you want to go back to conducting the school choir?

Monagh Sure – in a coffin.

Martyn How did you get the job?

Monagh Blackmail. Prostitution. Murder. It was easy. How long are you down in Dublin for?

Roy The duration.

Martyn We had to leave Belfast in a hurry. For a reason.

Monagh What was it?

Roy Fear.

Martyn Somebody sent us these. (*He shows the two bullets.*)

Monagh Jesus Murphy. What have you been up to?

Roy Nothing.

Martyn We wrote some material . . .

Roy I'll tell you about it later!

Monagh Maybe it was Cochrane. Maybe it was Kyle.

Roy No, we know it wasn't Marie.

Martyn British Army Intelligence. That's my theory.

Roy Gunk.

The **Woman** *sweeps by as Mrs Barker: tinted glasses. Cigarette. Glass of gin. An air of slightly slatternly superiority. Horsey baritone voice.*

Woman I've told you before about fraternising, dear.

Monagh These are friends of mine from Belfast, Mrs Barker . . . (*She makes a face at her departing back.*) We'll get a bus to my place. It's a rathole, but it's warm.

Martyn I think the rats have deserted ours.

Woman (*re-appearing*) You'd swear I was running a charity. (*Sitting down, she drains her glass and holds it up to* **Monagh**.) Tell Eamon to fill that for me, dear. You can bring something for your little friends, if you like.

Monagh Roy Fletcher. Martyn Semple. Mrs Barker. (*They nod to each other.*) The usual?

Roy Large.

Monagh Of course. (*She goes off.*)

Woman From the North, are you? Bloody silly place to live.

Martyn We've just moved, actually.

Woman Good for you. How did you like my cabaret?

Martyn   Very entertaining.

Woman   I could draw a bigger crowd with ballad sessions, but I can't stand that droning slush they all sing.

Martyn   I know what you mean.

Woman   Of course the acts I'm forced to use are practically unemployable, but they do for the yokels here to gawp at. I suppose that's a Presbyterian name?

Roy   Pardon?

Woman   Ronald Fletcher, wasn't it?

Martyn   Roy.

Woman   I'll tell you what I wish for you lot up North. I wish you'd get on with the bloody killing. Speed it up, hurry it along. Finish each other off, we'll be glad to see the end of you, Protestants and Catholics both, you'll be doing the world a service.

Monagh *re-appears with a tray containing the drinks.*

Monagh   Mrs Barker has considerable experience in horse trials.

Woman   She's such a pert little thing, I don't know why she's never managed to get herself a man.

Monagh   I didn't like to mention it before but I'm a female impersonator and this is my wife and mother-in-law. (*She downs her drink.*)

Woman   I've told her often she'd have a much better chance as a comedienne. At least she's got a natural ability for that.

Monagh   She's never done flattering me.

Woman   No point in pretending, dear. You're over the hill to start up as a pop singer. It might be different if you had outstanding talent. But you don't even have decent tits, do you?

Monagh   Your own could do with a bit of re-pointing.

Woman   Mine are no longer necessary, dear.

Monagh   Her husband was in the property market, you see – she inherited the Irish Stock Exchange.

Woman   I suppose you two belong to Paisley's crew.

Martyn   We're not involved . . .

Roy   I'm Protestant. He's Catholic. Satisfied?

Woman   It's nothing to me, dear, the British are welcome to the whole crowd of you. I just hope they never try and fob you on to us.

Monagh   We wouldn't touch your kind with a green, white and orange barge-pole, dear.

Martyn   Monagh . . .

Woman   You've crippled our tourism, you've blemished the name of Ireland throughout the world, and you're not even a part of it.

Pause.

Monagh   What do you mean by that?

Woman   I'm only stating facts, dear.

Monagh   I'm more Irish than you are, you overbearing old windbag!

Roy   Cool down.

Monagh   She's not telling me I'm not Irish!

Roy   What does it matter, who cares?

Woman   You can label yourself with any name you like, dear, I'm talking about real life.

Monagh   If you'd had a no-warning bomb in your fiberglass grotto here, you'd know all about real life, and hell slap it into you.

Woman   Don't be tiresome.

Martyn   Easy on.

Monagh   What does she know about it? What does she know about us? She's got no allegiance to anything except her cruddy cheque-book. (*To* **Woman**.) You want to know why they're down here?

Roy   Let's go.

Monagh   They got live bullets through the post! How'd you like that with your cornflakes?

Martyn   Come on, Monagh, we're going home.

Woman   You're one of life's born losers, dear, and there's nothing more I can do for you.

Monagh   You can stuff it up your horse-box for a start!

Roy   Out.

He manhandles her off. We hear her shouting: 'Piss off, I'm sick of this, sick of it, the old bitch' . . . etc.

Martyn   Don't mind her, Mrs Barker, she's overwrought.

Woman   She ought to know better than to take on a tough old boot like me.

Martyn   First thing tomorrow morning, she'll be on the phone to apologise.

Woman   Tell her not to bother, dear. I'd already decided to drop her. Quite apart from her singing talent, she's a bloody awful entertainer. She won't stoop to sell herself. And you have to, dear. It's a whore's game at one remove.

She goes. Blackout.

Monagh's *flat. In the darkness a television flickers on
soundlessly, its back towards the audience. In the eerie fuzz of its
light,* **Monagh** *is revealed on the sofa in front of it, watching.*
Roy *enters with drinks. He gives her one, and leans on the back
of the sofa, sipping.*

Monagh We should have waited for Martyn.

Roy He'll soft-soap your woman, he's good at that.

Monagh I'm just sorry it had to happen five minutes
after you arrived.

Roy You can't afford to fall out with these people.

Monagh That's her way of getting rid of everybody –
needling them till they blow their tops.

Roy It was a nice little gig to have.

Monagh God! The back of my neck to my kidneys is
just one long throb.

Roy *puts down his drink and begins massaging her neck and
shoulders.*

Monagh Aah . . . sublime. (*She closes her eyes and he
continues for a moment in silence, watching the television.*)

Roy What *is* this?

Monagh Some documentary about the troubles.

Roy They never give it a rest, do they? (*He watches,
still massaging.*) That's near Cecilia Street, I went to
school there.

Monagh Not much of it left now.

Roy Look – that was that bar off York Street.

Monagh That's the Dublin Road.

Roy Is it?

Monagh Oh God knows, I've lost track. When will it
ever end?

Roy You don't have to watch it.

Monagh It won't just go away if you switch it off, you know.

Roy It'll not be stopped by wallowing in it either. (*He stops massaging.*) How's that?

Monagh You haven't lost the touch.

Roy It's grown more sensitive over the years.

Monagh With practice, no doubt.

Roy (*moves round the sofa to her side*) It's a gift of nature. (*He makes to kiss her.*)

Monagh Hold on, Roy, this wasn't included in my five-year plan.

Roy Come on, Monagh ... (*He reaches for her.*)

Monagh Sit down. (*She pushes him on to the sofa.*) It isn't real, what's happening to us, I can't keep track. We'd all been drifting along teaching for seven years. The next thing you know, Kyle's running around with bombs, you and Martyn are a pair of hunted balladmongers, and I'm getting the bums' rush from a lounge bar.

Roy Listen, sprite. Something fell into place tonight.

Monagh You haven't called me 'sprite' for five years.

Roy Listen to me. You were good tonight. Real charisma.

Monagh You're fantasising, Roy.

Roy It took me completely unawares. You knocked me out.

Monagh Are you trying to talk your way into bed?

Roy Not unless that's the price of admission.

Monagh There are five thousand singers better than me in this town alone, and that's not counting the ones over sixteen.

Roy Look, will you forget this neurosis about age, the youth cult's a thing of the past. There's a huge maturity market now.

Monagh Sounds like the fatstock sales. Where do you get these phrases from?

Roy All I'm trying to suggest is – why don't the three of us work as a team? We can develop a whole strategy together, a concept. An image.

Monagh You mean, like you write the songs and I sing them?

Roy We co-ordinate everything – writing, singing, clothes, records, marketing, promotion. We aim the whole thing towards television. That's where we ultimately score.

Monagh Gee, kids – let's just do the show ourselves!

Roy Monagh Enterprises.

Monagh Right here in this battered old country.

Roy What do you say?

Monagh I was going to play a game with myself for five years. Sing around the clubs and hotels. Live a bit wild. Get out of the old necropolis. (*She gestures towards the television.*) Take a vacation from real life. You can't, of course. That was my five-year plan.

Roy Scrap it, sprite. We're going for the Great Leap Forward.

He kisses her on the lips, then on the ear, then the shoulder. Meanwhile, her attention is caught by the television programme again.

Monagh Bloody English politicians . . .

Roy Ah, hell's teeth!

Monagh   Look at them, they're always so
sanctimonious. They get on like a crowd of doctors. It
never seems to sink in that they're part of the disease.

Roy   Could this maybe wait, do you think?

Monagh   They treat us like some remote tribe of
savages.

Roy   They're not far wrong.

Monagh   So that's your considered opinion of your
fellow-citizens?

Roy   It's got nothing to do with me, all that gunk
there.

Monagh   Apart from earning yourself a bullet in the
mail.

Roy   Ah, come off it.

Monagh   Who sent them, Roy?

Roy   Search me – some clown probably got the
address wrong.

They get engrossed in the television programme again.

Monagh   What's that?

Roy   M1 carbine.

Monagh   You'd think it was a form of sport they were
dealing with. There's an Armalite rifle. (*They're watching
footage of a gun battle.* **Monagh** *winces and looks away.*) How
does little Marie Kyle live with all that? She's in the
thick of it. I can barely watch it on television. She was
always such a mouse. I was supposed to be the hard-
bitten woman of the world.

Roy   She was born with blinkers on, same as the rest
of them.

Monagh   All except Roy Fletcher, mighty man of steel.

Roy Knock it off.

Monagh You really hate your country, don't you?

Roy I can think of better places to be born.

Monagh Too late now, sprite, you're stuck with it, and you better start facing up to the fact. (*Pause.*) Are you staying the night?

Roy I want to.

Monagh Just don't kid yourself we're a winning concept.

Roy It's the old firm. In earnest this time. I still love you, Monagh.

Monagh Excuse me for calling in question one or two of your terms, Mr Fletcher. 'Still' for example. And 'you'. And particularly 'love'. And of course 'I'.

Roy Just give me a chance.

Monagh Certainly. Let's twist again like we did last summer.

Pause.

Roy I suppose this is one of Playfair's programmes.

Monagh Why so?

Roy You seemed in quite a hurry to switch it on.

Monagh We can dispense with that sort of crack for a start. We're in the maturity market now, right? That's where we all make our own breakfast and find our own way home. Okay? (*Pause.*) You really liked the act?

Roy I thought you were sensational.

She kisses him. He reaches for her.

Monagh Wait.

She switches the television off. Blackout.

A recording of **Monagh** *singing 'I For One' fades in towards the end of the song. Then a disc jockey voice is heard saying:* 'A first record there from a lady by the name of Monagh, with a number called "I For One" which I for one rather fancy myself, here's hoping you for one like it too for one. The time coming up to nine forty, the weather cold and cloudy, but stay tuned for more of the best in music . . .' *The song is faded up again as it comes to an end.*

Agent's office. Lights up on the **Man**, *as a booking agent, sitting at a desk.* **Monagh** *standing on the other side of it.*

Man   Monagh, my sweet, look at you, you're a walking talking daydream. Come here and make an old man happy. (*He kisses her cheek.*) My God, you're a public incitement to divorce.

Monagh   Did you ever just try saying hello, Cyril?

Man   No oul' lip now, I've got two bookings for you, and I expect you to show grateful, sit down there and look demure.

Monagh   Is it television?

Man   A television spot for new talent plus a live variety spot and it adds up to good money. How's the two boyos?

Monagh   Eager to please, Cyril. Tell me about the television.

Man   They're hard-working lads and they're sound and you know what – they should be trying their stuff in the Song Festivals. You tell them from me – Song Festivals.

Monagh   They've entered a number in the National Contest for Eurovision.

Man   Certainly Eurovision, but there's plenty of smaller fry besides. There's Castlebar in this country, there's loads of them on the continent, Majorca, Knokke-la-

Zoute, Monte Carlo, you tell them from me, there's
money in it.

Monagh   What's the live gig, Cyril?

Man   Now it sounds not – very – exciting, but it's a
first-class bill of professional artistes and, believe me,
very well respected as a booking in the business. It's a
Christmas Night concert in the Women's Prison.

Monagh   Good God. How did this come about? I
suppose you've a lot of business colleagues in there?

Man   Any more of this cheek and I'll give the booking
to my sword-swallowing act.

Monagh   I'm not ungrateful. I'm just wondering what
they do to you if they don't like your performance.

Man   Sure it's full of those Republican girls from
Belfast – they'll be delighted with you and your act.

Monagh   Captivated, in fact.

Man   My God, what a wit.

Monagh   So what about the *good* news, the television?

Man   From what I've been told, it's a showcase series
for new performers, professional, all professional – and
you're on the first one. Can those fellows of yours come
up with the right sort of song, do you think?

Monagh   I'll make damn sure they do.

Blackout.

Roy *and* **Martyn**'s *flat. Light up on* **Roy** *sitting at an old
upright piano, improvising moodily.*

Roy   What have you got?

Light up on **Martyn** *downstage in a rocking chair, smoking a
pipe, leafing through a big notebook.*

Martyn Not a lot. 'Fallen Arches'. A song for broken-hearted chiropodists.

Roy Where did that thing come from?

Martyn I bought it this morning.

Roy You don't smoke.

Martyn I thought I'd give it a try.

Roy It looks ridiculous. (*He plays some gloomy chords and runs.*)

Martyn I've been toying with the theme of a secret agent. Espionage.

Roy You've got spies on the brain.

Martyn My lover . . . works undercover, kind of thing.

Roy Sounds obscene.

Martyn He dresses to kill, gives me my fill. That sort of idea. His shoes are made from an alligator. He shoots first and asks questions later.

Roy We're not writing for Bessie Smith.

Martyn True. (*He doodles.*) Nobody's likely to track us down here. I can't even remember the address myself half the time. (*He doodles more.*) I mean, who would send a death threat on account of a few ballads?

Roy Will you quit talking about it?

Martyn Secret society. Swear an oath that you'll be true. Learn the password – I love you.

Roy The demo tape came back again, incidentally.

Martyn Thanks but no thanks?

Roy They're interested – songs show promise – not quite out of the ordinary enough – try them again – they remain ours etc.

Martyn What about trying London?

Roy No, that tape's had its chance. We're just not in focus yet. We need stuff that's ballady and romantic – plus a dash of drama.

Martyn Secret heart.

Roy She's good at drama, she thrives on it.

Martyn Secret sorrow . . . secret joy . . . secret love . . . that's been done.

Roy Keep going. (*He doodles on the piano.*)

Martyn My heart has its orders . . . from up above . . . a top-secret mission . . . to win your love . . . no, to capture your love . . . de-dah-dah-dum . . . something our engagement . . . then I found out . . . you're a double-agent!

Roy You keep coming out with these duff gag lines.

Martyn That's not a gag. It's wit.

Roy We don't need wit. We're creating a product for a nation of half-wits.

Martyn How *is* Monagh, anyway?

Roy She was late for the gig again last night.

Martyn Have you been tiring her out?

Roy Fat chance. She treats me like a brand of convenience food. Just pop it in the oven for fifteen minutes, when you're feeling peckish, ladies.

Martyn Sounds ideal.

Roy Well, that's not how it feels. She's cold-bloodedly destroying me, if you want to know. You and her both seem to think that I'm some kind of a mechanical robot.

Martyn Small wonder, the way you get on.

Roy *looks over his shoulder at* **Martyn**. *They stare at one* *another for a moment.*

Roy   Say that again.

Martyn   Small wonder . . . it's tearing me asunder.

Roy   Right. We're in business.

The lights stay on them as they work away quietly at the idea.

Television studio. Lights up on **Monagh**, *facing a television camera; the* **Man** *is the cameraman. The* **Girl**, *as a floor manager, enters wearing a headset and carrying a clipboard.*

Girl   We're ready to go now, love. Just do it bit by bit the way I said, while he lines up his shots. I'll give you a hand cue to start and stop. Okay?

Monagh *nods. The* **Girl** *cues her to start. Music.*

Monagh (*sings*)
 I have seen the cover
 That you've been living under
 To leave your former lovers high and dry . . .

Girl (*signalling*)   Fine, love. Keep your position.

They wait.

Flat.

Martyn (*looking up in the air*)   Small wonder . . . what does it apply to? 'My Small Wonder'. A song for midgets.

Roy   This could be the one to break her, you know. I've a feeling it might.

Martyn   Oh small wonder, you and I . . .

Roy   You need a romantic ballad to break nearly any female act.

Martyn   . . . *No* small wonder, you and I.

Roy   It just needs some sort of twist, to make it really commercial.

Martyn   Play me what you've got.

Roy (*playing and singing*)   Oh, small wonder . . . (*Speaks.*) That's all.

Martyn   That's the hook.

They go back to work.

Television studio.

Girl   Ready. (*She cues music and* **Monagh**.)

Monagh (*sings*)
In disguise, small wonder,
For each time we're together
Every girl around
Gives you the eye . . .

Girl (*signalling*)   Hold.

They wait.

Flat.

Martyn   Wonder. Wonder. The seven wonders of the world. There must be something there. The eighth wonder. Oh, small wonder, the eighth one . . . no, *call our wonder* the eighth one of the world . . . We can . . . do what? We can fly . . . no, we can reach so high. Higher . . . than the sky. No small wonder you and I! Genius!

Television studio. The **Girl** *cues* **Monagh** *and the music.*

Monagh (*sings*)
    You've given yourself away
    You've said too much that I
    Can read between the lines
    Your face and hands complete the picture –

    Oh, small wonder,
    You and I,
    Meeting in the park, touching in the dark –

    Call our wonder
    The eighth one of the world
    We can reach so high
    Higher than the sky
    No small wonder, you and I . . .

Girl (*signalling*)   Is there much more of it, love?

Monagh   Fifty whole per cent.

Girl   Well, catch your breath for a couple of minutes.

Flat.

Roy (*still at the piano*)   I know what Monagh's problem is now. She can't cope with being a free agent. She can't handle it. That's why she does all these lame things. So as somebody'll rush up and give her a hand. She acts the self-reliant woman but she's crying inside for somebody to run her life for her. Trouble is, it's not me. It's that television jock, Playfair. She's still hooked on that creep. She's just using me as a home help.

Martyn   Okay, I've got a lead on the verse.

Roy   What about the chorus?

Martyn   It's finished.

Roy   It's only started.

Martyn   You never listen!

Roy All I hear is you sitting there mumbling to yourself.

Martyn I'm only after going through the whole thing.

Roy Where is it?

Martyn *tears a page from his notebook, plants it down on the piano and returns to his seat.*

Martyn It'll sweep the country, this. From the jukebox in every sleazy waterfront drive … to the ballroom in every Fifth Avenue hotel. (*Pause.*) Will Monagh like it, do you think?

Roy She doesn't like anything much. Except that turd Playfair. He can do no wrong.

Martyn I thought it was over years ago.

Roy She says he wanted a divorce. But the wife wouldn't play along. And so on and so forth. You wouldn't think a woman of her intelligence would fall for that. But she wants to badly enough. So she does. Bitch. (*He fights his distress.*) What about the verse?

Martyn Shaping up. Spies may be all round us, jealousy may hound us.

Roy You and your bloody spies!

Martyn Watching for the signs that say we're through. Some day they may discover … love has got our number … and even something something can come true … miracles! And even miracles are sometimes true. Bullseye!

Roy Bullshit.

Television studio.

Girl (*cueing*) Go.

Music.

Monagh (*sings*)
Spies may be all round us
Jealousy may hound us
Watching for the signs that say we're through
One day they may discover
Love has got our number
And even miracles are sometimes true . . .

The **Girl** *signals to stop. They wait.*

Flat. **Roy**, *with tears on his cheeks, gets up suddenly and heads for the door.*

Martyn   Where're you going?

Roy   I'm going for a walk.

Martyn   That's only the half of it.

Roy *leaves,* **Martyn** *sighs, and grimaces with exasperation. Then gets engrossed again.*

Martyn   Making me your bride. Nothing left to hide. Live life side by side. (*Pause.*) Assuming you prefer your onions fried.

Blackout on flat.

Television studio.

Girl   Straight through to the end now.

She cues **Monagh**.

Monagh (*sings*)
You've given yourself away
You've said too much that I
Can read between the lines
Your face and hands complete the picture –

Oh, small wonder,
You and I,
Meeting in the park, touching in the dark,

Call our wonder
The eighth one of the world
We can reach so high
Higher than the sky
No small wonder, you and I.

Girl   Okay. Lunch!

Blackout on television studio.

Bookshop. **Martyn** *is looking through some poetry collections.*
Marie *enters.*

Marie   Surprise.

Martyn   Marie!

Marie   So this is where you've run to?

Martyn   What are you doing here?

Marie   Visiting friends. Selling books. What about
you? Here. (*She gives him a Sinn Fein pamphlet from her
satchel.*) Thirty pence, please.

Martyn   Roy and me are getting established, with the
songs. We've got a couple of records out, with Monagh.
We're doing an entry for Eurovision at the minute.
Listen, I'm sorry about the ballad. We had to leave
Belfast in a bit of a rush.

Marie   Very wise. I'm surprised at what's become of
you, Semple.

Martyn   Me?

Marie   Fletcher always was a wee Orange pimp, under
the skin.

Martyn   Easy on, Marie.

Marie   You're in his pocket, that's the thing. I thought
you told me your grandfather carried a gun in the
twenties.

Martyn   The past is over and done with, Marie. We're in the Common Market now.

Marie   You amuse me.

Martyn   Men have been on the moon. It's a small world.

Marie   Don't delude yourself, you can't just turn your back on generations of the dead. Don't imagine you'll get away with it that easy.

Martyn   I'm in favour of a united Ireland as much as the next man.

Marie   What are you doing reproducing this pseudo-American slop, then?

Martyn   What? What has that got to do with it?

Marie   Everything, that's all. The whole state apparatus of this country, North and South, is designed for one function – sell-out. Selling out the resources, the heritage, the culture, the very soil itself to foreign speculators.

Martyn   Come off it.

Marie   You're a cog in that machine, you and your Common Market and your Eurovision Song Contest.

Martyn   For God's sake, Marie, that's completely wired up. I mean, people enjoying songs, a harmless entertainment . . .

Marie   Nothing that mediocre is ever harmless.

Martyn   You've lost touch with real life.

Marie   You've lost touch with who and what and where you are. Don't think you can escape for ever into mass-produced catchpenny idiocies.

Martyn   Pop songs are like the folk music of our generation. There's nothing political about it.

Marie   That's really rich, coming from you, in your position.

Martyn   What are you talking about?

Marie   I'm talking about why you did a flit.

Martyn   Somebody posted bullets to us.

Marie   You're damn lucky they didn't arrive at a higher velocity.

Martyn   Why do you say that?

Marie   Considering what you were mixed up in.

Martyn   Us? We'd no involvement in politics whatsoever as you know.

Marie   Don't act all innocent. You took to the wing the minute it appeared in print.

Martyn   Whatever you're on about, Marie . . . I think maybe I'd rather not know.

Marie   You're not bluffing, are you – you really don't know what you've got yourself into. There was an article in a Protestant paper. Naming you two. It said you'd both been supplying entertainment to their drinking clubs. As a means of gaining information about them. On behalf of the British Army. The proof was that you were also doing work for the IRA. You're in dead trouble, Martyn.

Martyn   But none of it's true!

Marie   Oh? You did no work for the Protestants, then?

Martyn   We wrote a few comedy numbers for a cousin of Roy's, that's all.

Marie   You're the original babes in the woods, aren't you?

Martyn   What'll happen? What should we do?

Marie   These things aren't forgotten.

Martyn   We literally didn't know. I suppose there's no point in even trying to refute it now.

Marie   Not much.

Martyn   Good God, Marie, surely *you* never believed it?

Marie   I wouldn't put anything past Fletcher, but I was sceptical all the same. Even the Brits have more gumption than to employ the likes of you.

Martyn   I can't get over it.

Marie   Well, the best of British luck, as they say. I hope it's got more to offer than British justice. (*She makes to leave.*)

Martyn   Don't run off – what about a drink?

Marie   Sorry – I've another three shops to go round.

Martyn   See that girl over there?

Marie   What about her?

Martyn   Just before you came in, she shouts up to the woman at the cash register – Audrey . . . where the hell's *The Savage Mind*? I thought it would make a beautiful skit. Two assistants shouting across the heads of the customers – Where's *The Female Eunuch*? I don't know, but there's a couple of Trollopes under the counter . . . (*She smiles.*) You remember the old college revues?

Marie   Of course I do, why wouldn't I?

Martyn   You were some stage manager.

Marie   You were some comedian.

Martyn   We put in a lot of happy days and nights together, Marie.

Marie   It was half a lifetime ago.

Martyn   Seven years, that's all.

Marie   Some seven years.

Martyn   It's tragic to let it just completely vanish, all the same.

Marie   You have to grow up sometime, Martyn.

Martyn   You've time for a quick jar, come on.

Marie   No. I'm away. Incidentally, the Irish History section's over there.

She leaves. **Martyn***, left alone, tears the pamphlet in half. Blackout.*

Prison hall. The band plays the introduction to 'Somebody Out There'. Light up on the **Woman***, as a prison governess.*

Woman   Since the proceedings are now drawing to a close, I think the time has come for me to express the appreciation of all inmates and staff to our show-business guests for coming here tonight. You've given most generously of your time and talents to bring the pleasure of good entertainment into our lives, and I can assure you on behalf of all the inmates most especially of how much this kind of thing means to them. But I think you'll find them ready to express their gratitude for themselves in the customary manner, in just a moment. We all hope to see you back with us again soon – in your professional capacities, of course. And now for the last item on the agenda (*She consults a piece of paper.*) a song by Monagh, her latest one, which I'm sure we all hope will do very well.

Music. Follow spot on **Monagh** *entering.*

Monagh (*sings*)
  Somebody out there loves you, sugar

Somebody out there wants to know you
Give them your smile, give them the eye
They'll run a mile to be your girl or guy
Somebody in here needs some friendship
Somebody in here wants to love you
Don't be afraid of it
You can make the grade of it
Someone in there can surely see
That the somebody out here is me!

Lights come up on **Roy** *and* **Martyn** *in their flat, singing the song at the piano.*

Life can be hard
Times can be lean
Life can get lonely too
But don't give up
Don't get mad
Don't be had
Because there's somebody out there
Yes, there's somebody out there
Yes, there's somebody out there
Somebody out there . . .

The lights have narrowed down to two small pools, one on **Monagh**'s *face, the other on* **Roy** *and* **Martyn**'s *faces. They all three stare fearfully out into the surrounding darkness, as they sing the final repeated line.*

Blackout.

Act Two

Roy and **Martyn**'s *flat.* **Roy** *sitting in an armchair leafing through a contract.* **Martyn** *preparing to photograph him. Table set for dinner.*

Roy We're on our way, Sempo. No question about it.

Martyn Hold it.

He takes the photograph. **Monagh** *enters with a soup tureen.*

Roy Fletcher and Semple. Hereinafter referred to as the composer/author of the one part.

Monagh Soup. (*She's ladling it out.*)

Martyn Nifty machine, isn't it? (*The camera.*)

Roy Look at that beautiful document.

Martyn The Rolls Royce of cameras, these are.

Monagh Soup!

Roy Oh, right. (*He goes to the table.*)

Martyn The man in the shop was telling me.

Roy Sit down.

Martyn *sits. They all three eat their soup.*

Martyn What time tomorrow?

Roy Ten a.m. sharp in his office. Hereinafter referred to as the publisher of the other part.

Martyn They wouldn't just sit on the songs?

Roy They'll be sending the demos all over. I'm telling you. From now on we're a brand name, in with the big ones.

Monagh Oh, for the love of God!

Roy What's up?

Monagh   Will you please talk about something other than cursed songs! Just for once! There's a whole world to choose from.

Strained pause while they eat their soup.

Roy   Any news from home?

Martyn   Home?

Roy   How's your mother?

Martyn   My mother?

Roy   Is she keeping well?

Martyn   I dunno.

Pause.

Roy   That was a nasty business over the weekend.

Martyn   What was?

Roy   The bombing.

Martyn   Which one?

Roy   You watched it with me on TV.

Martyn   The big fire?

Roy   The bombing!

Monagh (*getting up, clearing soup bowls*)   I can hardly bear to tear myself away from this. (*She goes off.*)

Roy   Bitch.

Martyn   I think she feels left out.

Roy   She won't even let up for a celebration.

Martyn   Did I show you the book of desert photographs I bought?

Roy   Yeah, you did. (*He starts browsing through the contract again.*)

Martyn   Stunning lunar effects.

Roy   Sure. The language here's really historical. Look
at this. (*He reads.*) '. . . in respect of gramophone records,
piano rolls and all other devices for audibly reproducing
the said work for sale or hire in the United Kingdom of
Great Britain and Northern Ireland, and the Republic of
Ireland . . .'

Monagh *has re-appeared with a steaming chicken which she
dumps on the table.*

Monagh   How about carving the said chicken.

She goes off again. **Roy** *puts the contract in his pocket, gets up,
and starts to cut into the thigh of the chicken.*

Martyn   I think you'll like the wine I've chosen.

Roy   This is tough.

Martyn   It's young but it's got quite a lot of body. (*He
goes off to get it.*)

Roy   Yeccch . . .

Monagh *re-appears with plates.*

Monagh   What's wrong?

Roy   It's all bloody inside.

Monagh   What do you mean?

Roy   It's all red.

Monagh   It's been roasting for hours.

Roy   We can't eat that. Was it frozen?

Monagh (*sings*)   Don't get the bird – Get Brady's!

Pop! as **Martyn**, *re-entering, draws the cork from the wine.*

Roy   You mustn't have thawed it out fully.

Monagh   You're the expert, of course. You wrote the
jingle for the commercial, you would know all about it.

Roy I'm only pointing out the obvious.

Monagh You've a genuine talent for that.

Roy We'd better put it back in the oven.

Monagh Carve it up. We're eating it.

Roy It's raw inside.

Monagh It's medium rare.

Roy It's still bleeding!

Monagh Give me. (*She grabs the carving knife and fork from him and begins hacking at the chicken.*)

Roy You can get food poisoning that way, you know. It's stupid. You needn't carve any for me, I'm not eating that.

Monagh Shut your hole!

She grabs the chicken and flings it at him. It hits him in the chest, but he catches it and juggles it from hand to hand back on to the plate. Then he clamps his burnt hands to his sides under his armpits, and bends over in pain.

Monagh It's all yours! If you don't want to eat it you can always set it to music!

She storms out. **Martyn** *holds up the wine bottle.*

Martyn Châteauneuf du Pape. Last year's.

Roy I won't be able to play the piano.

Martyn Keep the air off them. Here, I've a couple of hankies. Give me.

Roy *extends his right hand, keeping the left under his arm.*
Martyn *bandages the palm.*

Roy That's why she did it, she's trying to wreck my career.

Martyn Maybe we should have gone out for a meal

after all.

Roy   What'll we do about Friday?

Martyn   She'll have cooled off by then.

Roy   I'm talking about me!

Martyn   Other hand please.

Roy *extends his left hand and* **Martyn** *bandages it.*

Roy   How am I going to play?

Martyn   Sure the keyboard tracks are already recorded.

Roy   So they are. So they are. Thank God. That's a piece of luck.

Martyn   It's going to be an enormous number, wait till you see. (*He finishes bandaging, and pours some wine.*)

Roy   I don't know what I'm supposed to do.

Martyn   Have you ever thought of composing something personal? (*He hands* **Roy** *a wine glass.*) Expressing the pain of your own feelings? In musical form?

Roy   I make no demands. Whatsoever. None.

Martyn   Something like a rhapsody. Or a fantasia.

Roy   What do *you* think I should do?

Martyn   I've been thinking about it for some time now, Roy. Why don't we write a concept album?

Roy   I'm not talking about bloody music, I'm talking about Monagh and me! (*He swills down the wine.*)

Pause. **Martyn** *sips.*

Martyn   Really quite fruity, yes?

Roy   I want help, I want advice, I want to hear what I'm supposed to do.

Martyn How do I know?

Roy You're the one with the divorce.

Pause.

Martyn We made an agreement never to talk about that.

Roy I don't recall signing that one.

Martyn There was an understanding.

Roy Well, it's just been buggered. I'm a war victim, I'm in no mood to observe the niceties. You've been through all this, there must be something you've learnt.

Martyn If you wanted advice on passing exams, you wouldn't go to the village idiot, would you?

Roy You've never bothered much with women since it, have you?

Martyn Abstinence makes the heart grow stronger.

Roy You never even try to score.

Martyn At least I've still got skin on my hands.

Roy What the hell did she do to you – bite it off?

Martyn She didn't seem to agree with me, and the subject's closed.

Roy You must still get the itch, so what do you do about it?

Martyn Hold it under a cold tap.

Roy I want to know.

Martyn What's the odds.

Roy I want to know what you do about sex!

Martyn What do you think, I take care of it myself.

Pause.

Roy Jerk off, you mean?

Martyn My hands and I are consenting adults. What passes between us in private is our own little affair.

Roy Jerking off – that's repulsive.

Martyn Your whole sexual vocabulary's repulsive.

Roy How can you do it? It's disgusting.

Martyn It's right up to date. Fast. Efficient. Hygienic. Available twenty-four hours a day. No fuss. No complications. Everybody does it.

Roy I don't bloody do it.

Martyn You're a romantic idealist. The last one still alive.

Roy I've got the same needs and appetites as any other normal healthy man . . .

Martyn And what a wonderful advertisement for them you make. Just at the moment. (*He indicates the chicken.*) A morsel of roast flesh?

Roy *grimaces.* **Martyn** *takes a piece and eats it, sipping the wine.*

Martyn 'Love At First Smite'. A song for masochists.

The introduction to the music of 'Aren't You The Lucky One' starts. The lights on **Roy** *and* **Martyn** *fade out.*

Recording studio. The strip-lighting comes on. **Monagh** *is standing inside a recording booth, wearing headphones. Grouped around the microphone in a downstage corner is the vocal trio (***Man***,* **Woman** *and* **Girl***) who sing backing harmonies. Their voices are heard* au naturel, *but those of* **Monagh**, **Martyn** *and* **Roy** *are heard through the studio speakers. The music stops abruptly.*

Roy (*off*) All right, are you all quite happy enough

out there?

Trio   Sure. Yes. Fine.

Roy   Monagh?

Monagh   Never jollier.

Roy   Okay. Stand by. Here we go.

The music starts.

Monagh (*sings*)
He called on the phone,
He told me how everyone
Hoped I'd be there,
For I was so droll, the life and the soul
Of each social affair,
I dressed in my finery, played to the gallery,
A queen on her throne,
But then he smiled and went to the corner where
You sat alone
But
Oh my, I was the lucky one,
They all wanted to be by my side,
While you were left as the lonely one
In the shadows it's easy to hide
But nobody knows how I'm crying besides . . .

(*Speaks.*) Oh shit! I just can't sing this po-faced drivel!

The music stops. **Monagh** *bursts out of the booth.*

Monagh (*to the vocal trio*)   I'm sorry, folks.

Girl   Never fret, love.

Monagh   I knew I'd bungle that shagging line. I could feel it coming.

Woman   It's a mouthful.

Roy, *hands still bandaged, enters from the cubicle followed by* **Martyn**.

Roy   Now listen, everything's basically fine . . .

Monagh (*still to the trio*)   That's good to hear, isn't it.
And there was us thinking that maybe, after several
hundred bungled takes, things were getting a teeny bit
fraught.

Roy   We're nearly home.

Monagh (*still to the trio*)   It's like chewing feathers,
inside that booth.

Roy   It was going well. It just needs – livening up.

Monagh (*to the* **Man**)   Do you like this number?

Man   I can't remember.

Monagh   It gives me the runs.

Roy (*to* **Martyn**)   You talk to her. (*He goes.*)

Martyn   If you'll just do the last verse again, the
engineer can drop you in for it.

Monagh   Thank God for that.

Martyn   Try singing it this time.

Monagh   Try lighting your fire with it next time.

She goes back into the booth. **Martyn** *exits.*

Roy (*off*)   We'll play you into the last verse, then.
Stand by.

The music comes up.

Monagh (*singing deadpan*)
    You told me you envied me,
    Footloose and fancy-free,
    Loved and admired
    For you felt insecure, so shy and unsure of what
    Others desired,
    The party was breaking up,
    The morning was waking up,

I still couldn't leave
And then he came and whispered and led you a-
Way by the sleeve
But
Oh my, I was the lucky one,
They all wanted to be by my side
While you were left as the lonely one
In the shadows it's easy to hide
But nobody knows how I'm crying inside
Because it was you that he chose for his bride –
You know it's funny but true –
Aren't you the lucky one too
Aren't you the lucky one too
Aren't you the lucky one too.

The lights have gradually reduced to a single one on **Monagh** *in the booth, which blacks out at the end of the song. Meanwhile,* **Roy** *and* **Martyn**, *with overcoats on, are seen entering a pub and sitting on stools.*

Pub.

Martyn   Tragic.

Roy   It's all because of Playfair, he has her demented.

Martyn   Time for reappraisals, Roy.

Roy   Don't fret, she'll grow out of it.

Martyn   It's not just Monagh, it's the whole conundrum. We always seem to be on the run, I need to find some bearings.

Roy   Meaning what?

Martyn   We're living here and now. Ireland in the seventies. I want to try and feel at home with that.

Roy   Once we've made it, you'll feel at home with the universe.

Martyn I'm talking about intangibles. Sensibility.
Identity. Actually, I've been meaning to mention this to
you for some time. I'm putting together a volume of
verse for publication.

Pause.

Roy You've never really stopped being an English
teacher, have you?

Martyn Sneer. Go ahead. You're an inverted snob.

Roy You should be devoting every working hour to
songs, same as I do.

Martyn The songs have just become a job for me.
Let's be honest, they're only ephemeral trivia. I want to
write something important, something about real life.

Roy We're not going progressive at this stage.

Martyn You know what we are? We're pushers.
We're dealing in mild narcotics. (*With dramatic emphasis.*)
We're the bland leading the bland.

Roy What have you been reading?

Martyn There's more to life than that, Roy.

Roy Listen, we're in business selling a legitimate
product like any other law-abiding citizen. We're putting
together decent commercial songs without any artsy-
fartsy pretensions – and we're going to work at it till we
get to the top.

Marie Kyle *has entered with the* **Girl**, *as a friend, in tow.*

Martyn Hello, Marie.

Marie You'd swear there was one of us following the
other.

Martyn What brings you here?

Marie We've been doing a radio programme.

Roy   I thought your crowd was banned from the air.

Marie   An Irish language programme. So far as I know we're still allowed to breathe the air.

Roy   It's a pity you don't extend that right to your victims.

Martyn (*hastily*)   Monagh's just been recording one of our numbers for a radio show.

Marie   Children's Hour, is it?

Roy   She's doing another prison concert next week, with a bit of luck you'll be able to attend it.

Martyn   Listen. We used to be good chums. The four of us. The old college gang.

Marie   Where have you been for the last seven years? The country's been at war, you know, a lot of chums are in prison. A lot of chums of mine have given their lives.

Martyn   The thing of it is – Roy and I just aren't politically involved.

Roy   We don't swallow the sort of fanatical gunk that you use to justify murder.

Marie   I know where I stand. On eight hundred years of history, eight hundred years of repression, exploitation and attempted genocide . . .

Roy   I live in the twentieth century, love.

Marie   . . . this time we're going to put an end to that for all time. There's unfinished business in this country . . .

Roy   You know, the twentieth century – aeroplanes, spin dryers. Pinball machines.

Marie   . . . and you're involved as much as any other Irishman which is right up over your ears whether you want to be or not.

Roy You can keep your history. You belong in it.
They should build museums for you instead of prisons.
The rest of us want shot of it. (*To* **Martyn**.) Let's go.
(*He leaves.*)

Martyn I mean, we could still be friends, without
having to agree about all this. We used to just discuss it
over a beer.

Marie You're both like two spoiled brats! Irresponsible
children!

Martyn (*going*) You've let yourself get bitter, Marie.
(*He leaves.*)

Marie (*shouting after them*) There's fifteen thousand
British troops fighting an imperialist war on the soil of
your own country! When are you going to wake up?
What are you going to do about it?

She walks off with her friend. Blackout.

Street. The **Girl***, as Playfair's wife, is standing smoking a
cigarette, waiting.* **Monagh** *appears.*

Girl (*extending her hand*) I'm Sylvia Playfair, Miss
Cahoon. Thank you for agreeing to meet me.

Pause.

Monagh I'd like to sit down somewhere.

Girl No, I'd sooner just say my piece and be off.
(*Pause.*) I want you to stop seeing my husband. He
himself wishes to end the affair, but he can't bring
himself to hurt your feelings. So the initiative has to
come from you, I'm afraid.

Pause.

Monagh You're being frightfully British about this.

Girl I don't enjoy . . .

Monagh Did he send you here?

Girl The sole reason I'm here is that you're distracting him from his work. As you know, he's the only broadcaster in Belfast who's trusted by both sides. What you don't know is that he's been acting as a go-between. A mediator. It's very important that he succeed. A good deal more important, frankly, than causing you distress.

Pause.

Monagh Yes. I'm living a disposable life.

Girl You have a career.

Monagh Aren't I the lucky one.

Girl May I ask you what you plan to do?

Monagh Well . . . I rather thought I might try and change the course of Irish history. Assassinate the Queen, maybe. Sit down in the middle of Belfast and set fire to myself. I have to warn you, though, I'm not very good at plans. I'm still making plans for my twenty-first birthday party. And that was eight years ago. (*She tries to smile.*) I still haven't decided what to wear.

Girl I think a letter would be best. I'd prefer you not to visit him again.

Monagh You do a very classy line in hatred.

Girl I don't feel any hatred for you. I've wasted very little time thinking about you at all. I've wasted very little time on any of his girlfriends. Only when it's called for. Thank you for talking to me. Good luck with your career.

She goes. As the light fades on **Monagh***, we hear the recording of her singing:*

Monagh (*recorded song*)
  But oh my, I was the lucky one,

They all wanted to be by my side
While you were left as the lonely one
Out in the shadows it's easy to hide,
But nobody knows how I'm crying inside
Because it was you that he chose for his bride –
You know it's funny but true –
Aren't you the lucky one too
Aren't you the lucky one too
Aren't you the lucky one too.

During this, lights come up on:

Roy *and* **Martyn**'s *flat.* **Martyn** *at the door holding an open letter.* **Roy** *standing at the piano. They stare at one another in silence.*

Martyn   What should we do?

Roy   Ignore it.

Martyn   We'd better clear out.

Roy   Burn it, we're not going through that again.

Martyn   We'd be okay in London.

Roy   We're starting to happen here. We can't just jettison that because of some twisted screwball.

Martyn (*looking at the envelope*)   It's got a Belfast postmark.

Roy *sits down at the piano and plays a few jagged chords.*

Martyn   It was posted only the day before yesterday.

Roy   Will you stop drivelling on about it!

Martyn   I'm trying to keep my lunch down.

Roy *gets up, takes the letter, looks at it, gives it back, sits down again.*

Martyn   You're always talking about London.

Roy   Ultimately. When we're ready for it. When we've got an established reputation as a hit-making team. (*They cast around silently.*)

Martyn   We could take it to the police.

Roy   Waste of time.

Martyn   The typing might give them some kind of lead. (*He looks at the letter.*)

Roy   So what? What could they do about it?

Martyn   (*reading it out in a menacing accent*) 'Just so you know to expect a visit one of these days. Don't think you're safe hid for you're not. We have got your number.'

Roy   It's like some form of leprosy.

Martyn   'Unclean, Unclean.'

Roy   The whole country's a pestilential swamp.

Martyn   Stagnant. Sick. We'd be far better off out of it.

Roy   They're not intimidating me out of my own job and home.

Martyn   Home? Home is just a place where you can hide away. As the songwriter puts it.

Roy   I've no reason to hide. (*He plays a defiant phrase or two.*) What have you got?

Martyn   You're joking.

Roy   Come on, cough it up.

Martyn   I can't write a song with a death threat in my hand!

Roy   Look, we've got to keep delivering product. (*He notices* **Martyn** *listening.*) What is it?

Martyn   I thought I heard a noise.

They both listen. Silence.

Roy   There's nothing. (*He plays a jaunty fragment of tune.*)

Martyn   In one ear and out the other one.

Roy   What is?

Martyn   It's an idea for that tune. Something like, every time my girl and I go walking, I try to win her love with my sweet talking, but I something might as well not bother, for all my words and sighs and little white lies go in one ear and out the other. Then the hook, (*Sings.*) In one ear and out the other one, in one ear . . .

Roy   Bit awkward.

Martyn   It needs the right beat. Disco.

Roy *tries out some half-hearted phrases on the piano.* **Martyn** *continues slowly deliberating out loud.*

Martyn   Honey don't spoil my fun. Our conversation's just begun. Put away that big bad gun. But she didn't see what I meant. She pulled that trigger and the bullet went. (*Sings.*) In one ear and out the other one, in one ear . . .

Roy   Cut that out!

Martyn   It's a possible bridge.

Roy   It's not funny.

Martyn   What's eating you?

The door is knocked loudly, off. They pale visibly.

Martyn   We're not expecting anybody.

Roy   Maybe it's Monagh.

Martyn   You said she was up with Playfair for the weekend.

Roy   Maybe it's the postman.

Martyn   With another letter.

Roy (*moving*)   I'll go.

Martyn   Don't be mad.

Roy   It's just somebody at the door.

Martyn (*calling*)   Who is it, please?

Silence.

Roy   They didn't hear you.

Martyn   Look out the window.

Roy *goes off.*

Martyn   Do you recognise them?

Roy (*off*)   I can't see anything.

Martyn *goes off. Pause. Sound of the door being opened and closed. They come back.*

Martyn   Who would it have been?

Roy *shrugs.*

Roy   What'll we do?

Martyn   Maybe it was somebody canvassing. Or collecting.

Roy *picks up the letter and scrumples it.*

Roy   We'd better get packed for London.

Blackout. Music.

Stage. **Monagh** *in a follow spot with a hand mike.*

Monagh (*sings*)
  The banks are blowing up throughout the land
  I'm catching all the pennies in my hand
  They're falling twice as hard as I can stand
  The breakdown man is greatly in demand

When I was a young girl
I climbed the highest trees
I crawled out on the rooftops
Upon my hands and knees

So take me higher Daddy
Take me higher please
Show me how your elevator climbs
Don't think you can satisfy me
Till you fly me
Higher than you did the other times

I always wanted mountains
Hills just wouldn't do
I gotta get above the clouds
Where nothing spoils the view

So take me higher Daddy
Take me higher please
Lift me till my head can scrape the sky
I can't stand this world below me
Don't let go me
Show me some escape before I die

I don't want no miner
I need a steeplejack
I want to keep going up
Till there's no going back

So take me higher Daddy
Take me higher please
Take me on an escalator ride
Don't you see you just frustrate me
Elevate me
Lately I've been so dissatisfied

Oh, take me higher Daddy
Take me higher please
Show me how your rocket-ship can roar
Down here the devils hound me
Crawling all around me

Pounding on my walls and on my door . . .

I need a steeplejack
I need a steeplejack
I need a steeplejack
I need a steeplejack.

Blackout.

A & R office. The lights come up on the **Man** *– as a record
company A & R boss, Spalding – seated behind a desk.* **Roy** *in
front of it in his overcoat.*

Man   Where's your partner, Roy?

Roy   He's down with the 'flu.

Man   Our lovely London weather, eh?

Roy   He's really sorry not to have met you.

Man   There's interesting potential in some of these
demos. How long have you two been writing together?

Roy   Just nine months professionally.

Man   You'll appreciate that a company like ours needs
to be sure of a steady output of good product.

Roy   That's guaranteed, no problem.

Man   I tell you what we'll do, Roy. Send me in all
your product, for the whole nine months, every little
thing you've done, the entire catalogue. We'll talk it
around in here, and you and your partner pop in again
on the thirty-first.

Roy   Fine.

Man   I'll arrange for you to be paid a small retainer to
cover this. No commitment either way, of course. If we
should decide to use any of the songs, that'll be treated
as a separate matter. How's that?

Roy Great.

Man Lovely. One other thing, Roy, and I must be honest. I should lose the lady if I were you.

Roy Monagh?

Man In cabaret, in the right dress, if you'd had a few gins, maybe. On record, not a hope. Too old, too ordinary, and twopence a dozen.

Roy We all work together, you see. It's a package.

Man You've got a contractual arrangement, have you?

Roy It's just an understanding.

Man I don't see any problem in that case.

Roy We're friends.

Man Suit yourself. It's your career.

Slight pause.

Roy Is there somebody particular you'd like us to write for?

Man Let's be quite clear, Roy, that the company isn't at this stage making you any sort of offer. Any offer that might materialise would be contingent on the outcome of these propositions I've laid before you.

Roy I realise.

Man But if we were to get to the actual point of doing business – I'd be asking you to supply material for a couple of young acts. A couple of schoolgirls we've recently signed. Dynamite voices. Lovely little things too. I think one of them's going to be very big.

Pause.

Roy That sounds exciting.

Man We *were* hoping to break them over the summer. But to be perfectly honest, Roy, we don't have the songs

yet. It's a tough end of the market, solo females is, well,
you know yourself.

Roy   I think there's a change due though . . .

Man   Talk it over, see what you come up with, Roy,
give me a little tinkle in three weeks, all right?

Blackout.

Roy *and* **Martyn**'s *flat.* **Martyn** *sitting in pyjamas and
dressing-gown holding a telegram with one hand, pouring a glass of
orange juice and vodka with the other, chuckling to himself.* **Roy**
enters, throwing off his coat.

Roy   It's not good.

Martyn   (*holding up his glass*)   I give you Fletcher and
Semple . . .

Roy   They don't want Monagh.

Martyn   . . . who have just been chosen, my friend . . .
to represent Ireland . . . at the Ettelbruck Song Contest.

Roy *stares in silent disbelief.*

Roy   Says who?

Martyn   (*holding up telegram*)   Dublin.

Roy   What with?

Martyn   'Crybaby'.

Roy   Where is it?

Martyn   Luxembourg.

Roy   When?

Martyn   Twenty-seventh to thirty-first of this month.

Roy *takes the telegram, peruses it.*

Martyn   They're flying us over. All expenses paid.

Roy My knees are shaking.

Martyn Have some of this.

Roy I thought you'd the 'flu.

Martyn I've begun to recover.

Roy *drinks*.

Roy I've never heard of it, have you?

Martyn It's in Luxembourg. We can go to Paris. The Louvre. The Rive Gauche.

Roy I wonder if it carries any weight.

Martyn It's a free holiday.

Roy This is serious!

Martyn 'Crybaby'? You call that serious?

Roy It's a bright catchy song.

Martyn (*sings mockingly*) 'Don't be a crybaby, if you wanna be my baby . . .'

Roy It's a Europe kind of song, that's why they chose it. If she could win this thing, it might change his mind.

Martyn Whose mind?

Roy Spalding. The A & R chief.

Martyn I forgot all about that, what did he say?

Roy He liked the songs.

Martyn You mentioned something about Monagh.

Roy He wants us to get rid of her.

Pause.

Martyn What did *you* say?

Roy No dice. I told him we're a team. It's a package

deal. Take it or leave it.

Pause.

Martyn   What was he offering?

Roy   Nothing – yet. He wanted us to show him everything we'd written, the whole collection. Then he'd let us know at the end of the month.

Martyn (*rising*)   I'll get it all together.

Roy   What's the point?

Martyn   It's the third biggest record company in England, that's the point. It's arriving at long last, a guaranteed salary. Prestige. A civilised life-style. Instead of this.

Roy   We're not breaking up the team.

Martyn   There is no godforsaken team! We're in London, she's in Dublin.

Roy   Once we get fixed up . . .

Martyn   She doesn't care. She's stopped even trying. She's not concerned.

Roy   We're starting to happen. This song contest's a real chance to prove it.

Martyn   A chance to finish it, you mean. Amicably. We've got her on the air, got her into records, and now she has the chance to see Ettelbruck and die. A fitting conclusion to a fabulous partnership. No regrets, still the best of friends, you can even marry her if you like.

Roy   This has nothing to do with my personal feelings, Martyn, I want you to realise that.

Martyn   It's the biggest chance we're ever going to get, Roy.

Blackout. The band plays the tune of 'Crybaby'.

Pub. Soft lights come up on the **Girl** *– as Meryl Shanks, a journalist – sitting on a bar stool taking notes, with* **Roy** *and* **Martyn** *on either side of her holding drinks,* **Martyn** *laughing.*

Martyn   Stripped stark bare! Not a stitch! Caught red-handed wasn't the half of it. And Roy and me clutching big beakers of bubbly.

Roy   If it hadn't happened, we might still be teaching.

Martyn   But the gem of it is, he takes a long look at Monagh – that's the girl – draws himself up, and says, 'Never in my career have I encountered such bare-faced effrontery.' (*He laughs. Pause.*)

Girl   Marvellous.

Martyn   So then we started writing songs full-time.

Girl   In Belfast?

Roy   Right.

Girl   You mean there's an actual music scene there – as such?

Martyn   Oh yeah. There's a couple of first-rate studios.

Girl   What about – you know – clubs and things?

Martyn   There's a certain number of clubs, yeah.

Girl   Ooh. One rather forms the impression here in London that they've all been blown up long since.

Martyn   No, not at all. There's a certain amount of terrorist involvement in show business, of course.

Girl   Ooh. Really.

Martyn   You know, illegal clubs, racketeering, intimidation. All that stuff.

Girl   Did you experience any of that?

Martyn   Not a lot, apart from two death threats.

(*Uneasy pause.* **Roy** *exchanges a look with* **Martyn**.) It
happens to a lot of people. Social workers. Journalists.
Anybody. Rumours and smear stories.

Roy   We really got properly started in the business in
Dublin.

Girl   Is that why you moved to Dublin?

Roy   What?

Girl   The threats?

Martyn   The thing of it is, Meryl . . . we need to be a
bit careful.

Roy   We'd rather not go into it.

Girl   Fine.

Slight pause.

Roy   Actually, the others'll be arriving soon, we'd
better get back to the flat.

Girl   Ooh. Yes. (*She starts off.*)

Martyn (*as he follows*)   The Fletcher and Semple Story,
End of Part One!

*Blackout. The band plays 'Crybaby' bright and fast. Stops
abruptly.*

Roy *and* **Martyn**'*s flat. A burst of laughter: lights up on a
party scene. The* **Girl** *and the* **Woman** *– as Meryl Shanks and
Mrs Smiley, a music industry publicist from Dublin – are seated
on the sofa.* **Roy**, **Martyn** *and the* **Man** *– as Spalding – are
standing. All have drinks. Their laughter peters out.* **Monagh** *is
speaking from beside a drinks trolley.*

Monagh   So then they moved in on a big fat close-up.
You know, the pitted pores and the mouth grazing the
microphone and the big cow eyes mooning straight into
the camera. At which point a fleck of spittle appeared

on his fat lip. A large globule of white slime, squatting
right there in full view, looming closer and closer.
Whereupon . . . the middle finger of his hand entered
the picture . . . all hairy, and knobbly with rings . . . and
he flicked the spittle away. I nearly spewed all over the
set.

Man   He's an artiste who's worked a long time to get
to the top.

Woman   His voice is adorable, isn't it.

Man   His first album went gold a few months back.

Woman   It's so warm and soothing.

Pause.

Man (*to* **Monagh**)   You get the same programmes as
we do, then?

Monagh   Pardon?

Man   In Northern Ireland . . . you get our television
programmes, do you?

Monagh   Now and then – if the wind's in the right
quarter.

Roy *appears with a bottle.*

Roy   Another drink, Mrs Smiley?

Woman   I will in a minute, lovie.

Roy   Mr Spalding?

Monagh   Why don't we all just help ourselves when
the need arises? (*She liberally does so.*)

Roy   Certainly. Everybody feel free.

Woman   Do you know, I haven't set foot in Belfast for
eight or nine years, it must be.

Man   During the war was my only time there.

Girl (*to* **Monagh**)   It's amazingly brave of you to live there.

Monagh   Never give it a second thought, do we, lads? Dodging your way through a hail of bullets to fight for the last loaf of bread in the shop . . . it comes naturally to us.

Girl   Really, though – it's very hard for us to imagine what it must be like.

Monagh   I'll tell you what it's like . . .

Roy   We all live in Dublin now, you see.

Monagh   You know these items you see in the papers every so often. The latest world record for staying underground buried alive in a coffin. I don't know whether you've noticed . . . but the cretin who does it is always an Irishman. Comes naturally to us. Breathing through a straw, crapping into your absorbent underpants. That's what it's like.

Slight pause.

Woman   I think you must be a Scorpio, Monagh.

Monagh   Cancer. Lovie.

Martyn   Are you keen on astrology, Mrs Smiley?

Woman   Oh, I follow my horoscope religiously, isn't it terrible?

Monagh   With the moon lodged in the lower bicuspid.

Roy   I hope ours were favourable for the week ahead anyway – for the Song Contest.

Monagh   I've read them. I read all the papers in the plane coming to London. They all said the same thing. On no account go anywhere . . . this week . . . because there's nowhere left worth the trip. Not even the moon. Especially not the moon. Why don't you two ever write a song about the good old moon?

Martyn   I could never think of a good rhyme for it.

Monagh (*singing*)   By the light of the silvery *moon* . . . I love to *spoon* . . . with my honey I'll *croon* . . . love's *tune* . . .

Roy   Okay, Monagh . . .

Monagh   . . . Honey*moon* . . . keep a-shining in *June* . . . your silvery beams will light love's dreams, we'll be cuddling *soon* . . . by the light of the *moon*.

Martyn   Yeah, that pretty well cornered the market.

Monagh   I wish to God they'd never gone near it. It's polluted now. Everybody was so excited, I wasn't excited, I cried my piggy little eyes out. It was just a dirty beach. One of them even said that . . . just a dirty beach they'd brought with them in their heads. It gives all the songs a new twist, doesn't it? (*Sings.*) Somewhere there's music, how high the moon . . . (*Speaks.*) high as a wrestler's jockstrap. (*Uncomfortable silence as she pours herself a drink.*)

Man   I shall have to be off, I'm afraid.

Woman (*rising also*)   Would you ever be able to drop me at my hotel, Mr Spalding? It's not very far.

Man   Certainly, a pleasure.

Roy   We'll be seeing you in the morning, then, Mrs Smiley?

Woman   Aren't they adorable fellas, these two rascals?

Man   I like their spirit, I must say.

Martyn   Thanks for dropping in, Mr Spalding.

Man   My pleasure, Martyn, nice to meet you. Give me a little tinkle when you get back from the Continent and I'll let you know what's what. All right?

Martyn   The minute we're back.

Man   Nice to meet you all.

Woman   Yes, indeed. Cheerio, lovies.

Girl   Bye.

Roy and **Martyn** *escort the* **Man** *and* **Woman** *off.*

Monagh   What kind of a name is Meryl?

Girl   Ooh. Well. My eldest sister was given Beryl, then the second one was Cheryl, so I suppose I just had to be Meryl.

Monagh   Any brothers?

Girl   Not actually, no.

Monagh   That's a blessing. (*She pours a drink.*) Mrs Smiley is a publican for the Irish music industry.

Girl   Yes. Quite. A publicist, you mean.

Monagh   No, I mean a publican. She sustains the flow of drink at a constant level. It's her one redeeming feature.

Girl   She didn't actually clue me in – fully, I mean – on just what was happening.

Monagh   God himself would be hard put. What rag do you write for?

Girl   I'm a freelance.

Monagh   When you think about it, we've had quite a Biblical crowd here tonight. A scribe. A pharisee. A publican. Jesus Christ. And God the Father Almighty. I gather it's the entry into Jerusalem.

Girl   And which part do you play?

Monagh   I'm the shagging donkey.

Girl   Yes, I gather that the Spalding man is probably going to offer a contract to your friends?

Monagh We gather alike.

Girl They were telling me a perfectly amazing story about receiving death threats.

Monagh Where they now? So you've been getting the whole thrilling saga of their turbulent rise to fame?

Girl How exactly did it come about?

Monagh It's not unusual. It happens every day. Innocent people. Some of them get more than threats. Some of them get shot. Some of them even go and bloody die. (*She grabs the whiskey bottle, sees that it's empty and tosses it away.*) It's Hunt-the-Booze Time. The private supply. Bet you I know where they've got it. (*She wanders off.*)

Girl It was just random threats, then, was it?

She follows **Monagh** *off. Stage empty for a moment. Sound of final farewells and door being closed from off.*

Roy (*entering*) Where is she?

Martyn (*entering*) Where's Meryl?

Roy *sinks down on the sofa.*

Roy What the bloody hell is she trying to do to me?

Martyn I never dreamed she'd take it this hard.

Roy Her whole behaviour was just an attempt at sabotage.

Martyn She's had it, Roy.

Roy She's ruined her chances with Spalding, that's for sure.

Martyn She damned near ruined ours.

Roy They must be in the kitchen.

Martyn (*picks up empty bottle*) She got through practically all of this single-handed. That's what she'll be after.

*The **Girl** appears in the doorway.*

Roy   God only knows what she's telling that bird-brained reporter.

Martyn   Hello there, Meryl.

Girl   I'm afraid that girl, your friend, seems rather distraught.

Martyn   Is she in the kitchen?

Girl   We were just talking, and then she literally ran off into the night. Into that sort of waste ground at the back.

Roy   We'd better go after her.

Girl   Would it seem awful of me to slip off? I'm rather late for another appointment . . .

Roy   That's okay.

Martyn   We're sorry for what was inflicted on you.

Girl   Ooh. I loved every minute. Really did. I'm sure I can place a piece about you both.

Martyn   That's terrific, Meryl.

Girl   Perhaps we can talk again sometime.

Martyn   Certainly. Anytime.

Girl   Well, bye.

She exits. **Martyn** *follows.*

Martyn (*off*)   Safe home.

Roy (*from door*)   Cheers.

Martyn *re-enters.*

Roy   We'd better get some torches.

Blackout. The band play 'Crybaby'.

Parking lot. The beams of two torches flicker across the dark stage.
Roy *and* **Martyn** *are heard calling* **Monagh**'s *name from off. They enter, flashing the torches into the corners of the stage; one of them picks out* **Monagh**, *huddled on the ground, staring straight ahead. They train both torches on her.*

Roy   Are you all right? What's wrong?

Monagh (*voice dead*)   He was filming. There was shooting. It was in the paper.

Martyn   She's raving.

Roy   No, it's Playfair. Something's happened. Monagh. It's Playfair, isn't it.

Monagh   He was hit. They shot him. He's dead.

Pause.

Roy   Help her up.

They hoist her to her feet and help her off in silence. The torchlight flickers disappear.

Stadium. Flood of light. The band plays a fanfare. The **Woman** *sweeps on in a gaudy full-length dress, carrying a mike, grinning hugely.*

Woman   An elo, dir Dammen en dir Hären, ass de Moment komm, wo deï distinguëert Dammen en Hären vun onsem Jury hîrt Schlussurteel ofzegin hun. Mir werden also elo geschwenn wessen, wien de Gewenner vun desem allereïschten Ettelbrecker Internationalen Gesangsfestival ass. Dir sit bestemmt eens mat mir, wann ech soen, dass net nemmen eent, mais vill vun deenen Lidder, deï mir bejëert hun, de Preis verdengen. Eise Jury huet et bestemmt net lîcht. Wahrend de Jury nun sein Endresultat vîrbereet wöllt de Willi Zero ons nach e besschen ennerhâlen, an zwar sengt hien ons dat Lidd: the Zig Zag Song!

She goes off, as the **Man**, *loudly dressed as Willy Zero, runs on with a hand mike. The band strikes up. As he sings, he tacks back and forth across the stage, swerving his knees from side to side.*

Man (*sings*)
Sing hello the Zig Zag song
Sing bye-bye the Zig Zag song
It's a song that all can sing
Come along and let it ring

Sing it low the Zig Zag song
Sing it high the Zig Zag song
Do the Zig Zag as you go
Now the chorus goes just so:

La-la-la-la-la-la-la
La-la-la-la-la-la-la
La-la-la-la-la-la-la
La-la-la-la-la-la-la

Zigging Zagging up and down
Zigging Zagging round the town
Oh, la-la-la-la-la-la-la
La-la-la-la-la-la-la

Now you know the Zig Zag song
All join in the Zig Zag song
To and fro the Zig Zag song
All begin the Zig Zag song

Sing it low – Zig Zag song
Sing it high – Zig Zag song
Do the Zig Zag as you go
Now the chorus goes just so:

La-la-la-la-la-la-la
La-la-la-la-la-la-la
La-la-la-la-la-la-la
La-la-la-la-la-la-la

And that's how you do the Zig Zag song!

He zig zags off and the lights fade out. The band plays on in double time in the darkness.

Airport lounge. Bright harsh fluorescent glare. A row of moulded plastic seats. **Roy** *on the end one reading a newspaper.* **Martyn** *behind him. Both dressed in very flashy showbiz formal wear – ruffled shirt-fronts, floppy bow ties, huge cufflinks – but all of it ravaged by several days without sleep. They talk and move like sleep-walkers.* **Monagh** *is further down the row, sprawled out, her head lolling on her chest.*

Martyn It's all there. Everything. (*Reading.*) 'Terrorist Girl Who Calls The Tune'.

Roy Christ!

Martyn (*reading*) 'Songwriters Roy Fletcher and Martyn Semple . . . a somewhat unusual start to their careers . . . traditional-style Republican martyr-ballads – on commission . . . "We don't talk much about it these days," says Martyn, 29, wryly . . .'

Roy She must have pumped Monagh for it. Evil bitch.

Martyn Wait till Marie Kyle sees it.

Roy (*thrusting paper aside*) Ah, to hell. What's the time?

Martyn (*looking at his watch*) Just after seven.

Roy A.m. or p.m.?

Martyn I don't know. (*More frightened.*) I don't know. What was it like coming in?

Roy Twilight.

Martyn Either way. There's no windows.

Roy Maybe there's a strike or something.

Martyn They won't let her on the plane like that, Roy.

Roy *moves down and slaps* **Monagh** *on the cheeks.*

Roy   Monagh. Pull out of it. We have to get on the plane now. Monagh. (*She moans a little but doesn't move.*) Her handbag's full of pills.

Martyn   Not as full as she is.

Roy *returns and sits again.*

Martyn   We're not in the right place, Roy.

Roy   The airport. It's the airport. There's only one.

Martyn   Where's the plane, then?

Roy   It doesn't go till ten.

Martyn   P.m. or a.m.? (*Pause.*) We're early.

Roy   The money's spent. I don't even feel tired any more.

Martyn   I feel corroded. My flesh. I wish they'd turn the lights off.

Roy   That Swiss song was gunk.

Martyn   What was it about, anyway?

Roy   How do I know? Cuckoo clocks.

Martyn   You could tell it would win. It was the elbow routine. The crowd fell for that.

Roy   We should have walked it.

Martyn   After her shoe came off – I couldn't watch any more.

Roy   She mixed up the chorus and the verse. It was just like gibberish. The band didn't know what to do. They limped on behind her but she was all out of key. You couldn't describe it as singing at all. It was just a prolonged howl. I had to go and help her off at the end.

Pause.

Martyn Hey, we never opened our telegrams. (*He takes four greetings telegrams and a larger packet from his case … He opens the first one, glances at it.*) I think we ought to change our style, you know. Get back to the roots. (*Reads:*) 'Monagh my sweet may your Crybaby cry all the way to the bank. Cyril.' (*He tosses the telegram back in the case.*)

Roy What roots?

Martyn Something ethnic. The heritage of the past. (*He opens another telegram, glances at it.*)

Roy Cecilia Street Primary School. Rock 'n' roll. Football. The pictures. That's my roots.

Martyn I mean further back than that. The country's history. The old culture. The tradition. (*Throws telegram into case.*)

Roy That's got nothing to do with me. It's got nothing to do with you either.

Martyn I'd an uncle who was a fluent Irish speaker. I was pretty good at it at school too.

Roy You're no more a Gaelic speaker than I am.

Martyn You? You've never learnt a word of it.

Roy I picked up a few phrases once from a tourist brochure. It was in a Chinese restaurant in Cork.

Martyn (*opening another telegram*) Extraordinary people, the Chinese, I've been reading them up, you know. I've been thinking them over.

Roy They write lousy tunes.

Martyn A quarter of the world's people. And nobody owns anything. It's all held in common. They all work for each other. For the common good. (*Throws telegram in case.*)

Roy The Japanese are a different story, however.

Martyn The only thing that bothers me is – I've yet
to hear of a Chinese joke. I don't mean Chinese laundry
jokes – chop-chop flied lice all that stuff – I mean one
of their own. A Red Chinese gag. They don't appear to
have a sense of humour. The way we do. It's a serious
drawback, that, in my opinion. It could very well end
up endangering world peace. (*He opens another telegram.*) Of
course I might be mistaken. I might have it wrong. The
way they see things – maybe *we're* a Chinese joke. (*He
throws the telegram into the case.*)

Roy You don't even like folk songs.

Martyn Some. Not all.

Roy I hate them.

Martyn This'll ruin us, Roy. We'll be blacklisted.

Roy They won't blame us. The song was all right. It's
the end of the line for her, though.

Martyn Maybe we should get her to a doctor.

Roy She'll be all right. It'll pass off. Anyway, all the
money's spent.

Martyn We've got a present. (*He begins to pick at the
tape on the remaining package.*) I feel as if we've been here
for days already. Years. Maybe the whole airport's been
hijacked. Maybe all the ground staff are pinned down in
their offices. By terrorist guns. The control tower
paralysed. All the planes flying round and round stacked
up above us. Running out of fuel. Any minute now
they'll start falling out of the sky like asphyxiated flies.
(*Pause.*) It hasn't turned out the way we thought it
would, Roy.

Roy Not much.

Martyn It's not the way we dreamed it would be.

Roy   Not yet.

Martyn   How long are we going to have to wait in this place?

*He rips the tape off the package. Simultaneously – Blackout. Explosion. A noisy drum intro. The band strikes up. A red spot comes on. Showing **Monagh** on her feet, smiling brightly, with a hand mike. **Roy** and **Martyn**'s seats are toppled over. In the red glow, we see them on their knees, hands and faces covered in blood, groping about blindly.*

Monagh (*sings*)
Laugh and the world laughs with you,
Cry and you cry alone,
If you plan to make me love you,
If you want me for your own –

Don't be a crybaby
If you wanna be my baby
For when you're smiling
You're the apple of my eye
Don't heave a sigh baby
There's no earthly reason why baby
You know that loving is something
Money can't buy
You know that loving is really something
Money can't buy!

Blackout.

Nightshade

For Kate, as ever

Characters

Quinn, *forty-six*
Delia, *his daughter, sixteen*
The Dean, *his brother-in-law, forty-seven*
Vance, *twenty-four*
Miss Gault, *forty*
Dr Dempster, *sixty-two*
Albert Bell, *fifty-six*
Vincent Kane, *thirty-one*
Male Employee
Female Employee

Nightshade was first performed at the Peacock Theatre, Dublin, on 9 October 1980, with the following cast:

Quinn	T.P. McKenna
Delia	Lise-Ann McLaughlin
The Dean	Michael Duffy
Miss Gault	Maureen Toal
Vance	Colm Meaney
Dr Dempster	Kate Flynn
Albert Bell	Geoffrey Golden
Vincent Kane	Niall O'Brien

Directed by Chris Parr
Designed by Bronwen Casson
Lighting by Tony Wakefield

Act One

The place is a city within the British Isles. The time is the immediate future.

The setting is formalised and symmetrical, with the disproportion of a dream. There is a great back wall like the facade of a mausoleum, with the name JOHN QUINN *carved across it. Underneath are the words* MAGICIAN AND MORTICIAN (MAGICIAN *is over the stage right area, and* MORTICIAN *over the stage left). There are heavy outer doors in the bottom corners of this wall. At its centre is a shiny black curtain, lustrously swagged and tucked, which can be drawn up to reveal what is – figuratively as well as literally – an inner stage.*

Before this curtained inner stage is a broad arc of platform, the circumference of which is stepped – three steps leading down to what remains of the mainstage area. This raised platform will serve as a kind of all-purpose public room. The remaining mainstage area (which serves for various private rooms) is furnished as follows: mid-way down, on extreme left and right, there are identical steel-and-chromium office desks and chairs. To the immediate left and right of centre, hard by the platform steps, there are identical large leather reclining armchairs. The vicinity of these armchairs is **Quinn***'s home, which is next door to his funeral parlour.*

Each side wall has three identical interior doors, evenly spaced. They should be used at random, as should the outer doors in the back wall. The action is fast and continuous, a constant traffic, the fitful opening and closing of possibilities. The staging and lighting should be as magic as possible: discoveries, disappearances, transformations; one foot through the looking-glass, at least.

Darkness first. Then the curtain rises on the inner stage to reveal **Quinn***, in topper and tails, lighting a cigarette. Disposed about the public room and the steps, listening, are the shadowy figures of* **Vance***,* **Kane***,* **Bell***, the* **Dean***, the* **Male Employee** *and the* **Female Employee**, *some of them holding plates and drinks.*

Quinn You don't need me to tell you people . . . miracles can be made to happen. The impossible takes a little time, that's all. One year in this case. We showed them how – (*He opens his matchbox again, but this time pulls a red handkerchief out of it.*) – matchless, that's the word for it. Double your fleet of motors. Triple your turnover. A new branch in the New Year, how do we do it? Business sense. Hard graft. Team work – (*He is stubbing out the cigarette on the hanky, and now holds up the hanky unmarked.*) – a performance not to be sneezed at, in this day and age. With the country in rags and tatters all around us – (*He produces a soup plate.*) – and plenty of other firms in the soup, as well you know. With Mr Wolf at the door. But not round this way, friends. We're living in the modern world – (*He drapes the hanky over the soup plate.*) – we're perfecting the tricks of the trade round here. And that spells growth! (*He whips the hanky away; the plate has sprouted flowers.*) Expansion. An unmitigated success, in fact, and it was us together that pulled it off. You and me and nobody else. So now, a toast – (*He drapes the hanky over his left hand.*) – to a great year gone by, my friends, and a better one yet ahead. Because we're only starting out, you see. This is just the warm-up. You've seen nothing yet. There'll be branches sprouting all over. Buildings out of thin air. Business like you've never seen. One fine day we'll be taking over this city – here's to it! (*He whips the hanky away to reveal a glass of wine which he sips. Applause from the others. He throws the hanky into the air and it turns into a snake. He bows.*) Thank you, you're very kind. And now by way of a modest grand finale – my assistant and I have prepared a little surprise. Presto!

Gong. **Quinn** *hauls from the inner stage wings a tall magician's box, and opens it to reveal* **Delia** *inside, dressed in a black satin tap-dance outfit and spangled tights. Music starts off.* **Delia** *steps out, and* **Quinn** *turns the box round to show the inside empty,*

*tapping on the inside walls. He then ushers **Delia** into it again,*
closes it up and turns it a full 360 degrees. Drum roll. **Quinn**
takes a short plank, slots it into the side of the box, and pushes it
through. Then a second and a third as the drum roll builds. He
then holds up a large ornamental sword, slots it in, and pushes.

There is a frightening scream from inside. Blood spurts out and
runs down the front of the box. The music stops. **Quinn**
suddenly tears the box open in a frenzy. **Delia** *stands inside,*
clutching her stomach, face contorted in pain. Music starts again,
very loud. She suddenly springs out with a dazzling smile, into a
quick tap routine, and dances off. The music stops, the curtain
falls on the inner stage, **Quinn** *having moved down into the*
public room. There is a moment's awkward silence.

Quinn   Well now, there's your cue, everybody! Time
to work off all that grub, what do you say? The dance
floor beckons, who's game for a stagger around?

All except **Kane** *and* **Bell** *move off, chatting.*

Quinn   Save one for me now, ladies, don't forget the
old boss!

Vance (*lingering at his elbow*)   I didn't know you were a
magician, Mr Quinn.

Quinn   Oh, just my party piece, Vance.

Vance   You do it most professionally.

Quinn   Isn't she rare?

Vance   Your daughter, is it?

Quinn   A born comedian. Every professional man
needs a recreation, Vance.

Vance   Indeed.

Quinn   I do the odd social evening. For the church or
Masonic Lodge or that. Children's parties.

Vance   Very impressive.

Quinn   Simple stuff on the whole.

Slight pause.

Vance   She's a lovely girl.

Quinn   A gifted child, you know. Years ahead of herself, in the brain-box.

Vance   Is that so?

Quinn   No credit to me, I'm afraid. She's forever trying to put one over on her old man, eh?

Vance   Yes.

Quinn   What about yourself?

Vance   In what way?

Quinn   Any hobbies?

Vance   Well. Driving.

Quinn   After you, Vance, go ahead.

They go off. A band can be heard from an adjacent ballroom playing 'That Old Black Magic'. **Kane** *and* **Bell** *are left sitting on the steps. Pause.*

Kane   The first four hours are the worst.

Bell   You'd wonder where he gets all the energy from.

Kane   Listen, if you were coining money at the rate he is . . . you'd be sawing through ladies, rings round you.

Pause.

Bell   Say what you like, Vincent – but there'll never be a go-slow in the funeral business.

Kane (*looking at the side of his right foot*)   Oh Christ.

Bell   What's up?

Kane   I've got blood on my shoe from that motorway job.

Bell   It's never even been entertained. In the whole seventy years of the union's existence.

Kane   I only bought them last month.

Bell   You can dye them.

Kane   This is exactly the sort of thing, you see. People need waking up. A fellow gets his face stove in on his steering wheel, and who's expected to scrape it into the plastic bag? His own mother wouldn't go near it. Let alone the other driver. We're talking about people who can barely face it when their pussy-cat pukes on the Axminster.

Bell   All in a day's work.

Kane   People who blench at eating rabbit pie. While we're out scooping their son's intestines back into the stomach cavity, with all due reverence and dignity, of course.

Bell   All part of the job, Vincent. It's a public service.

Kane   Don't talk to me about public service. We're invisible men to the public.

Bell   The very idea of industrial action is just outlandish.

Kane   The funeral service managements have been getting away with murder.

Bell   Quinn's not the worst.

Kane   It's money on the table I'm looking for.

Bell   He's open to reason.

Kane   We'll see. We'll see what he can pull out of the hat in real life. (*Pause. He stands up.*) I must have a word with the new assistant.

Bell   A slippery-looking customer.

Kane   You never know, he might come in very handy,

the same Vance. C'mon, we'd better join the bunfight.

Bell (*rising*) All the same, Quinn had me fooled there for a minute – with the blood coming out of the box.

Kane The daughter had *him* fooled.

Bell D'you reckon? She's a bit of a practical jester, right enough.

Kane Nutty as a fruitcake, if you want my opinion. She's a worse case than the da.

Bell Not a word of the wife, for over a year now. Isn't it mystifying?

Kane Aye, Agnes outdid the pair of them there. She was the escapologist.

They follow the others off. As they go through the door, the band music peaks and finishes. **Dr Dempster** *appears at the desk stage right, in her white coat, facing* **Delia**, *who is wearing a street coat over her tap outfit.*

Dempster Is it your father's pills?

Delia I think it's meant to be me as well.

Dempster Why, what ails you?

Delia He wants you to check up on me.

Dempster You shouldn't be walking the streets like that, you'll catch your death.

Delia There's a lot of it about.

Dempster Don't you smart-talk me, madam.

Pause.

Delia He's frightened that I'm going to turn out like my mother.

Dempster He needn't be.

Delia Was she clinically insane, do you think?

Dempster   We're not discussing your mother.

Delia   You wouldn't happen to know where she is?

Dempster   That's quite enough! (*Pause.*) You're entitled to grieve for what has happened. But grief is no licence for cheek and misconduct.

Delia   Yes, Doctor.

Dempster   Your mother came of fine stock. Four generations of bishops and high-court judges, that's how strong her mind was . . .

Delia   Why the past tense?

Dempster   . . . but she was also possessed of a delicacy of feeling. I'm saying no more, run on home now.

Delia   She'll never be dead as long as I draw breath.

Dempster   Don't flatter yourself, madam. There wasn't a trace of show-off in her, nor self-centredness either. You're a Quinn. Through and through.

Pause.

Delia   Is that what you want me to tell him?

Dempster   You can tell him I'm a medical doctor and I can't prescribe a cure for a spoilt child.

Delia   It's an odd phrase, that. Like failed priest. Or fallen woman.

Dempster   His pills are with the receptionist.

Delia   I hope your own father is keeping better.

Dempster   Not particularly, thank you.

Delia   Just think, Dr Dempster – your hands were the first that were ever laid on me.

Dempster   On you and scores of others, young lady.

Delia   Oh, I know. It was nothing personal.

Delia *exits.* **Dempster** *frowns, then follows. Muzak starts.*
Quinn *appears upstage left, holding aloft a remote-control switch.*
Vance *is at his shoulder.* **Quinn** *presses the switch and the
muzak stops abruptly.*

Quinn   Eh? (*He starts the muzak again, smiles at* **Vance**,
then stops it again.) All right?

Vance   Throughout the premises?

Quinn   Two separate circuits. Organ hymns for the
Selection and Reposing Rooms. This one everywhere
else.

Vance   I congratulate you, Mr Quinn.

Quinn   Tasteful, you see. Dignified. But nothing
mournful about it.

Vance   Yes.

Quinn   Mournfulness is the first thing to avoid,
Mervyn. Now, that suit, for example.

Vance   Too dark?

Quinn   In actual fact, it appears black.

Vance   There is a grey line . . .

Quinn   I see it indeed, and it's a nice-enough looking
suit, but you take the point. Appearances. Clients don't
want reminded. Black ties, armbands, doleful faces – no,
not nowadays, the client wants normality. Mind you, I'm
not saying you turn up on the doorstep in a loud check
singing 'Yankee Doodle Dandy'.

Vance   I understand.

Quinn   But you're not a glorified gravedigger either.
You're a respected family adviser, along with the doctor
and the solicitor. A professional man. So you dress and
act accordingly.

Vance   Point taken.

Quinn *leads the way to the desk stage left.*

Quinn   Now then. You're on your way to a First Call. What are you taking along with you?

Vance   The arrangements briefcase.

Quinn   Containing?

Vance   Arrangements forms, list of charges, coffin and casket brochures and photographs.

Quinn   Good. So you're in the house. I'm the client. And I'm raving and howling uncontrollably. Heels kicking the settee. Tears tripping me. Over to you.

Vance   Please accept . . . our deepest sympathy. For your tragic loss. Rest assured, we will do all in our power to ease the burden . . .

Quinn   Hopeless.

Vance   Ah.

Quinn   Weeping and bawling redoubled. You see, Mervyn, it's not just learning our business that counts – but also learning what isn't our business. A crucial distinction. E.g. Efficient disposition of the deceased – our business. The private emotions of the bereaved – no business of ours.

Vance   You ignore them, then?

Quinn   An attitude of polite neutrality. You neither sympathise nor reproach. Like the doctor and the lawyer. Non-judgmental.

Vance   What if the client goes on crying?

Quinn   Describe your demeanour coming into the room.

Vance   Businesslike . . . efficient . . . dignified?

Quinn   Overriding all that . . . you have authority. Relaxed professional authority. To the client, you see, that's bracing. Calming.

Vance   Authority and relaxed.

Quinn   But – let's say the storm still rages on. Now, there's invariably another party in the room, a bit calmer. A neighbour, maybe, or relative. You say to them – I shall wait outside to let Mrs Brown have the chance to compose herself. You convey authority. Along with the sense that you're in no hurry. You are a reassuring figure of professional expertise who is at their disposal. It never fails.

Vance   Of course, yes, it makes sense.

Quinn   You'll find, by the way, that type of client will tend to be down the ladder a bit, educationally speaking.

Vance   The emotional kind?

Quinn   The higher the educational level, the more composed the client.

Vance   Stands to reason.

Quinn   The lower the noisier. As a matter of fact, that had a lot to do with your getting this job, Mervyn.

Vance   How do you mean?

Quinn   Your degree. When you take over the new branch, you'll be servicing a different sort of parish than down here.

Vance   Suburbia.

Quinn   New estates. Skilled workers, in the main. It's a maxim in the business – the funeral diector should always be just one degree higher than his parish. Otherwise no authority. You'll get on very well up there.

Vance   With the benefit of your experience, Mr Quinn.

Quinn We all share a big responsibility, Mervyn. To the profession. That comes first.

Vance Quite.

Quinn You see, we haven't always enjoyed the high standing in society that is ours today. Even in my young days, the so-called undertaker was socially ostracised by and large. He was an agent of doom. Of course there was a shocking amount of charlatanism and amateurishness in those days.

Vance From a strictly business point of view – the profession seems to me to be almost in its infancy.

Quinn That's the God's own truth, Mervyn. And it has everything to do with the excitement of the job. We're in the pioneering phase. But . . . it's fatally easy to get carried away. You must never forget – you're first and foremost a professional adviser. And only secondarily a salesman.

Vance Sales are what makes profits, of course.

Quinn Take it from me, there's only one way to make a worthwhile profit. Give the customer what he wants. And charge him only for what he gets. I can't abide crookedness in any shape or form, Mervyn. You wouldn't believe the rackets some people get up to in this business. It harms the profession's image, but there's more than that to consider. There's the man upstairs. (*He gestures to heaven.*) He's the sleeping partner in this enterprise. I firmly believe in keeping on the right side of him, Mervyn.

Vance Absolutely.

Quinn It might be out of fashion in some quarters, but not round this way. (*Pause.*) Where were we?

Vance You were mentioning sales.

Quinn So I was. The point being, our main product

is service. That's what we're selling to the public first
and foremost, not the hardware. We're not just glorified
reps for the florist and the coffin factory.

Vance   Though I'd be interested to hear about the
arrangements that you have with them.

Quinn   We'll get to the small print in due course,
Mervyn.

Vance   Sorry.

Quinn   I just want to impress on you the values in this
profession. As I see them. You'll have noticed this. (*He
indicates an embroidered text in a frame on the desk.*)

Vance (*reading*)   'And the light shineth in darkness; and
the darkness comprehended it not.' Beautifully worked.

Quinn   My wife was a fine needlewoman. In her
young days.

Vance   Mrs Quinn? She did this?

Quinn   The firm's motto, Vance. We're bringing light
into the gloom of superstition and fear. We're letting in
warm sunshine to the dark corners. That's the service
we offer the client, and believe you me, he deeply
appreciates it. We get thank-you letters by the lorry-load.
So much for the critics.

Vance   Critics?

Quinn   Oh, there's always people ready to criticise in
any walk of life. The smart set. The same sort that's
richly amused by our calling. The sort that has a good
old snigger every time it's mentioned.

Vance   Up until the moment when they find they have
a corpse in the lounge.

Quinn   Crudely put, Mervyn, but the point is sound
enough. Anyway. That's enough nattering for the
moment. I want you to read through these – invoices

for the past few months. And this is the Diary. All the
details of every funeral we handle are entered here, as
they arrive – like a log-book. That'll fill you in on the
pattern of business we handle.

Vance Splendid.

Quinn And by the way – don't hesitate, if you see
room for improvement anywhere. Speak your piece. It's
liberty hall round this way.

Vance Thanks.

He gets involved in the invoices. **Quinn** *begins to work at the
desk also.* **Albert Bell** *has meanwhile come in through the outer
door and passed on through to the public room, where he sets up
two trestles. On his way back out he encounters* **Delia** *arriving,
in her school uniform, carrying a large Bible.*

Delia Hello, Albert.

Bell Is it young Delia or what?

Delia The very self-same.

Bell I hardly know you this weather, you're growing
up too fast.

Delia Are you still at the wrestling game, Albert?

Bell Ah, just the odd bout, to show the young fellows
how it's done (*Indicating her Bible.*) What's this here, are
you turning into a Bible scholar now?

Delia (*handing it to him*) It's for a school project.
Though I recommend it if you're looking for a good
read.

Bell (*looking through it*) Pictures and all.

Delia There's even a bit of wrestling for you, Jacob
versus the Angel. Speaking of which, is Quinn around?

Bell So far as I know, Delia.

Delia Would you tell him from me that Miss Gault is

on her way to see him . . .

Bell Oh Lord, are you in her bad books again?

Delia I don't know but I'm trying to avoid her . . . (*The door opens.*) . . . oh shit, too late . . . (*But it's* **Vincent Kane** *who enters.*)

Kane This body out here is growing a beard.

Bell Don't fret, I'm coming.

Kane Hiya, Delia.

Delia Hello, Mr Kane.

Kane That was a great number you did at the firm's do.

Delia Thank you.

Kane You know, you and me should team up, I've won prizes for my *paso doble*. (*He suddenly sweeps her round the floor in a comic Latin embrace.*)

Bell It's a credit to you, with feet like them.

Kane Light, bright and nimble, old hand.

Delia (*giggling*) Listen, I've got to get out of here . . .

Bell Don't embarrass the child.

Kane This is no child, this is a star of the dance!

Vance *appears. Awkward silence.*

Delia Oh, well. Midnight strikes again. (*She takes the Bible from* **Bell**.) My pumpkin awaits. (*She exits.*)

Vance Sorry, I was just wondering about the Mulligan remains – have they been collected yet?

Bell We're taking them through now to the Embalming Room, boss.

Vance I thought I'd just keep the Diary straight.

Kane   Yes, you do that, Mr Vance.

He and **Bell** *start out, but as they reach the door,* **Miss Gault** *appears in it. She is brought face to face with* **Vance** *as she enters.* **Kane** *and* **Bell** *go on out.*

Gault   Vance!

Vance   Hello, Miss Gault.

Gault   What on earth are you doing here? I hope that nobody . . . I mean, you haven't lost anyone, I hope.

Vance   No, I work for the firm.

Gault   For Quinn's?

Vance   Mr Quinn has engaged me as his personal assistant. (**Kane** *and* **Bell** *re-enter, carrying a 'shell' or temporary coffin. They pass by* **Gault** *and* **Vance** *en route to the public room.*) While I get to know the business.

Gault   Physics was your subject, as I recall.

Vance (*deadpan*)   The law of falling bodies. (**Kane** *and* **Bell** *plant the 'shell' on the trestles, and depart.*) I switched to Business Studies.

Gault   How do you like it?

Vance   It's a good firm. There's a branch opening in the New Year which I'm to take over. It's a business with a lot of growth potential.

Gault (*deadpan*)   For the daisies, certainly.

Pause.

Vance   I trust you haven't suffered a bereavement yourself, Miss Gault?

Gault   No, no, just visiting, thank God. I was hoping to have a word with Mr Quinn.

Vance   Certainly. You'll find him in the office there.

Gault   Good. Well. Nice to see our former pupils

prosper.

Vance   You're looking very well yourself, Miss Gault.

Gault   Am I?

Vance   I see you've let your hair grow.

Gault   You've had yours cut, Vance.

Vance   Mr Quinn recommended it.

Gault   Good for him. Well, very best wishes in your new employ.

Vance   I'd like to drop in at school some day.

Gault   Do.

He exits. She proceeds down to **Quinn**'s *desk.*

Quinn   Miss Gault! (*With a flourish, he reveals a deck of cards spread in his right hand.*) Come in. Take a seat. Pick a card.

Gault   Any card?

Quinn   That's the style.

Gault (*as she takes a card and sits*)   You seem full of beans, Mr Quinn.

Quinn   Speaking of which – coffee?

Gault   Thank you, no.

Quinn   A glass of sherry, perhaps?

Gault   Well – maybe I'll have a coffee after all.

Quinn *presses the buzzer on his office intercom.*

Quinn   Back in the deck. I'm not looking.

Female Employee (*on intercom*)   Yes, sir?

Quinn (*to intercom as* **Gault** *replaces the card*)   Gillian, will you bring in one coffee, please, and will you refer all calls to Mr Vance. (*As he shuffles the deck.*) Tell me one thing, Miss Gault – how do you manage to look years younger every time I see you?

Gault You're the magician, not me.

Quinn (*giving her the deck*) Find your card. That's a most handsome dress, if I may say so.

Gault Thank you. (*After giving the cards a perfunctory riffle.*) It's not here.

Quinn How very mysterious, are you sure? The Lost Card, eh?

Gault I've come to talk about Delia, Mr Quinn.

*The **Female Employee** enters with a coffee tray which she places on the desk.*

Quinn Thank you, Gillian. Hang on, what's that stuck behind your ear there? (*He plucks a card from her head. She proceeds on out without any particular reaction, being used to this.*) My goodness, the Queen of Hearts.

Gault Very impressive. She's become a serious problem.

Quinn Ah.

Gault Her behaviour has grown increasingly wayward. To the point where she's seriously disrupting the work of her whole class.

Quinn Up to her tricks again?

Gault That certainly seems an apt way of putting it. If she were in a lower form, I'd be asking you to remove her from the school. Since she has less than a year to go, I'm reluctant to do that. However, her behaviour is quite intolerable and will have to change.

Quinn A rueful plight, Miss Gault, to be handicapped by your own special gifts.

Gault The girls from the upper school went on a

museum visit last Thursday. They're doing a study
project on Ancient Egypt.

Quinn Aha. That'll be why she was quizzing me
about mummification.

Gault Doubtless. On account of Delia's behaviour,
they were asked to leave the museum.

Quinn Horseplay.

Gault Amongst other things, she threw herself across
one of the exhibits shouting, 'Mummy, Mummy, it's
you, it's you!' (*Pause.*) It's not funny when you have to
repair the damage of such behaviour. Which I think
you'll agree qualifies as hooliganism rather than
precocity.

Quinn So far as any damage done – I'll have a
cheque made out at once.

Gault That won't be necessary. However . . .

Quinn Words will be spoken.

Gault She herself doesn't suffer, you see. The gifted
ones don't. It's the dimwits who are influenced by her.
They can't afford to slack.

Quinn I did send her to see Dr Dempster, as a matter
of fact.

Gault Not a psychiatrist by any chance?

Quinn Oh, no, no. Just our GP. The family doctor. A
fine sensible woman. I knew she'd be able to offer a
good private heart-to-heart natter. Delia misses her
mother, you know.

Gault May I ask if there is any news of Mrs Quinn?

Quinn Not a whisper, I'm afraid. For over a year.

Gault The police have found no trace of her?

Quinn Oh, the police drop their enquiries on a

missing person after six months. How's your coffee?

Gault   Finished, thank you.

Quinn   Let me get rid of that cup for you. (*He picks up the tray, then removes the empty cup, sets it on the desk in front of him, and drapes the napkin over it.*)

Gault   Forgive me for asking this, but how exactly did it happen?

Quinn   One windy day – the sun shining out of a clear blue sky – she went down to the florist's.

Gault   And?

Quinn   That's all. (*He taps the napkin-covered cup twice on the desk. Then instead of a third tap, he smashes the napkin down flap. It is as if the cup had gone through the desk.*)

Gault   (*trying her best to ignore this*)   You mean she just vanished?

Quinn   *brings the unbroken cup out from under the desk and sets it back in its saucer.*

Quinn   She was mad about flowers, Agnes. A passionate gardener. Though she really loved wild flowers best, oddly enough. But she was a great help to me. Particularly with the florist's orders. Sprays, wreaths, crosses, chaplets etc. I was only a few months in business, on my own account. Before that I was a Branch Manager with Fullerton's. She went out this day with several orders, just as usual. She never arrived at the florist's. And she never came home again.

Gault   You don't have any . . . any idea . . . ?

Quinn   Amnesia. Most likely. She could be anywhere. A different name . . . sleepwalking, in a way. Some day, some little thing, could jolt her wide awake. Who knows?

Pause.

Gault   I suppose we're all like that, one way or another.

Quinn   Beg pardon?

Gault   I'm sorry, I was . . . I mean, it must be terrible for you. A nightmare.

Quinn   No, no, nothing of the sort. You learn acceptance in this job, Miss Gault. There's no room for melancholy in our trade. It's a real vocation, you know. In fact, it's a way of life.

Gault   I've never thought of it quite like that.

Quinn   So long as you're here, let me show you round the premises.

Gault   Well, I'm afraid I really don't have the time just now . . .

Quinn   Miss Gault – surely not squeamishness from a lady of your sophistication?

Gault   Somehow my thirst for knowledge just stops short of funeral parlours.

Quinn   No shock-horror round this way. Nothing macabre. Nothing up our sleeves. Just dealing in a decent businesslike manner with an everyday law of nature.

Gault   Perhaps another time.

Quinn   Promise?

Gault   Yes. All right. (*She rises.*)

Quinn   Another time, then. (*He escorts her to the door.*) And I hope you'll come through to the house for dinner after. I'll ring you later in the week to arrange a day, will that suit?

Gault   That's fine.

Quinn   Very good. (*They exit together.*)

Delia *is discovered in the armchair stage right, with the Bible open on her lap.*

Delia The smooth man. That was Jacob. Esau was the hairy one. 'Behold Esau my brother is a hairy man, and I am a smooth man.' (*She starts looking through the Bible.*)

The **Dean** *is discovered, upstage right, standing holding a scrap of paper, in a public-speaking posture.*

Dean You know, this occasion puts me in mind of the first funeral I ever officiated at. (*To himself.*) No, perhaps I'd better re-phrase that. (*Public again.*) At any rate, I well recall the days when the coffin would always be carried all the way to the graveside. There might just be one hired limousine to take the older folk, with everyone else on foot. So there I was, with a chronic bunion, hobbling along, still a good mile from the cemetery gates. And greatly relieved when the undertaker said to me, Excuse me, Reverend, but would you like a lift? Having graciously accepted this kind offer, the next thing I know is, I've become one of the pallbearers. What he meant by a lift, you see, was a lift of the coffin. (*Pause. To himself.*) Sounds laboured . . . a lighter touch . . . (*Public again.*) You know, this function takes me back to the days of what I believe you in the trade call a walking funeral . . . (*To himself.*) No, that'll never do. (*He gets engrossed in rewriting.*)

Light full on **Delia** *again.*

Delia (*reading*) And Jacob was left alone. And there wrestled a man with him until the breaking of the day.

Gong. The curtain rises on the inner stage, revealing a little wrestling ring. **Vincent Kane**, *in wrestling shorts and boots, is asleep in a corner. Into the opposite corner climbs* **Albert Bell**, *also in wrestling gear, but with the added features of a silver hood and tiny angel's wings.* **Delia**'s *back is to them throughout the scene, which is of course occurring in her imagination.*

Kane (*springing up*)   God Almighty!

Delia   That's one interpretation.

Bell *wrestles* **Kane** *into an arm-lock.*

Kane   Who is this? Why does he want me to wrestle? I'm no wrestler.

Delia   I wouldn't exactly say that. Look at this – 'He took his brother by the heel in the womb' – and that was only the start of it.

Kane *suddenly slips free. He and* **Bell** *circle.*

Delia   A smooth man.

Bell   A slippery-looking customer.

Kane   So that's who he is – Esau, the brother?

Delia   That's another interpretation.

Kane *lunges,* **Bell** *falls, but manages a deft scissors which pins* **Kane** *to the floor.*

Delia   There was the business of his birthright too.

Kane   He made me an offer.

Delia   You robbed him blind.

Kane   A mess of pottage.

Delia   Some bargain.

Kane   Fair and square. I gave him my lentils.

Delia   Just what is pottage, anyway?

Kane *pushes* **Bell** *in the face and gets free. They circle.*

Delia   Then you swindled him out of the father's blessing.

Kane   The mother put me up to that.

Delia   Dressing up in goatskins to make yourself hairy.

Bell *gets a hold on* **Kane**, *picks him up and holds him above his head.*

Delia   And when Esau heard the words of his father, he cried with a great and exceeding bitter cry, and said unto his father, Bless me, even me also, O my father.

Bell *throws* **Kane** *to the ground.*

Kane   Leave me in peace!

Delia   After that you ran away to your uncle's house and got rich.

Kane *gets up, staring at* **Bell**.

Delia   Now it's fourteen years later and you're travelling back home. Tomorrow morning you have to face your brother Esau again. Tonight you're on your own. And it's yourself you have to wrestle with.

Kane *grabs* **Bell** *and holds him in a neck-lock.*

Delia   That's my interpretation, for what it's worth.

Kane   I will not let thee go, except thou bless me!

Delia   You're a terrible man for the blessings.

Kane   Tell me, I pray thee, thy name!

Delia   And when he saw that he prevailed not against him, he touched the hollow of his thigh; and the hollow of Jacob's thigh was out of joint, as he wrestled with him.

Bell *wrenches free and claws a hand down* **Kane**'s *thigh, leaving a red track.* **Kane** *howls with pain. The inner stage is flooded in red.* **Bell** *lifts* **Kane** *up, kisses his head, lifts his arm in victory to the sound of triumphant music.* **Kane** *embraces him as the curtain falls on the inner stage, as the light goes out on* **Delia**, *and as that on the* **Dean** *comes up again. He is now holding a drink.*

Dean   The mystery to me is – why was it not

contested? Now that's the bit I don't understand, John. Why did Dr Dempster not contest it, do you think?

Quinn *is discovered upstage of the* **Dean**, *unpacking a parcel.*

Quinn   Maybe the fight's gone out of her, Dean – now that old boy Dempster's finally passed on.

Dean   It's a matter of what was rightfully hers, though.

Quinn   Maybe the peace and quiet is enough to do her, they were at each other's throats right up to the last.

Dean   Twenty-seven years she nursed the old boy and I doubt if ever a soft word passed between them. He used to brag that he'd outlive her, you know.

Quinn   Damned near did, too. He was a stubborn old cuss all right.

Dean   And at the end of the road, sweet fanny adam. He leaves every penny to the younger one in New Zealand, that ran away as a schoolgirl.

Quinn   The doctor got the practice.

Dean   Didn't she work her passage to get it, for half a lifetime?

Quinn   By the way, Dean, how's the new verger doing?

Dean   Very little life about him, John.

Quinn   The old fellow was great value.

Dean   A heart of corn, and a man could do the needful without always needing it pointed out to him.

Quinn   But not the new chap.

Dean   The labourer is worth his hire, John. What can you expect? If you don't pay the rate for the job?

Quinn   This is the modern world.

Dean   The going rate, I don't care if it's serving lunches or serving summonses or serving the Lord. A fair day's pay is called for, and the church is not providing it.

Quinn   Result – a drop in standards.

Dean   Low recruitment. Mediocre material. You have to pay the rate for the job if you've got the slightest hope of growth. Otherwise goodnight.

Quinn has now unpacked the parcel: it contains a straitjacket. He goes to the door.

Quinn (*calling*)   Delia!

Dean   What about this new assistant of yours?

Quinn   Mervyn Vance? Only first-class, Dean. A natural-born funeral director if ever I spotted one. He'll go places, I've no doubt about that. (*Calls.*) Delia!

Dean   The incentive's there, you see, John . . .

Quinn   Where has that girl got to?

Dean   It makes all the difference.

Quinn   Pardon me for a moment, Dean. (*He exits.*)

The **Dean** *scrutinises his scrap of paper again.*

Dean (*after reflecting for a moment*)   So the good man's brother comes up to me and says, you'll maybe be wanting a lift, Reverend? Little realising just what he meant, I of course replied . . .

Delia (*entering*)   Thy name shall be called no more Jacob but Israel.

Dean   What's that?

Delia   Nuncle.

Dean   Well well well, and how's that favourite niece of mine, eh?

Delia Who do you think was Jacob's opponent in the wrestling match?

Dean Jacob? Jacob and the angel is it you mean?

Delia In Genesis he's described just as a man.

Dean Is that so? For your school homework, is it?

Delia I think the angel comes from a later reference in Hosea, 'Yea he had power over the angel and prevailed.' On the other hand, both of them actually suggest that it could be God himself, 'I have seen God face to face and my life is preserved.'

Dean Of course those old stories are a bit of a mishmash, you know.

Delia That one's the best in the book, I think. A wrestling match with the God inside.

Dean You've certainly been reading it up anyway.

Delia I'm working my way from cover to cover.

Dean Good for you, child. You'll be wanting to concentrate on the Gospels, of course.

Delia No, I prefer the Old Testament. It seems more true to life.

Quinn (*re-entering*) Talk about a vanishing act – I've been searching high and low and you're here all along.

Dean Something of a Bible scholar to boot, John.

Quinn Here, look at this that I got today.

Dean Chapter and verse off pat.

Delia *examines the straitjacket.*

Delia What's the trick?

Quinn It's an old escape dodge. See these loops? You keep hold of them while the jacket's being laced up. Then you let go the slack – and goodnight Harry

Houdini. Want to try it?

Delia   Why not?

Quinn   Watch this now, Dean. (*He puts the straitjacket on* **Delia**.)

Delia   The thing is, Dean – was it the Father or the Holy Ghost? . . .

Dean   What's that?

Delia   . . . who was the wrestler in the family?

Dean   Oh, I see! Well now, what you have to remember is, those were the primitive days, Delia. Ancient Tales of the Patriarchs. A ragged band of desert nomads. Simple folk. The understanding of God being very elementary.

Delia   A personal God.

Dean   Absolutely.

Delia   A God you could get your mitts on. Feel him squirming in your gut. Face up to him in your own reflection.

Dean   Then again, a lot of those old yarns were just made up to explain the meaning of a well-known place-name.

Delia   Penuel.

Dean   What's that?

Delia   The place they wrestled at was Penuel.

Dean   There you are.

Quinn   There you go. Try that.

Delia   Face of God, it means. (*She starts to wriggle.*) I have seen God face to face. Wrestled him to the ground. First he cripples you. Then he gives you his blessing. (*She goes into a fury of writhing and twisting. Finally* *she wrenches the straitjacket off, flings it to the ground and begins to cry bitterly.)*

Quinn Dilly dearest, it's all right, don't be frightened . . .

She stops crying as suddenly as she started, and picks up the straitjacket.

Delia I just wondered if my mother might be in need of one like this. (*She hands the straitjacket to the **Dean** and goes to the armchair stage left, where she curls up. Pause.*)

Dean Highly strung, John . . . (*Embarrassed even more by the unwitting pun.*) I mean, a sensitive nature.

Quinn Just a slight panic. I'll go and talk a while to her.

Dean I'll toddle on, then.

Quinn Wait, though . . . there was something you came round to discuss.

Dean It was only the talk.

Quinn The talk?

Dean The talk for the Association of Funeral Directors.

Quinn Oh, there's just a few words called for. Along with the prayer.

Dean It's a question of hitting the right note, though.

Quinn No problem, Dean.

Dean I'll stop by tomorrow again.

Quinn Do indeed. Good night now.

*The **Dean** exits. **Quinn** crosses to where **Delia** crouches in the chair.*

Quinn Dilly, love? Is the old man forgiven?

Pause.

Delia   You never sing that any more.

Quinn   What, 'Dilly Dilly'?

Delia   Used to work wonders on the childish grief.

Quinn (*singing*)
Lavender green, dilly, dilly,
Lavender green,
I'll be your king, dilly dilly,
You'll be my queen . . .

Delia   You're a bit rusty on the lyrics.

Quinn   And after that you'd always demand a story.

Delia   You'd a terrible memory for those as well.

Quinn   Fairy tales, Bible stories. Anything.

Pause.

Delia   Tell me 'The Sleeping Beauty'.

Quinn   What, now?

Delia   Don't panic. I'll keep you straight.

Quinn   'The Sleeping Beauty' . . . right. Let's see.
Once upon a time.

Delia   So far so good.

Quinn   There was a king and queen. To whom was
born. A little princess. And . . . they invited to her
christening party . . . some of the fairy folk.

Delia   Seven. Seven fairies.

Quinn   Seven fairies, who all brought her gifts. Of
various kinds.

Delia   Beauty. Wit. Grace. Playing, Dancing and
Singing.

Quinn   That's only six.

Delia   The seventh was held in reserve. The seventh would be the kiss. But the curse had to happen first.

Quinn   The curse, that's right. From some bad old fairy they'd all forgotten about, who lit on the king and queen and declared, as soon as this child pricks her thumb on a spindle, she shall die. And then the seventh spoke up and said, this curse I cannot cancel. But my gift is – the princess will not die – but only sleep.

Delia   For a hundred years.

Quinn   For a hundred years, and then a prince will come along. And waken her with a kiss. So the princess grew up, until she was a lovely girl of sixteen.

Delia   The king having banned spindles from the palace. But sure what use was that. The wound has to happen first. There always has to be the wound. Before there can be the kiss.

Quinn   So one day the princess found this room in the attic, and there was an old lady spinning. This old lady hadn't heard about the king's command. The princess asked to try her hand at the wheel . . . and rightaway pricked her thumb . . .

Delia   First he cripples you. And then he gives you his blessing. If you're lucky.

Quinn   Eh?

Delia   Tell me the rest.

Quinn   So the princess fell into a deep sleep. Well – a hundred years passed by.

Delia   Don't forget the forest.

Quinn   Was there a forest?

Delia   The fairy caused a forest to grow around the castle, to protect the princess as she lay asleep. When the prince finally appeared, hunting, the trees leaned

back to let him through, closing behind him again. He
didn't know what lay ahead – but he couldn't go back
either. He must have wondered what in the name of
God was going on.

Quinn   At last he came to the door of the castle and
pushed it open on its rusty hinges.

Delia   She couldn't stand the smell, Quinn.

Quinn   Was there a smell?

Delia   The smell of white lilies and dark heavy clothes.
Polished wood and sanctity and guilt and grief, the smog
of the funeral industry.

Quinn   You know, we should be rehearsing for the
Association's do . . .

Delia   She couldn't bear it and she ran away.

Quinn   No . . .

Delia   She might have taken me with her at least.

Quinn   Don't be hard on the old man, Dilly.

Delia   Talk to me about it!

Pause.

Quinn   Too much imagination, you see. The work put
a strain on her, there's no doubt. She'd no professional
objectivity. She suffered alongside every client. You can't
afford to do that, any more than a doctor or a nurse. A
load on your mind like that . . . she didn't want to
abandon us. She loved us.

Delia   A hundred years is a long time.

Quinn   Don't you fret. It'll be all right. (*Pause.*) Hey.
(*He stands up.*) Come on and we'll fit up the box, eh? For
the skeleton joke – eh? Eh?

She wearily follows him out. **Bell** *and* **Kane** *enter, carrying a
coffin, which they set beside the one already in the public room.*

Vance *is escorting them.*

Vance   No, I'm afraid he left a message that he wouldn't be in at all.

Kane   He was meant to be meeting a delegation this afternoon, it was arranged a week ago.

Vance   Well, if it's anything I can deal with, Vincent . . .

Kane   It's union business, Mr Vance.

Vance   Which reminds me. (*He takes an envelope from his pocket and hands it to* **Kane**.) My membership application.

Kane   You're joining?

Vance   Oh, yes.

Kane   You realise Mr Quinn won't have any truck with the union?

Vance   Really? We've never discussed it. Oh, excuse me, lads . . . (**Dempster** *has entered.*) Good afternoon, can I be of service?

Dempster   Yes, you can go and tell Quinn that Dr Dempster wants to see him.

Vance   I'm sorry, Doctor, but Mr Quinn is out of the office today. Perhaps I can be of help?

Bell *and* **Kane** *quietly slip out during this.*

Dempster   Who are you?

Vance   I'm Mervyn Vance, his assistant manager. If it's in connection with the interment of your father, Doctor, I assisted Mr Quinn in all the arrangements . . .

Dempster   You don't look old enough for this work.

Vance   I'm doing my best to learn.

Dempster   Except for your eyes, they're old enough. They look as if they're peering out of a crypt. I'm here to order another funeral, as it happens.

Bell *and* **Kane** *re-enter, carrying another coffin: they place it alongside the other two during the following, and exit.*

Vance   Certainly, Doctor. If you care to come this way, I'll be glad to make a note of the particulars. (*He leads her to the desk, holds the chair for her to be seated, and sits down himself.*) Now then.

Dempster   The particulars are few. The funeral in question is my own.

Pause.

Vance   Yes. (*He opens a drawer and takes out a form.*)

Dempster   What's that?

Vance   Just a standard form, Doctor.

Dempster   What kind of form?

Vance   Well – it's what we call an N.Y.D. form.

Dempster   Meaning?

Vance   Not Yet Deceased.

Pause.

Dempster   You know, Death has been personified in many different ways throughout history, Vance. I might have known that today's version would be a cryptic little bureaucrat.

Vance   The form is only a convenience for us, Doctor. Just to ensure that everything's cut and dried.

Dempster   A singularly unhappy turn of phrase.

Vance   If you'd sooner dispense with it . . .

Dempster   Let's just allow the N.Y.D. to rest in peace, shall we. (**Vance** *puts the form away.*) I'm here because I'll be dead within a few months, and I wish to be disposed of in my own way. Not in Quinn's way or anybody else's. If there were some form of Do-It-Yourself funeral, that's what I'd choose. I could always jump into the sea, of course, but it's not really my style unfortunately. Temperamentally I seem to be drawn to the slower and messier forms of suicide. Like thirty-five years of solitary drinking, say. Though it wasn't all suicide in my case, actually. There was also an element of murder involved.

Pause.

Vance A cup of coffee, Doctor?

Dempster Quinn's wife used to be his assistant, you know.

Vance Yes.

Dempster Speaking of murder.

Vance I gather she was of a rather nervous disposition.

Dempster She lacked your equanimity.

Vance I'm trying to learn the methodical and professional way to do the job.

Dempster You certainly have a prize teacher. And I expect my precise instructions to be conveyed to him, is that understood?

Vance Of course.

Dempster I'm presenting various organs to medical science. If nothing else, my liver will serve as an awful warning to drunken students. However, I want the rest interred in my family's plot in the cemetery. Buried on symbolic grounds, you might say. The Last of the Dempsters. So – you will collect my carcass from the hospital, deposit it in a plain wooden box without ornamentation of any kind, conduct it to the cemetery and bury it. There are to be no religious rites, no other people present, either here or at the graveside, no processions, obsequies, or hypocrisies of any sort. Is that all quite clear?

Vance   Perfectly.

Dempster   My solicitor will pay the bill. Cash on delivery.

Vance   Very well.

Bell *and* **Kane** *have entered with another coffin, which they place beside the other three.*

Dempster (*rising*)   So that's that. Goodbye, Vance.

Vance   Goodbye, Doctor, and thank you. (*He walks towards the door with her.*)

Dempster   I don't expect to be seeing you again. Though you, of course, will have the pleasure of seeing me.

The **Dean** *enters through the outer door.*

Dean   Well, Doctor, is it your good self?

Dempster   I'm glad to see you, Dean, I have something for you.

Dean   Did I hear right that you're giving up the practice?

Dempster   I suppose that's a way of putting it, what do you say, Vance?

Vance   If you'll excuse me, please, I must attend to other business. (*He signals to* **Kane** *and* **Bell**, *waiting by the coffins in the public room, and they all three exit together.*)

Dean   I know it's none of my business, Doctor . . .

Dempster   . . . but?

Dean   Well, I was most distressed about the terms of your father's will. I think you deserved better from him.

Dempster   Why?

Dean It's a matter of what was rightfully yours. You wouldn't think of contesting it?

Dempster *has been fishing in her handbag.*

Dempster Ah, here we are. (*She produces an engraved, gold-plated trowel.*) It's the ceremonial trowel used at the laying of the cathedral foundation stone. Presented to my great-great-uncle as architect. My father was most emphatic that you should have it after his demise.

Dean Well well well, that was thoughtful indeed.

Dempster You can hold it in reserve for the topping-out ceremony. If the building ever gets finished. How long has it been now, ninety-six years?

Dean It's a matter of hard cash, Doctor. The money wasn't all there when they started, and it's not too easily raised nowadays. There again, building costs these days, for that sort of structure . . .

Dempster So you think the family money should have come my way?

Dean Indeed I do.

Dempster What about your own family money?

Dean Beg pardon?

Dempster That you and Agnes loaned to Quinn? To open this death-factory with?

Dean It's been put to good use, Doctor. John has a very fine business brain, as well you know.

Dempster Not to mention a smooth tongue.

Dean Oh, no, it's soundly invested.

Dempster Except that it's tied up in your sister's name, and now she's vanished.

Dean An unforeseen tragedy, Doctor.

Dempster An act of God, I suppose.

Dean Oh John does a grand job, he would always see me right.

Dempster You still have no news of Agnes?

Dean Not a whisper, no. (*Pause.*) What brings you here, Doctor?

Dempster He's quite Uriah Heepish, that young man, isn't he?

Dean Young Vance, is it?

Dempster I was giving him instructions for my funeral.

Dean God grant they'll not be needed for a long while yet, Doctor.

Dempster Not too long, I have cirrhosis of the liver, I'm entering a hospice this afternoon. (*As he makes to speak.*) Spare me the pieties, Dean. I made it clear to Vance that I want no mumbo-jumbo when they bury me, and I'm making you personally responsible on that score.

Dean You'll be a heavy loss to us, Doctor.

Dempster I won't be the least loss to anyone. My father and I lived like wrestlers, always grappling for the upper hand. Though it was my mother's ghost in me that he was really wrestling with. At any rate it was a stupid waste of two lives. No sooner does he go down at last for the final time, than I'm pulled down directly after him. You could concoct quite a sermon out of that, Dean. I spend my whole life waiting for my father to die. And it's that very life – that life which I spent – that I'm now dying of in my turn. Yes, you could draw all kinds of homilies from that. However, not over my graveside, if you don't mind.

She exits. He follows. The muzak starts, very loud. **Vance** *enters, holding aloft the remote-control switch, and abruptly switches it off.*

Vance   That system will have to be replaced. It switches on if somebody slams a door.

Kane *and* **Bell** *have followed him with another coffin, which they place alongside the ones already there.*

Vance   Is that the lot?

Bell   Just the one more, boss. (*He exits again.*)

Vance   They're not really up to much, are they?

Kane   The public never notices, Mervyn. Nobody wants to be bothered with the dead these days.

He exits too. **Vance** *inspects the coffins.*

Vance   The fact is, they could be made for a third of the cost. And still look twice as good. There's so much pointless workmanship in them. The whole concept needs to be rethought.

Bell *and* **Kane** *re-enter with the sixth and final coffin, which they place alongside the others.*

Kane   That applies to more than just the coffins.

Vance   You know, I'm interested to hear how chaps like you get started in this business.

Bell   In my young day you took any job that was going, and thankful to get it, Mr Vance. Although personally I like the work. You feel you're doing something for people.

Vance   That's certainly true.

Bell   Actually, I was put in mind the other day of a story my granny told me once. She recalled a man knocking at the door of her cottage when she was a young widow. It was a boiling hot day and he asked for a drink of water. My granny told him to step on in. I

can't, he says, my mother's out here. So my granny told
him to bring the mother in too. No, he says, I have her
in the wheelbarrow, you see – I'm just on my way to
the graveyard to bury her. (*He chuckles.*) The ma's body,
in the wheelbarrow. At least we've progressed a bit since
then, eh? Beautiful premises, like this place. We're a bit
more civilised about it now.

Kane   The only difference now is, you're pushing the
barrow for him and getting a pittance in return.

Bell   Right enough, the money's not great.

Vance   Hence the national pay claim?

Kane   If it's rejected this time, the union's ordering a
work-to-rule to commence in ten days' time.

Bell   We'd prefer to avoid it if we could, Mr Vance.

Vance   Why?

Kane   The bodies will pile up in the mortuaries, that's
why. There'll be corpses starting to putrefy in people's
back bedrooms.

Bell   We don't want to cause distress to the public.

Vance   Why not?

Kane   Eh?

Vance   Surely it's the public who are at fault by your
own account.

Bell   I don't quite follow you there, Mr Vance.

Vance   Society would prefer to forget what our work
entails, right? The one way to remind society would be
to withdraw our labour. Suddenly people would have to
push their own barrows. I guarantee you that funeral
fees would triple overnight, no problem.

Kane   We're not after that. The managements are
making fat profits as things are, they can afford to meet

our claim.

Vance You'd be surprised. And anyway, within a year, the issue will arise again, and again and again after that. No, best to call an all-out strike and have done with it, I'd say. A bout of quick drastic surgery is better than years of ineffective medicine.

Pause.

Kane I take your point all right.

Vance Good. It seems to me a business that needs a bit of a shaking-up.

Bell Vince – we ought to collect that order from the printer's.

Kane Sure.

Vance I'll come with you, I want to ask that printer a few questions.

They exit. **Quinn** *and* **Miss Gault** *appear from stage right, holding large glasses of sherry.* **Miss Gault** *is laughing.*

Quinn Share the gag, come on.

Gault (*suppressing her laughter*) No, really, it's just a very silly thought. (*They pass on into the public room and she sees the line of six coffins.*) Aha. Death Row.

Quinn This is our Selection Room.

Gault *bursts out laughing again.*

Gault I'm sorry, I'm sorry – this is awful – but I keep on thinking it's all like a high-class whorehouse.

Quinn (*mock shock*) Miss Gault!

Gault I know, I'm sorry, but it's all the carpeting and the chandeliers and all those names – interview rooms and preparation rooms, not to mention the reposing rooms. (*They both laugh. Pause.*)

Quinn I love that laugh of yours, you know.

Gault You what?

Quinn The way you laugh with your whole body.

Gault I don't suppose there's much of that goes on around here.

Quinn Not amongst the clients, no. The rest of us stay cheerful, though.

Gault You're certainly full enough of life. How can you go on like that surrounded by all of this?

Quinn You could ask the same of a surgeon.

Gault Only a very incompetent surgeon.

Quinn The fact is, this work enhances life. It makes you more aware than most of your blessed five senses. It sharpens your hunger for life.

Pause. They are standing quite close together. **Gault** *breaks away.*

Gault And this is the firm's showroom? I suppose these are the latest models?

Quinn Just our standard coffin types. These are the elms – Park, Consul, Ascot – and these ones are the oaks – Crown, Royal, and Doric.

Gault Good God, they sound like brands of cigarettes.

Quinn What could be more appropriate?

Gault Spoken like a non-smoker.

Quinn Apropos of which, we have a range of cremation urns as well.

Gault But why would anyone want to choose a coffin? What does it matter?

Quinn Your final resting-place. It may as well be a decent one.

Gault But it's only your old cadaver.

Quinn Think of how much you owe it.

Gault It's curious, but I've never really thought about my own death. I mean the actual physical event as opposed to the abstract idea.

Quinn All the music you've heard. And the birdsong and the sea. The food you've eaten and the spring sun on your face ... the smell of the ground. Your body gave you the world. The least you can give it back is a nice box.

Pause.

Gault What an extraordinary man you are. (*He kisses her. She responds, then moves away.*) We'd better go.

Quinn You're magnificent.

Gault Please ...

Quinn A vibrant strong lovely woman.

Gault Don't be so foolish.

Quinn A miracle, Miss Gault. You can't stop me feeling that. (*They kiss again. She is more responsive, but breaks off again.*)

Gault This is grotesque. This room ...

Quinn We'll go through to the house.

Gault I really don't think we should.

Quinn You promised.

Gault Apart from anything else, you're a married man.

Quinn No.

Gault Well, your wife may have disappeared, but you're still ...

Quinn I'm not married.

Gault What do you mean?

Quinn I'm a widower. (*Pause.*) Agnes passed away six months ago.

Pause.

Gault How do you know?

Quinn The police. In North London, it was. Traffic accident. She'd been working as a hospital cleaner. No identification. All they found in her handbag were the orders for the florist, with my name on them.

Gault How desperately sad. I'm truly sorry.

Quinn Life was a torment to her. In many ways it was a merciful release.

Gault Why didn't you tell me before?

Quinn Only her brother and I know. The Dean, that is. We arranged for a private cremation. I wanted to keep it from Delia.

Gault But she'll have to be told.

Quinn No. Not yet. She's too vulnerable. When she's older. Stronger. I'll break it to her gradually.

Gault So you've borne it all alone for six months?

Quinn I've got professional status in these matters, don't forget.

Pause.

Gault Shall we go through to the house now?

He nods. She goes to him. As they kiss, the lid of the coffin nearest them is flung back and **Delia** *sits up.*

Delia OVER MY DEAD BODY, SUNSHINE!

Gault *backs off, hands to mouth, gasping, then runs out.*

Quinn, *deathly pale, goes after her. As* **Delia** *climbs out of the coffin,* **Vance** *runs in from stage left, wearing a long black woollen overcoat.*

Vance　I heard a disturbance, what happened?

Delia　Oh, nothing serious – my father was just groping my headmistress, and I was watching from a coffin.

Vance　Where's Mr Quinn?

Delia　I think he's chasing her down the street now. Have you ever tried out one of these coffins?

Vance　Not in person, no.

Delia　You owe it to your clients, Vance. They're very badly insulated. Even Jonah was better off inside his big fish.

Vance　Why are you such a frantic little fart?

Delia　How'd you like to kiss my arse?

Vance　Quite a lot, in fact, from what I've seen of it.

Delia　You're a Jonah. You know what that is, don't you? A carrier of evil luck. Like a rat carries plague.

Vance　You've heard bad news, is that it?

Delia　You've got a Jonah for a soul. Peering out through your fish eyes.

Vance　Everyone has it in for my eyes around here. (*She falls to her knees and starts to shiver violently.*) What's wrong?

Delia　I'm cold. I can't walk.

Vance　Here.

He takes off his coat and wraps it completely round her, raising her to her feet. She starts to faint. He lifts her in his arms. Music starts from off, very loud. The curtain rises on the inner stage. He

carries her up on to it. The curtain falls again, the music stops,
and **Quinn** *is discovered, downstage right, in evening dress.*

Quinn   Fellow Association members – and ladies – the
Dean's tale of getting a 'lift' has put us all in mind I'm
sure of similar embarrassing moments. The best laid
plans and so on. I know the reddest face I ever had was
at an out-of-town affair once. It was a place I'd never
been before in my life. The deceased had only recently
moved there, you see. Well, I got the cortège off on
time . . . but before too long I knew we were hopelessly
lost. The street directions made no sense at all. The
mourners were all strangers as well. I had to stop the
whole cortège and ask some passers-by the way. Nobody
seemed to know. We just drove round, hour after hour,
more and more desperate, more and more lost . . . (*He
starts to cry. Music from off. He pulls himself together.*) But
anyhow, by way of a modest grand finale, my assistant
and I have prepared a little surprise. Presto!

Gong. Curtain rises on the inner stage, with the box as before and
Delia *posed beside it in her tap outfit.* **Quinn** *joins her, opens
the box, pushes it round to show it's empty, tapping on the walls;
then he ushers* **Delia** *in and closes it. Music continues. He
pushes the box round again.*

Quinn   Nothing up our sleeves, folks! No skeletons in
our cupboard!

*He opens the box. There's a skeleton inside. He closes it,
pretending shock, opens it again,* **Delia** *is inside holding a prop
dagger. She steps out, sticks it in his heart. He sinks slowly to the
ground. She tap-dances downstage. The curtain falls on the inner
stage. The music stops. She is in a small pool of light.*

Delia   Once upon a time the damsel and the
christening. The spell and the spindle and the castle in
the forest. Which brings us nearly to the end. What is
she, lying there, with her damaged thumb, in a pure
dreamless sleep? The prince jangles in, trailing mud,
smelling of horse. He has come from a world of furious

transactions. His body is all itches and sniffing, ready to kiss. Who is she? A stateless person. An unresolved chord in the waltz of time. He shuffles round the catafalque and peers at her. One kiss would crack this nimbus open, for time to flood her veins again. He bends over the pale, perfect lips, ready to kiss. He looks. He ponders. He hesitates. And, of course, is lost.

Blackout. Music: the waltz from Tchaikovsky's Sleeping Beauty.

Act Two

*The naked corpse of a young girl (played by the **Female Employee**) lies on a bare trolley on the stage left side of the public room, in a pool of light.*

Quinn *is discovered in the armchair stage right. Beside him is a clothes-rack full of elegant dresses. As he talks, he pulls out an impossible number of women's scarves from a top hat on his knee.*

Quinn There's no telling where it might end. Once upon a time it was all winding-sheets and shrouds, nothing but white, now we have the client's own night-wear, at the very least. With a custom-designed dressing-gown over that. Pastel shades. Quilted paisley pattern or suchlike. Why not a smart suit? Or a favourite sports outfit? People want to show their best to the world, it's natural. Nature didn't provide too well. A few clumps of hair. People want to look pleasing, it's only natural.

The curtain rises on the inner stage. **Gault** *is standing with her back to the audience, wearing a stylish, hip-clinging dress, with a flower pattern in warm, sensuous colours. She's reflected in triple mirrors.*

Gault How do I look? On reflection?

Quinn Pleasing. *(But he's looking straight ahead.)*

Gault It's not really the sort of thing that I can get away with.

Quinn It's perfection.

Gault You think it's all right?

Quinn Come and choose some scarves.

She comes down. The curtain falls on the inner stage.

Gault How did you talk me into this, Quinn?

Quinn Look at these.

Gault   I don't feel right about it.

Quinn   She would have wanted them worn.

Gault   Not by me.

Quinn   Why not by you? You suit them. Down to the ground. Look at this . . . (*He has taken a silk dress off the rack and is holding it up against her.*) . . . eh? Eh?

Gault   She certainly had dress sense.

Quinn   Try it on.

Gault   I couldn't take something like this.

Quinn   Listen. It's yours if you want it. Go ahead.

Gault   Can you unzip me? (*He unzips her and she steps out of the first dress and into the second as they continue talking.*) What about Delia?

Quinn   She's due home soon.

Gault   I meant what will she think about this?

Quinn   She thought it was very sensible.

Gault   You've discussed it with her?

Quinn   She phoned me. (*He finishes zipping her into the second dress.*) There you go . . . (*He turns her round.*) Magical. (*He kisses her, his hands moving over her body.*)

Gault (*breaking away*)   For God's sake, Quinn . . . this whole thing is sick, it's ghoulish.

Quinn   It's all right.

Gault   I'm not her, you know! You can't make me into her by dressing me up in her frocks!

Pause.

Quinn   I was going to give the most of them to charity.

Gault   I'm sorry, that was uncalled-for.

Quinn   I just thought, maybe . . . one or two . . .

Gault   Of course. And I'm grateful.

Quinn   It's not right to leave them hanging like that.

Gault   But it must be so painful . . .

Quinn   No, no . . .

Gault   Seeing them worn . . . it must remind you of her so vividly.

Pause.

Quinn   She was forever at odds with her body, Agnes.

Gault   She was very attractive.

Quinn   She shrank away from it. There was an element of the angel in her, you see, trapped in her.

Gault   What do you mean?

Quinn   As if it had flown too low. And some brute creature caught it by the heel. Wrestled it to the ground. Tore its wings. So that it was trapped in the earth. Pining for home. She was always at loggerheads. She rarely wore a new dress for long, two or three times, that's all, they were never a part of her . . .

Gault   She always looked so elegant and stylish, when I saw her. Though perhaps a little bit . . . fretful . . .

Quinn   Delia wants back.

Pause. **Gault** *takes the silk dress off.*

Gault   I don't see how.

Quinn   She wants to do the exams. Talk to her at least.

Gault   I can't see what possible good . . .

Quinn   Just see her. Please.

Gault (*after a moment*) Very well, but she'll have to make an appointment.

Quinn *takes another dress off the rack.*

Quinn How about this?

Gault Gorgeous colours.

He throws it across one of her arms and takes another dress off the rack.

Quinn This one too? (*He throws it across her other arm, takes down another.*) And this?

Gault Steady on . . . (*He throws it across her shoulder, takes another.*)

Quinn This one?

Gault Quinn! (*He throws it across her other shoulder, takes another.*) Will you stop it!

He throws it over her head, she starts laughing, he throws the remaining dresses at her, she runs off laughing, he follows her. **Bell** *comes in stage left to where the dead girl lies on the trolley, carrying a sheet, and pursued by* **Kane**.

Kane Will you knock it off?

Bell I'm not finished.

Kane What do you think a work-to-rule means?

Bell I can't leave her like that, Vincent.

Kane She was brought in like that. (**Bell** *covers the girl's body with the sheet.*) I have to warn you, brother. You're in persistent contravention of union instructions.

Bell Away to hell out of this.

Kane You think I like it? You think I'm a freak?

Bell I sometimes wonder.

Kane Get it into your thick skull! It has to be nasty

and it has to be solid. Otherwise all the hardship is
squandered.

Bell   It's downright callous.

Kane   Of course it's bloody callous, it's war. And if
you don't have the stomach for it, stay at home and
draw your sickness benefit. Because if you go on
scabbing like this, old hand, you're going to lose your
card.

Bell   The point's already made, Vincent. If the
money's there, Quinn'll pay it to us.

Kane   The managements are all together, it's national.
Anyway, Quinn's finally lost his magic marbles.

Bell   The strain's definitely showing on him, that's for
sure.

Kane   Tranquillised to the eyeballs, I guarantee you.
His face doesn't fit right. Not that he ever shows it
round here. Who's that?

The **Dean** *has appeared through the stage left outer door.*

Dean   Good afternoon.

Kane (*crossing to intercept him*)   Hello there, Dean. Mr
Quinn's not in, I'm afraid.

Dean   The place appears remarkably quiet.

Kane   We're just knocking off, in fact.

Dean   At this hour?

Kane   We're involved in industrial action, Dean. Have
you not heard?

Dean   Lord save us.

Kane   Mr Vance is in the building, if you'd like to see
him.

Dean   Oh, yes. Thank you, I'll wait.

Kane *and* **Bell** *exit. The* **Dean** *moves irresolutely towards the* *desk stage left and pauses there.* **Delia** *appears, wearing a black hat and coat and carrying a suitcase.*

Delia Nuncle.

Dean Is it you, Delia? Are you all right?

Delia Fading fast, Dean. I'd better not sit down in here or they're liable to embalm me. Where are they all, anyway?

Dean Apparently on strike.

Delia What, against the man upstairs?

Dean Your father, you mean?

Delia Who art in heaven . . . you know, the sleeping partner. I can't see him negotiating, Dean. His wrestling days are long over. I can't even see him waking up, what do you say?

Dean Have you spoken to your father yet?

Delia I'm just this minute off the plane.

Dean Sit down here and rest yourself. (*He seats her at the desk.*) You gave us all an awful fright, running off like that. What possessed you, child?

Delia I was reconstructing the events leading up to the crime. Retracing my mother's steps, wearing her coat and hat. You should have told me about her, Dean. You did me wrong.

Dean Your father thought it best to spare you, Delia. He only meant it for your own good.

Delia A motive which has destroyed whole populations. Besides, it was really himself he was trying to shield. He was able to keep the knowledge of her death at arm's length so long as I was ignorant of it. It couldn't go on for long, though, could it.

Dean Pray God you'll find peace of mind now, the pair of you.

Delia   I want to know what you did with her ashes.

Dean   Your father scattered them, Delia.

Delia   Where?

Dean   I'm sure he would rather tell you that himself . . .

Delia   It'd cost you less, though, Dean.

Pause.

Dean   Well, now . . . you know how much Agnes loved her garden . . .

Delia   In our back garden? He scattered them there?

Dean   You have it all now.

Delia   He must have done it when I was asleep. Dead of night. By the light of the moon the mad gardener sows his barren ground with ashes . . . you surely must have seen he was cracking up.

Dean   Oh no, he'd been most composed the entire time. We had a service of course at the crematorium.

Delia   I visited there last week.

Dean   A devil of a place to find, in the middle of that heartless sprawl. It was tragic that Agnes should end her days in such a wilderness. Of course, she wasn't herself, she was oblivious to her predicament.

Delia   So why did she lift all the money before disappearing, Dean?

Pause.

Dean   What's that?

Delia   She went to London with all the firm's cash reserves stashed in her suitcase, including the borrowed money owed to you. Now, why was that?

Vance *appears.*

Vance   I'm sorry, I'd no idea you two were here. Welcome home, Miss Quinn.

Delia   Thank you, Jonah.

Vance   Can I assist you in any way, Dean?

Dean   What's that? Oh, there is, yes, I called in to tell you . . . it's Dr Dempster . . . she died early this morning.

Vance   Peacefully, I hope.

Delia   Punctually, at any rate.

Dean   Oh, she never came out of the coma.

Vance   Thank you for letting me know, Dean, I'll attend to it.

Dean   What about this strike business, though?

Vance   The doctor didn't want a funeral, so it should be quite practicable. I'll arrange for ambulance men to deliver her here. So far as the burial goes, there are still a number of private-sector gravediggers working normally.

Dean   Mr Quinn might feel that something more auspicious is called for, though.

Vance   The doctor's instructions were clear and definite, Dean.

Dean   Well, my doleful duty's done, so I'll run along. (*To* **Delia**.) Be a good girl now.

Delia   You be a good dean.

Dean   I'm in the running for the Bishopric, you know, so remember me in your prayers. Good day, Vance.

Vance   Goodbye, Dean, and thanks again.

The **Dean** *exits.*

Delia   Nice to see that business is still buoyant.

Vance   How was London?

Delia   If you ever have occasion to mourn, go and tramp the streets of Ponders End for three long winter weeks. It fits the bill. You'll cry yourself dry. Not that you'd ever have occasion to mourn.

Vance   I've missed your sunny disposition, Delia.

Delia   I sat in that grisly crematorium for a whole morning, watching the production line rumble and the furnace doors whirring open and shut. In the country wakes in the olden days, the mourners would get drunk and get up and dance with the corpse. That's the kind of last dance I'd choose. Not jitterbugging into cinders at the centre of an electric firestorm.

Vance   You think too much.

Delia   In the afternoon I went to a sex cinema. More joyless bodies. The funny thing is, a man tried to feel me up. But that was in the crematorium. In the cinema nobody gave me a second glance. How can you go on doing this, Vance?

Vance   Making a living, that's all.

Delia   Or is making a killing the choicer phrase?

Vance   Give yourself a holiday, accept the world as it is for a spell. Content yourself with what you've got.

Delia   Sleepwalk through life, you mean. I'm working at it, but I'm still inclined to bump into the furniture. Maybe you can steer me.

Vance   At your service.

Delia   Fancy you being sweet on the boss's daughter, what can have caused it?

Vance   One of these days I'll slap that little bum of yours.

Delia   Has Quinn been told of this strike carry-on?

Vance   It's only a work-to-rule, in fact.

Delia Pardon my slang. It's not likely to destroy the business, with luck?

Vance No, but your father's mismanagement might. Far from being buoyant, it's sinking fast.

Delia At last the good news.

Vance Scarcely.

Delia You're not worried about losing your job? A man of your talents and training could always find work . . . in film production, say . . . or party politics . . .

Vance I'm sorry my talents offend you.

Delia It's one thing I've learned from growing up here – there are many forms of dying and many degrees of deadness. I've seen white-haired corpses more alive than you are.

Vance If your notion of being alive is the self-regarding . . . wasteful destructive lunacies of your father and yourself, then I'm happy to remain moribund.

Delia Only you could make 'happy' sound like a swear-word.

Vance I'm getting a little bored at being the butt of everyone's insults.

Delia So that's why you called a strike, I've been wondering. You still haven't told me if Quinn knows about it.

Vance He's been told often enough, but he seems to be wilfully ignoring it. I don't understand what has come over him recently.

Delia You could never understand it. Although it's actually very simple. He's come to grief, that's all. He's finally come to grief.

She exits. The Sleeping Beauty *music is heard.* **Vance** *stands, disgruntled for a moment, then he crosses to where the dead* *girl lies on the trolley. He takes a white gown from a coat-stand and puts it on.* **Quinn** *appears, wearing a white gown. Music stops.*

Quinn   The purposes of embalming, Vance.

Vance   To delay decomposition, thus preventing the leaking of fluids and obnoxious smells. To prevent infection. To restore a lifelike appearance.

Quinn *has removed the sheet from the girl's body, and they are fitting a night-gown and quilted dressing-gown to her as he speaks.*

Quinn   Good. The aim being to eliminate any shocking visual memories. That sort of thing can cause an unnatural revulsion towards passing away.

Vance   Unnatural?

Quinn   Eh?

Vance   Surely a feeling of revulsion towards death is very natural.

Quinn *(pausing, looking at him sharply)*   I'm surprised to hear that coming from you, Vance. That's the sort of superstitious clap-trap the profession has been fighting hard to overcome.

Vance   But it's just a fact of human nature . . .

Quinn   Concerning revulsion of any kind, it's our job to dispel it. Because that revulsion will not just be directed at the event. That revulsion will be directed at everything connected with the event. Including the funeral director. *(He returns to dressing the girl.)* Incidentally, the term 'embalming' should never be used in discussions with a client.

Vance *(wearily)*   I know. Hygienic treatment. Temporary preservation. Taking care of the body.

Quinn   Good. Now, today I'm going to deal with Natural Posing. *(He starts combing the girl's hair.)*

Vance Before we start on that, Mr Quinn.

Quinn Well?

Vance How is the firm planning to survive this industrial action?

Quinn Put that out of your head, Mervyn. The profession has never had to cope with that kind of carry-on. Besides . . .

Vance It's into its third week now.

Quinn . . . my boys would never let me down. They all came with me from Fullerton's, you know, every one.

Vance Mr Quinn, the army is standing by to take over.

Quinn As a matter of fact, old boy Fullerton was raging. He had to close the branch down till he'd trained enough new staff. However. Natural posing. Now, the first thing is to deal with this prior to rigor mortis, right? Pillows. (**Vance** *lifts two pillows from under the trolley, and* **Quinn** *places them under the girl's head.*) The aim is for a natural, restful posture. So we try to avoid the old idea of the nose at dead centre and pointing up to heaven. Try to incline the head a bit . . . (*He does so with the girl's.*) Prop the chin up. Smooth down the lips into a nice relaxed position – if there's dentures you need to make sure they're properly seated. Now, the eyeballs shrink. So what you need is two wafers of cotton wool spread over them, so as to support the eyelid. Then you can set the eyelids to give the appearance of natural sleep. Coverlet. (**Vance** *hands him a flower-print coverlet from under the trolley, while* **Quinn** *tints the girl's cheeks with rouge. He then spreads the coverlet with the sheet over the girl, turns it down, and lifts the girl's arms out over it.*) The arms and hands can be very expressive, Mervyn. The only place they should never be is straight down the sides. There's a host of possibilities . . . one hand folded over the other . . . one over the other's wrist . . .

one on the breast, the other straight down ... or even folded on the breast, that's a favourite with religious people. (*He demonstrates each of these as he goes along.*) It's a matter of personal judgement. One thing that can ruin the whole effect, though, is stiff, straight fingers. Bend them to a natural pose – it takes a bit of pressure on the wrist and fingers. (*He does so.*) Now. You step back a few paces. To judge the general effect. (*He steps back, surveys the girl. The pose is grotesquely winsome and doll-like.*) You see? Magical. Peaceful. Asleep. (*A buzzer is rung off.*)

Vance   I'll get it. (*He goes.*)

Quinn (*oblivious*)   The artistic impulse comes into play here, Mervyn. You can work wonders. It's a creative area. You'll find it repays you to take trouble. Clients are deeply grateful. It reassures them, you see.

Vance *re-appears, carrying trestles, and leading an ambulance man (the* **Male Employee***) and* **Bell***, who are carrying a coffin containing the body of* **Dr Dempster**.

Vance   Through here, please.

Quinn   What's this?

Vance   Dr Dempster's remains, Mr Quinn. From the hospital. Just put it here. (*He has set up the trestles and they place the coffin on them.*) That's fine. Thank you. We're deeply grateful. (*He leads them out again, slipping them money.*)

Male Employee *and* **Bell**   Thank you, sir. Thanks, Mr Vance.

Quinn *removes the coffin lid.*

Quinn   Well, Doctor. I suppose they've put you through it. You're not yourself at all. You're looking distinctly unkempt. (*He fetches a quilted dressing-gown.*) Never worry. We'll soon get you to rights.

Vance *re-appears.*

Vance   No need for any preparation here, Mr Quinn.

Quinn   Vance, you can take that girl to the Reposing Room now.

Vance   Certainly. It's just that the doctor's instructions . . .

Quinn   Take care of that for me, please.

Vance   Very well.

He wheels the trolley off. **Quinn** *starts to comb the* **Doctor***'s hair.*

Quinn   We'll soon have you good as new. Smartly turned out. We're going to do you proud, Doctor. Do the honours. The full works.

Vance (*re-entering*)   Excuse me, Mr Quinn.

Quinn   Eh?

Vance   It's just that the doctor did ask for a simple burial.

Quinn   The doctor is an old family friend of ours, Vance.

Vance   Of course.

Quinn   The least of my obligations to her is a decent send-off.

Vance   Surely her instructions should be honoured, though.

Quinn   Permit me to know the thoughts of my own friends and how they should be honoured.

Vance   The doctor was very specific, I gave you the list of her demands . . .

Quinn   I've heard quite enough, thank you! You're not in charge here yet!

Vance   I'm sorry, I just thought perhaps . . .

Quinn   I know very well what you just think, Vance! I

know the game you're at behind my back! You just
think you can calmly take my business over!

Vance   That's not true.

Quinn   While I've been treating you like my own son,
you've been busy betraying me! I've nourished a viper
in my bosom!

Vance   You need help, Mr Quinn.

Quinn   Away to hell's gates out of this! I'm sick and
tired of your sleekit beady eyes!

Vance   Right.

He pulls off the white gown and flings it aside as he exits.
Quinn *returns to the* **Doctor***'s body. He lifts her up to fit her
into the dressing-gown.*

Quinn   It's only what's fitting, Doctor ... only fitting
... ministering to the body's needs ... you did it for us
in life ... my turn now ... (*The* **Doctor** *grunts with
amusement.*) No, you can't deny me that now ... not now
at this stage ... it's a question of proper care ...
professional expertise ... you and me, Doctor ... birds
of a feather now, eh? (*The* **Doctor** *gives a low laugh.*
Quinn *has the gown fitted now and is putting silk pillows
behind her head.*) ... all those arguments ... the plucked
flower, you remember that one?

Dempster (*a low murmur*)   I'm smiling for you, Quinn.

Quinn   A plucked flower ... you don't throw it on the
rubbish tip, now, do you?

Dempster   You never saw me smile before.

Quinn   You trim it ... place it in a nice vase, eh? ...

Dempster   It's irresistible when you're dead.

Quinn   And is the human body less than a plucked
flower? ... answer me that one, Doctor, eh? (*He begins
working on her face.*) You never would buy it, though ...

not from a coarse Christian the likes of me . . .
unqualified, unlettered, a bit of a common joker, a bit of
a joke for a posh girl like Agnes . . .

Dempster We're both smiling for you now.

Quinn I could make her smile . . . once upon a time
. . . she chose me, Doctor, in spite of all . . . you never
cured her of it . . . no cure for the heart, eh?

Quinn *works on at preparing the* **Doctor**'s *body in a
particularly garish way. Meanwhile* **Vance** *re-enters, to the desk
stage right, followed by* **Miss Gault**.

Gault So.

Vance Here I am.

Gault As promised. What's this I hear about a strike?

Vance It's not a full strike yet.

Gault Well, labour pains anyway.

Vance More like teething troubles. It's a work-to-rule.

Gault That must be a nightmare – I mean,
presumably people don't die conveniently during
business hours.

Vance The mortuaries are filling up.

Gault So how do you manage – a skeleton staff,
perhaps?

Vance (*mock reproach*) Miss Gault.

Gault Sorry.

Vance The school's looking very trim.

Gault I must show you round.

Vance I've already had a look. It's a curious feeling.

Gault Remembrance of things past?

Vance No, how long ago it all seems ... another incarnation.

Gault You, of course, developed early, Vance.

Vance Did I?

Pause.

Quinn (*still working away*) The love was there all right, but it wasn't enough.

Dempster Your pills are with the receptionist, Quinn.

Quinn To tell you the truth, I can't help losing heart a bit, Doctor ... just a little ... (*He cries quietly as he continues working.*)

Gault How is Mr Quinn these days?

Vance Rather out of sorts.

Gault The news of his wife was tragic.

Vance I believe she was very gifted.

Gault Really.

Vance You must have known her.

Gault Not personally.

Vance I imagine her to have been rather like Delia.

Gault I would guess that Delia takes after her father more.

Vance Does she?

Gault In character, I mean. Though she does look like her mother.

Vance You don't happen to know if there's a history of mental illness in the family?

Gault Vance!

Vance None of them seems quite normal.

Gault They may have their eccentricities ...

Vance   They're growing more screwball by the hour.

Pause.

Quinn   You were heartsore yourself, of course ... all your life long ...

Dempster   I'm ready to drink the earth now, Quinn.

Quinn   Don't say that.

Gault   I should think that kind of work would unhinge anyone.

Vance   No more than any other kind.

Gault   It would certainly drive me to drink.

Vance   It's like any other business.

Gault   You're not having second thoughts about the work, then?

Vance   Actually, I think I've just been sacked.

Gault   Sacked? By Quinn?

Vance   He accused me of treachery.

Gault   You must have done some evil deed, Vance.

Vance   I think I've been rather a good boy, on the whole.

Gault   Are you sure?

Vance   Scout's honour.

Gault *gets up, and gazes off.*

Gault   So what now?

Vance   I'll have to see.

Gault   See what?

Vance   What can be done. (*He gets up and moves behind her, gazing off too.*)

Gault   Few sights that weigh more heavily on the heart
. . . playing fields in February . . . in that failing
afternoon light . . .

Vance   Not a soul to be seen anywhere.

Gault   They're all curled up at home by now.

Vance   Sounds inviting. (*He begins to rub his fingertips
lightly up and down her back.*)

Gault   Stop it, Vance. (*She turns to walk past him but he
kisses her. They stagger round a bit together, bumping into the
desk, knocking a few things over. Pinned to the desk, she pushes
him back.*) No! (*Pause.*) Not in here.

Vance   Where better?

*They kiss again, pulling each other down. They fall in a tangle
out of sight, upstage of the desk. Triumphal music. The curtain
rises on the inner stage. Standing before the mirrors but facing front
is the* **Dean**, *now dressed in the full vestments of a bishop.*

Bishop   Glory be, John, you can embrace one of the
Lord's anointed, the call has come this very minute to
say that I've got the Bishopric!

Quinn   Dean, is that you I hear?

Bishop   Dean no longer, John, it's Bishop from here
on! Mind you, it was rightfully mine, no question. The
man on the spot, the man who's worked his passage.
You can be sure of nothing these days, though, it's all
politics these days.

Quinn   We have to call you Bishop now?

The **Bishop** *moves down to* **Quinn**'s *side; the curtain falls on
the inner stage.*

Bishop   You can take your time with the money now,
John, I know you've had a hard knock, you may be
down but you're not out yet. I won't be hurting for a
bob or two. You can pay me back in your own time,

when things pick up again.

Quinn   No shortage round this way, Dean . . .

Bishop   Dean no longer!

Quinn   It's all go round here. All in the black. Last year was a miracle.

Bishop   I won't sell you out, John, don't worry. We've come through thick and thin together, I'm not going to turn on you now. I know you're a good man, in spite of all. Is that the doctor you have there, isn't it a shame she didn't live to see this day?

Quinn   Should have been buried from the cathedral. By rights.

Bishop   Wouldn't have it. Strict instructions, you've never heard the like. She would nearly have had us throwing her out in a sack. The mind eaten away with the drink, you see. A sad case. Still – at least we'll pay our respects and give her a proper Christian departure.

Quinn   I'm not quite ready for you yet, Bishop.

Bishop   Time enough, John. Just you press on.

He settles down with a newspaper while **Quinn** *works on.* **Kane** *appears at the outer door stage left, backing away, as* **Bell** *advances on him.*

Kane   You're pushing us too far, old hand. You're cutting your own throat.

Bell   Let me by.

Kane   That's an official picket-line out there.

Bell   I don't care if it's the Red Army chorus, the old doctor's going to get her funeral.

Kane   It'll be your own funeral if you go in there.

Bell   Intimidation, is that the idea?

Kane Just face facts. Once you're out of the union, you're out of a job.

Bell Quinn's not going to sack me for doing my day's work.

Kane Wise up. He won't have any choice left if he wants to stay in business.

Pause. **Bell** *suddenly seizes* **Kane** *and holds him in an arm-lock.*

Bell I tell you what, Vincent – I'll wrestle you for it.

Kane Quit the high-jinks, this is no joking matter!

Bell Three falls, right? (*He lets* **Kane** *go.*)

Kane Fucking head case.

Bell Are you ready?

Kane Listen, Albert, this is your last and final chance, now you can't say you haven't been warned ... (**Bell** *seizes him in a bear-hug.*) Let go, you stupid bloody clown! ...

They wrestle round a bit and fall to the ground, **Bell** *gripping* **Kane** *in a scissors. Lights full up again on the stage right desk as* **Gault** *gets to her feet, smoothing down her dress.* **Vance** *also brushes himself off and moves behind her.*

Vance Almost dark now.

Gault You're dismissed.

Vance I thought you just were.

Gault Don't start crowing, Vance. You might have been any one of dozens.

Vance Perhaps I have been.

Gault Get out.

Vance That's not very civilised of you.

Gault   Don't ever come near here again.

Vance   If you say so, miss.

Gault   Now scram.

Vance (*as he exits*)   Cheers, then. And thank you. You were my very earliest ambition.

She stays at the desk as the light dims on her. **Bell** *gets up.*

Bell   That's one.

Kane *tries to run, but* **Bell** *grabs him in a neck-lock.*

Bell   Give up?

Kane   Drop dead!

Bell   Give up? Heh?

Two mourners – played by the **Male** *and* **Female Employees** *– walk by them, looking askance, and continue through to take their places beside the* **Doctor**'s *coffin.* **Bell** *nods to them as they pass.*

Bell   Good afternoon.

Kane *takes his chance to kick* **Bell** *in the shins, and gets free.*

Kane   That's you done for, Head-the-Ball. You're a dead man now. Curtains. You stubborn old cunt.

He exits. **Bell** *dusts himself off and limps into the public room, where* **Quinn** *has finished his preparations and removed the white gown. He is at one side of the coffin, the mourners at the other, and the* **Bishop** *at the head.*

Bishop   And why take ye thought for raiment? Consider the lilies of the field, how they grow; they toil not, neither do they spin. And yet I say unto you that Solomon in all his glory was not arrayed like one of these.

The **Doctor** *laughs.*

Quinn   Lie still, Doctor.

*The **Bishop** looks at him in some alarm.*

Bishop   But friends, what if your lilies are trampled
and bruised, what if they're parched and withered?
Then they must perforce be tended and nurtured by
skilful hands – like the hands of our dear departed sister
here today – Lily Dempster. For herself she took no
thought, what she should eat, what she should drink (*A
shadow crosses his face.*) . . . wherewithal she should be
clothed. Her thought was always for others – for her
late lamented father whom she nursed through a
lifetime's illness – and for countless others on whom she
bestowed her professional powers of healing. Now she
herself is a lily plucked and we gather here to lay her at
rest in the good earth. But her memory endures within
us as a fresh blossom which will never fade. In the
name of the Father and of the Son and of the Holy
Ghost, amen.

Mourners   Amen.

Quinn *presses his remote control switch and the organ muzak
starts. He then leans over and kisses the **Doctor**. **Bell** lifts the
coffin lid, and he and **Quinn** fasten it on.*

Quinn   Where are the other bearers, Albert?

Bell   It's on account of the strike, Mr Quinn.

Quinn   Get them in here on the double.

Bell   We'll manage fine. (*To the **Bishop**.*) Would you
take a lift, Reverend?

Bishop   What's that? Oh yes, by all means.

Bell (*gesturing to the **Male Employee***)   Sir?

*The **Bishop** and the mourner take the front of the coffin,
Quinn and **Bell** take the back. They carry it off, with the other
mourner walking behind. The organ muzak gets louder, then stops.
Delia is discovered at **Miss Gault**'s desk, sitting reading aloud
from an exercise book. **Gault** is standing, listening.*

Delia Because we are the tribe which has lost the
knowledge of how to die. In the boundless abundance of
knowledge by which we act, this supreme skill has
somehow been mislaid. Yet this one action – which we
all dread – is the only one that's forced upon us all
without exception. And we do it in shame and in
confusion. Other tribes, who knew much less, at least
knew this. They died with conviction and finesse. But we
are entirely in the dark. And the black void of our
ignorance spreads wider still. For a person begins to die
at the moment of birth. So dying is an action that we
perform throughout our lives. And so – at the heart's
core – we are the tribe which has lost the knowledge of
how to live.

Pause, as **Delia** *closes her exercise book and gives it to* **Miss
Gault**.

Gault As usual you write like an angel. And as usual I
have only just the foggiest idea of what you're on about.

Delia I tried to say it as baldly as possible.

Gault Yes, but I mean . . . I've always assumed, for
example, that death is something that happens to you,
not something you do.

Delia Surely killing is what's done to you. Dying is
what you do in response.

Gault The distinction doesn't mean a lot to a man
who's been hit by a bus.

Delia No, but the form of the killing is a local matter,
what I'm trying to say is – the nature of dying is a life-
long affair. Personally, I already feel most of the way
there.

Gault I do wish you could bring yourself to write
about something a trifle cheerier.

Delia This is my last word on the subject, I promise
you, Miss Gault.

Gault Thank God. In your case I'd give anything to read about what you did on your summer holidays. (*Pause.*) Or in your case, perhaps not. At any rate, you've really been applying yourself, Delia.

Delia Yes.

Gault I'm very pleased about that. You have the ability to do virtually anything you want with your life. Don't let it waste away in bitterness.

Delia I'll try and invent some use for it.

Gault I know the loss of your mother was a bitter blow . . .

Delia I've come to terms with my mother's death. More or less. I only wish my father could.

Gault How is Mr Quinn?

Delia I wish you'd visit him.

Gault I hope you fully realise, Delia . . . that your father and I . . . you're in no danger of getting me for a stepmother.

Delia It's all right. He just needs company.

Gault He's not ill in any way?

Delia He's bereft.

Pause.

Gault Well. I'll call in some evening.

Delia Thank you.

Gault This office gets so airless. I can hardly breathe. I'll walk you down to the gate. (*They both stand up.*) How are the tap-dancing classes?

Delia I gave them up.

Gault I suppose you don't have the time any more.

Delia I'm a big girl now.

They exit. **Kane** *is entering stage left, removing an overcoat. He looks round with immense satisfaction and then launches into a* manic *paso doble with his coat for a partner.* **Vance** *appears through the same door and watches.*

Vance Fancy footwork.

Kane Nothing to what went on at the meeting.

Vance Victory, I presume?

Kane Danced rings around them.

Vance That sounds like it calls for a drink.

Kane Too damn right, Mervyn.

Vance *leads the way to the desk.*

Vance I shouldn't really be in here.

Kane That circumstance has changed, brother.

Vance How so?

Kane All in due course. Break out that booze.

Vance I knew the Association would cave in eventually.

He's pouring the sherry and passing a glass to **Kane**. *They sit down and put their feet up on the desk.*

Kane Total collapse of stout party. There was a bit of bluster at the start about manning levels. So we obligingly tacked some persiflage on to the basic demands. That was all the face-saver needed. Twenty minutes later they'd conceded everything. Basic rate. Dirty money. Free funerals for members. The lot.

Vance Congratulations.

Kane Including the reinstatement of dismissed brothers, including your good self.

Vance   Quinn wasn't there, though?

Kane   They phoned him. Apparently he's taking a rest cure. The brother-in-law's in charge for the time being. He wants you to take control of the day-to-day running of the firm in the meantime.

Vance   You don't say.

Kane   Cheers, Mervyn.

Vance   Cheers to you.

They drink.

Kane   You had the right idea. It took the all-out strike to bring them round. If we'd started that way, the whole thing would have been over inside a fortnight.

Vance   We'll all have to work flat out to clear the backlog.

Kane   I forgot to say. They also agreed to letting Albert Bell go.

Vance   Oh yes?

Kane   The man was given every chance, but he's too damned headstrong for his own good.

Vance   No great loss. He worked at a snail's pace.

Kane   Don't I know it. The clients always liked him, though. Listen, this stuff's only fit to put in a trifle, come on out and I'll stand you a real drink.

Vance   You're on. (*As he clears off the glasses.*) By the way – something I've been meaning to ask you. What was Agnes Quinn like?

Kane   Agnes? She was an amateur princess. God rest her. She never had much truck with us mortals. Too smelly by half, that was the impression you got. Speaking of which, just what is the story with Quinn, anyway?

Vance Who knows? Maybe it's glandular.

They exit. Gong. The curtain rises on the inner stage. **Quinn**
stands dressed in a long Chinese silk dressing-gown, over rumpled
pyjamas. He is also wearing a wizard's hat, round black joke-
spectacles with a pointed nose and moustache attached, and black
lipstick. His props are on a small table beside him.

Quinn Hello there, boys and girls, welcome to the
wizard's den. There's a friend here with me you should
meet. (*He picks up a large wooden cutout figure of a boy.*) It's
Weepie Willie. What a misery. Blubbering and boo-
hooing all the day long, into his hanky. (*He picks up a*
large handkerchief and holds it over the dummy's face.) One day,
though, he cried so hard that he got completely carried
away – or at least his head did. (*He suddenly yanks the head*
off the figure, with the handkerchief wrapped round it.) Never
mind, we're all inclined to lose our heads from time to
time. We're all inclined to be absent-minded. The only
trouble was – Willie's head completely disappeared. (*He*
spreads the hanky with a flourish: the head is gone.) Well, the
doctors didn't like it a bit. He couldn't be allowed out
with no head on. So in place of a head they provided
him with a nice shiny balloon. (*He attaches an inflated*
balloon to the figure's neck.) Now, that was all very well, but
a balloon can't do too much. It can't pick its nose. It
can't hear the sea. It can't smell the ground. So Weepy
Willie wished very much that he could get back his
head. And he said to himself if only I could get my
head back in place, I'd never weep or cry again. And
no sooner had he said this to himself – than his wish
was granted. (*The balloon bursts and the head is magically*
restored in place.)

Quinn *picks the figure up and peers closely at it. He walks*
downstage tinkering with it. The inner-stage curtain stays up.
Delia *enters.*

Delia Christ, I thought you'd shot yourself.

Quinn Where's the sewing-machine oil?

Delia   We don't even have a sewing-machine.

Quinn   Willie's spring's all rusty.

Delia   What are you up to?

He has pushed the figure's head down into the neck; now he presses the catch which makes it spring up again.

Quinn   Just getting ready for the kiddies.

Delia   You mean the party at the children's home?

Quinn   I'm a bit rusty myself, I need to practise.

Delia   Quinn, that was last month.

Quinn   Eh?

Delia   You missed it. You forgot. It's long since over.

He takes off the hat and spectacles.

Quinn   I always do it.

Delia   It's all right.

Quinn   They depend on me.

Delia   They had a film show. You can do your act again next year.

He pushes the figure's head back down again. Then he sets it aside and slowly buries his face in his hands.

Delia   Let her go, Quinn. Don't fight it. Loosen your grip. It's crippling you. She was what she was. We have to live.

Quinn   *(removing his hands)*   There's a rat in this house, you know.

Delia   You won't listen.

Quinn   The old man's just a bit tired, Dilly.

Delia   Did you take all the pills the doctor left?

Quinn   It was the noise of it that kept me awake.

Delia What noise?

Quinn It was scrabbling and scuffling round the place all night, I lay listening to it in the dark.

Delia You imagined it.

Quinn No, they're breeding in the garden, there are holes down by the rowan tree.

Delia (*looking at her watch*) Time I was gone.

Quinn I'll set a trap. (*Knocking from off.* **Delia** *goes to answer it.*) Vance can manage for a week or two. I think maybe I've caught something. It has me run down.

Delia *re-enters with* **Albert Bell** *behind her.*

Delia It's Albert to see you.

Bell *goes to* **Quinn** *and shakes him gravely by the hand.*

Bell I'm very sorry for your trouble, Mr Quinn.

Quinn Eh?

Delia *has put on her black coat and hat, and now wheels on a small drinks trolley.*

Delia I'm just away. You could offer Albert a drink, Father. I'll be late back. Good night.

Bell Bye-bye, Delia.

Quinn *goes slowly to the drinks trolley.*

Quinn You put me in mind of Charlie Crayford, Albert.

Bell How do you mean, Mr Quinn?

Quinn You're a whiskey man, aren't you?

Bell If you happen to have a bottle of stout . . .

Quinn I'm very sorry for your trouble . . . that was Charlie's meal-ticket. (*He is pouring two whiskies.*) Help yourself to water, Albert. You remember Charlie?

Bell   Is that the Crayford worked for Fullerton's years ago?

Quinn   A little scrawny bird of a man. But a face the length of a wet Sunday. He got the sack in the end.

Bell   That's what I came to see you about, boss . . .

Quinn   Over-familiarity with the clients, that was the problem. From then on he lived mostly on funeral meats. You remember the grub in those days. The bereaved family was expected to lay on a feast for the mourners, you were judged by it – the amount of food and drink. Charlie Crayford would open his morning paper at the Deaths page. He'd go down the list like a punter with his racing sheet. Pick out a likely-looking prospect – a family in business, say, the father dead, roughly his own age. He'd turn up at the house in his working suit. Take the grieving widow by the hand – 'Sorry for your trouble, missus, I knew your husband well many years ago, a finer man never walked the earth.' Always the same act. They'd invite him back from the graveside with the other men and he'd sit down and gravely stuff his face. We'd see him time and time again at the better class of funeral – standing round the fringes, like a shrunken sort of a buzzard. Charlie Crayford. One of the most contented men I ever knew. (*He drinks.*)

Bell   I got a letter of dismissal, Mr Quinn.

Quinn   What's that?

Bell   I know it's not your doing.

Quinn   I'm not entirely myself at the moment, Albert.

Bell   If you could just see your way to giving me back my job.

Quinn   I've never been a great man for holidays, you see. Never took one in two whole years. Foolish really. The old engine gets run down, you see.

Bell I don't like troubling you this way. But I'm in a
bad fix, boss. I'd never get another job at my age. If
you could maybe just phone Mr Vance.

Quinn Another drink, Albert?

Bell I've worked for you twenty years. (**Quinn** *is
pouring more drinks.*) I'm the one stuck by you. I'm the one
did my job. They should all be getting their cards, not
me.

Quinn Help yourself to water.

Bell I won't be fobbed off, you made your pile out of
me, mister.

Quinn drops his glass, smashing it.

Quinn You don't entirely understand, Albert. The
cash flow. The cash flow problem . . . the fact of the
matter is, it all flowed away.

Bell What yarn are you telling me?

Quinn All flew away . . . flew to London. There's
nothing in the till. Don't talk to me about your job.
Talk to the banks. The banks own the lot of us.
Nothing I can do. There's no virtue left in me, Albert.

Pause. **Bell** *stands up.*

Bell You people. I know you for what you are. Oh
aye, cuter than a shithouse rat, all right. But you're the
real scum of this country.

He exits. **Quinn** *slowly covers his face with his hands again, as
though trying to hold it together. The light dims on him.* **Delia** *is
discovered sitting on the steps with* **Vance**, *stage left, smoking.*

Vance Your mother just doesn't add up.

Delia Nobody ever knows the whole sum, that's why.

Vance What did you find out from your search?

Delia A lot of the facts. A little of the truth. Which

would you prefer to hear?

Vance   I don't know ... whatever story you're telling
yourself at the moment.

Delia   All right. Half-way to the florist's, she decided
to write her life off. She had come to hate it that much.
She was a woman without resources.

Vance   Apart from being attractive and well-off, you
mean.

Delia   In a nutshell. Yes.

Pause.

Vance   Go on.

Delia   You don't see it because it's so far outside your
tiny scheme of things. I know what she felt. You burst
upon the world, expecting to astound it with your
astounding self. And you don't so much as ruffle the
water that your name's written on. On her best days she
probably felt like a minor curiosity. The rest of the time
it was just a superfluous life.

Vance   Why not suicide in that case?

Delia   She wanted out of the death factory, not into it.
Anyway – reincarnation is a better option. Another
town, a new identity, take it all from the top. She
cashed in the firm's chips – it was her money anyway –
and stepped on to the next plane. She found herself
sitting beside a divorced surgeon, a Mr Wright. He took
her home with him. He got her a voluntary job at the
hospital, helping out with a redecorating scheme. He
died beside her at the wheel of his Rover, on a blind
corner.

Pause.

Vance   The only thing I'm inclined to believe is the
surgeon's name.

Delia　Suit yourself. You did ask.

Vance　Does Quinn know all this?

Delia　Probably much more. He cremated the pair of them.

Vance　When did he find out?

Delia　The day after she died.

Vance　No wonder he's been indisposed.

Delia　You'd better make your peace with him, Vance.

Vance　Of course. I'm pretty sure the firm can be brought back into profit, you know – with careful nursing.

Delia　The same may not be true of Quinn, however.

Vance　What about you?

Delia　In the pink.

Vance　You've had a lot to cope with.

Delia　I'm a hothouse blossom. Forced and lurid. Fading fast.

Vance　Growing up.

Delia (*standing up*)　Is that what it's called?

Vance (*also standing*)　I've tried quite hard to disregard you, you know. But you're a bewitching little brat. (*He kisses her lightly.*)

Delia　First the wound and then the kiss. Don't worry, Vance, I'd already decided to indulge you. You're so dependably predictable. I can't foresee any possible way in which you could ever threaten me.

Vance　You mustn't flatter me so much.

Delia　You're a blessing in disguise, in a crippled sort of way. Come on, let's go home.

They exit. The lights come up full on **Quinn** *again, still sitting in the stage right armchair, drinking the whiskey.* **Miss Gault** *appears.*

Gault   Are you receiving?

Quinn   Eh?

Gault   The door was left ajar. I did knock. Perhaps you didn't hear.

Quinn   Join me in a drink, Miss Gault.

Gault   I won't be staying. How are you keeping?

Quinn   I don't drink. As a rule. It's for the rust.

Gault   The what?

Quinn   Lubrication.

Pause. She moves about restlessly.

Gault   As a matter of fact, I've already drunk my fill this evening. I won't be staying. Just looking in.

Quinn   That's kind.

Gault   I'm not the brightest of company, however. I'm feeling ever so slightly murderous this evening. (*She moves about again.*) There's something radically wrong with me, you see. My secret kink. Courting catastrophe. Flirting with fate. Playing Russian roulette with my entire bloody career. Meaning the only life that I've got. I shouldn't be telling you this, should I? (*Pause.*) I was the youngest headmistress, you know, in the country, when I was appointed. It even got into the papers . . . 'Beauty And The Beak'. Highly exhilarating, all that power and prestige. And I owed none of it to anybody but myself. Somewhere down the page, of course, there were also my aspirations as an educationalist. Amazing how soon it all ground down into the present hateful charade. Where's Delia?

Quinn   Delia's out tonight.

Gault She's a frightening little witch, your daughter.
She has a wonderful gift for provoking the worst from
her elders. It was her who made me aware of it – how
much I'd been turned into the standard caricature.
Bossy, nosey and stiff-backed. Headmistressy. (*She moves
about again.*) Anyway, I improve the shining hour by
dicing with disaster every so often. Last week that little
prick Vance came into my office. I let him have it off
with me on the floor. For example. Why do you
suppose I do it, to prove I'm real? Do I hanker after
disgrace and humiliation deep down, do you think? Or
is it just profound self-loathing that pricks me on? I
hope you're sufficiently shocked by all this. Perhaps it
bores you.

Quinn *bends down by the side of his chair and picks up a large
rat trap. Dusk has been gradually filling the space.*

Quinn I have to set this trap, it's getting dark.

Gault I'm going now. (*She moves to the door.*) You're the
only person I've ever told this to. I hope that somehow
strikes you as a compliment.

She exits. Pause.

Quinn On account of Agnes being dead, you see. It's
a jungle now, that garden. A nest of rats down by the
rowan tree. Not that I ever knew one tree from the
next, I never looked at trees. Not until she showed me
them. It was her creation, that garden. It's a wild jungle
now. I haven't set foot in it since she died, except that
night, with her ashes, I get a man in with a scythe,
every so often, he saw the holes. (*He gets up and moves
downstage. It has now grown quite dark.*) Because I heard a
rat last night. I didn't smell it. I wonder if you really do
smell rats, she would have known that, she knew all
that, she showed me a world of things. We went into
the fields on our wedding day to pick wild flowers for
her bouquet. She found a nightshade. 'That's poison!'
'No, it's not, that's not the Deadly sort, that's Enchanter's

Nightshade.' I never knew there were different kinds,
another was Bittersweet, she showed me it in the hedge.
(*He gets down on his knees to load the trap.*) I never knew
enough, never enough to comprehend her. She kept me
forever on approval, she would never entirely give me
her blessing. I could hear the sound of her crying from
down there, in the summerhouse, for nothing was good
enough, nothing free of pain, not with me, not with me,
maybe with him, for a spell, but she won't leave me go,
won't leave me go . . .

*The inner stage is suddenly flooded with bright light, spilling into
the darkened downstage right area as though a light has been
switched on in an adjacent hallway. The light silhouettes the figure
of a woman in a hat and coat. Simultaneously,* **Quinn** *springs
the rat trap on his own hand, cries out and reels upstage.*

Quinn   Dear God, Agnes love, will you ever give my
head peace!

*He collapses on the floor. The figure of the woman moves down to
the stage right wall and switchs on a light. It is* **Delia**. **Vance**
follows behind her. The curtain falls on the inner stage.

Delia   Father! What's that on his hand?

Vance   It looks like a trap of some sort.

Delia   Get it off.

Vance *prises the trap off while* **Delia** *puts her ear to*
Quinn's *chest and feels his brow.*

Vance   Is there heart failure?

Delia   I suppose there is. One way or another. But
then again, he never did have a good head for drink.
Lift him on to the chair.

*They lift him on to the armchair and recline it so that he is
stretched out.*

Vance   That hand's a mess.

Delia   Go and call an ambulance.

Vance *exits.* **Delia** *takes her coat off and drapes it over* **Quinn**. *She looks at him for a moment.*

Delia   Looks. Ponders. Hesitates. Is lost. (*She slowly bends over and kisses him. He doesn't stir.*) Tries a tentative kiss. Nothing happens. (*She moves downstage.*) The prince cleared his throat and shuffled his feet a bit. Did I get the year wrong? he thought. Is this the right address? (*A pool of light is growing on her face as the other lights fade away.*) And he thought, it's more like a dungeon, this, than a stately mansion. And he thought, it'll certainly take a lot of redecorating. And he thought, no point in trying to sneak back through that cursed wood. And he thought, what the hell – I suppose after a hundred years of suspended animation, you can't expect miracles. And he said, People really amuse me, though. It's so typical. It's disgusting. It's no joke. It's the living end.

Blackout. Music: finale from The Sleeping Beauty.

Pratt's Fall

(in two parts)

Pratt's Fall was first performed at the Tron Theatre, Glasgow, on 26 January 1983, with the following cast:

Godfrey Dudley	Lennox Greaves
George Mahoney	Sean Scanlan
Victoria Pratt	Elaine Donnelly
Serena Pratt	Anna Davidson
Professor of Celtic Studies/ Abbot/Dr Bridges/Cortez	Bill Simpson
Mr Rhys/Malachy/Proctor/ Magazine Editor/Eriksson	Bill Riddoch
Harvey Small/Monk 1/ Brendan/Gamble/Kilroy/ Mrs Small/Monk 2	Steven Whinnery

Directed by John Bruce
Designed by Colin MacNeil
Lighting by Gerry Jenkinson
Music by Shaun Davey

Setting

The time is the present, and the place sometimes the Map Room of a major metropolitan library, and at other times a room in a flat, a monastery library, a conference-hall stage, and an office in a map-publishing firm.

The all-purpose setting should be quite stylish and uncluttered, but largely in simulated surfaces – wood-effect wallpaper, polystyrene plaster, imitation leather. At the back is a wall of bookshelves, filled with biggish volumes, the width of the stage, flanked at each end by a classical column. A decorative arch curves above this, connecting the two columns, with the words IMAGO MUNDI *carved into it. In the centre of the space under the arch and above the books is a large reproduction-antique clock-face, showing ten to twelve; the rest of the space around this is filled with a frieze imitating the engravings on early printed charts (something like the frontispiece of William Blaeu's 'The Light of Navigation', 1612). The floor is tiled; centre stage the tiling forms a large compass rose, with the cardinal points marked. In the centre of the compass rose stands a large antique globe, supported on the shoulders of a kneeling figure of Atlas. This object is another fraud: a quadrant of the globe, slid back, reveals it as a cocktail cabinet. Upstage left is a low 'military' table (a reproduction of an old map of Ireland under the glass top), with two small armchairs round it and a plain bench along the wall, all quite formal. A single white carnation in a glass sits on the table, and there is a telephone attached to the wall. Downstage right is an old hatstand painted white, on which hangs a dark-grey man's three-piece suit, with a white shirt and a silver tie. A pair of polished black shoes to match is placed underneath. Upstage right is Victoria's desk, with papers, books, files etc. neatly disposed upon it. There are three office chairs nearby.*

Incidental music: 'The Brendan Voyage' (an orchestral suite for uillean pipes) by Shaun Davey.

Act One

Hesperides

Music. **Godfrey Dudley**, *a somewhat ponderous academic from the north of England, is standing by the hatstand, wearing spectacles, vest, boxer shorts and black socks, and staring abstractedly in front of him into an invisible mirror.*

Godfrey   Friends, family. Ladies and gentlemen.

Serena (*from offstage*)   Ten minutes, Godfrey!

Godfrey (*nervously*)   Just dressing! (*He removes the shirt from its hanger on the hatstand and starts putting it on, meanwhile speaking out front again.*) A few short words. Not being the sort likely to win a prize for public speaking. But today I have won the finest prize a man could oh shit, stupefaction guaranteed. (*Takes trousers off hanger, starts putting them on.*) Happiest man alive. As you cast your mind back over these past three headlong years. It's the opposite of the drowning man thing, actually. Far from it all flashing before my eyes, I feel as if I'm seeing the whole affair in slow motion. Perhaps I'm dehydrating. As the happiest dehydrating man alive, how has it ended up with you in the spotlight? I mean, people are inclined to forget you're actually there, especially when they're talking to you, but then since people only ever talk to themselves anyway, most of the time, like you here and now, oh Christ, I'm actually wishing Mahoney would turn up. Scandal, sensation! The ghost at the wedding feast. May I take this opportunity of saying, as a congenital bystander of very long standing, that I'm no different from all you other quivering voyeurs, lusting as always for somebody rash and ill-advised to create an incident, and let's give George his due, he treated the whole bunch of us to a downright bloody major international sensation of sorts, him and his map. Though it was me who put him on to Victoria, after all.

George Mahoney *enters.*

Mahoney   Very civil of you, Godfrey.

Godfrey   Not that it mattered . . . he would have gone to see her on his own regardless.

Mahoney *is bearded, with a small gold earring in his left ear, and dressed in a navy blue Guernsey sweater and ragged jeans. A Clydesider. Under his arm is a largish old calf-bound book held together with string.*

Mahoney   I don't feel quite so daft with you here to introduce me.

Godfrey   Oh, but Victoria's intrigued about it, George.

Mahoney   Is that right? What exactly did she say?

Godfrey   Well, she said of course, that she can't really say, not till she's actually examined the map . . .

Mahoney   No. Naturally not.

Godfrey   But she did say that it sounded intriguing.

Mahoney   Very good. Known her long, have you?

Godfrey   We were at Oxford together.

Mahoney   Oh, yes. In the motor industry, was it? Just kidding, Godfrey. She must be a high-flier, running a big Map Department. (*He's scanning the bookshelves.*)

Godfrey   Oh, her credentials are quite awesome.

Mahoney   The earth-mother type, eh?

Godfrey   There aren't many can touch her in the field of historical cartography.

Mahoney   As big as that? (*He has taken down an old British atlas and is leafing through it.*) Have you ever wondered why Bristols is old-fashioned slang for the female titular appendages?

Godfrey   Bristols?

Mahoney I daresay it's in the realm of etymology rather than cartography.

Godfrey Yes, I should think so. (*Pause.*) Nothing to do with Bristol cream, is it?

Mahoney Haven't a lulu, Godfrey, it only just occurred to me. Listen, maybe we should just leave the book on her desk there and call back later.

Godfrey No, no, she knows we're coming. She's probably been waylaid in the stacks briefly.

Mahoney We should all be so lucky, eh? Incidentally, I'm sorry I've had no luck finding a decent kip yet.

Godfrey There's no hurry, George, really.

Mahoney I'll be out of your hair the minute I find someplace.

Godfrey The room is yours as long as you need it.

Mahoney Very decent of you, Godfrey.

Pause.

Godfrey Funnily enough, I'm very deficient myself so far as maps go.

Mahoney How so?

Godfrey It's rather like being tone-deaf, I suppose. Actually I'm tone-deaf as well, but what I mean, though, is, my brain refuses to make the leap from the page to the landscape.

Mahoney It requires an act of faith, Godfrey.

Godfrey You see, I can appreciate all the lines of stitching and the little crosses and triangles and so on, in their own right. But when I straighten up, they just refuse to translate neatly into railway lines and churches and altitudes. What's worse is, I always need the road on the map to be facing the same way as the actual road I'm

standing on. Which usually entails turning the thing
sideways on. And then of course you can't read the place-
names anyway.

Pause.

Mahoney   So how did you come to teach Geography?

Godfrey   Oh, that was all academic. My PhD thesis
was the definitive study of azimuthal projections.

Mahoney   There's not many can say that.

Godfrey   Not many would admit to it.

Mahoney   I've often wondered about azimuthal
projections. What really lies behind them, I mean.

Godfrey   Infinite boredom, I'm afraid.

Mahoney   No, I'm interested.

Godfrey   No, really.

Mahoney   No, come on.

Godfrey   Oh, well. Let's see. Azimuthal projections.
Say you construct a plane at a tangent to either of the
two poles . . . you must have noticed I'm rather good at
that. Going off at a tangent, I mean. Anyway. As you
know, a completely accurate map of the world is
impossible. Because every method of projection incurs a
different form of distortion. So anyway. The two poles.

Victoria *sweeps in and deposits a few large portfolios on the desk.
She is a good-looking and assertive English woman, her briskness
overlaying a certain measure of shyness and reserve.*

Victoria   Well, Godfrey.

Godfrey   Oh, Victoria. Here you are. Hello.

Victoria   If you're after me to give another lecture,
forget it. I've still got that little Welshman of yours,
coming in here to argue about the Carthaginians being
extra-terrestrial visitors.

Godfrey   Oh, lord, not Mr Rhys. He's a monumental mason, you know.

Victoria   He also believes they built Stonehenge.

Godfrey   Actually, I don't think I've seen you since I was made Director.

Victoria   Of what?

Godfrey   Same old thing. Extramural Studies.

Victoria   What happened to the venerable Burke?

Godfrey   I'm afraid he came to grief. You know the vast amount of tea he used to drink.

Victoria   Yes, but I've never heard of it actually proving fatal.

Godfrey   No, no, it was the plug of his electric kettle. Killed outright.

Victoria   Well. Congratulations.

Godfrey   Erm, I wonder if I might perhaps, if you remember me mentioning . . .

Mahoney (*extending hand*)   Hello there.

Godfrey   George Mahoney . . . Victoria Pratt.

Victoria (*with one brisk handshake*)   The St Brendan gentleman?

Mahoney   The old map lady?

Victoria   I've taken a look at this ancient chart you say you found. (*She produces it from the top portfolio.*) It would appear to prove that America was discovered by the Irish.

Pause.

Mahoney   You mean it was ever in doubt?

Victoria   How much do you know about cartography?

Mahoney   I always thought it was the posh name for fortune-telling.

Victoria   We may sometimes depend on inspired guesswork, but not quite to that degree.

Mahoney   So what's your best guess in this case?

Victoria   That you're a practical joker.

Pause.

Mahoney (*raising his right hand*)   Not guilty. As Godfrey is my judge.

Godfrey   Well, I was actually right there on the spot when George made the discovery.

Victoria   Very well. Suppose you tell me about it.

Godfrey   Well. It was inside this book. (*He takes the book from* **Mahoney** *and hands it to* **Victoria**.)

Victoria (*reading*)   '*Navigatio Sancti Brendani.*'

Mahoney   'The Voyage Of St Brendan.'

Victoria   That much Latin I do have, thank you.

Mahoney   Hell of a good read, are you acquainted with it?

Victoria   It's the medieval romance which has him paddling across the Atlantic in a coracle.

Mahoney   Not a coracle, no. A curragh. Coracles are small, round and Welsh.

Godfrey   Rather like Mr Rhys.

Victoria   Of course. Foolish of me. Curraghs are the ones that are long, lean and Irish?

Mahoney   Check.

Victoria   I'm afraid I don't have much time for tall tales and folk legends, Mr Mahoney.

Mahoney   That's just where you and Christopher
Columbus part company, flower.

*She has been untying the string round the book which now separates
into sundered portions.*

Victoria   Your book appears to have been vandalised
at some point.

Mahoney   Too right, last Tuesday. It was pillaged by a
four-year-old Viking.

Godfrey   Ragnar Nilsson's brat, actually. That's how
the map came to light.

Victoria   Yes?

Godfrey   You remember Ragnar? Biology? Pigtails?

Victoria   Is this really material, Godfrey?

Godfrey   She called in, you see. Tuesday lunchtime.
With a petition supporting the hostel for battered wives.
While we were talking, her toddler wandered into my
spare room and tore up George's belongings.

Victoria   Yes?

Mahoney   Published 1649. It survives Cromwell,
Napoleon, the Famine, two world wars . . . only to fall a
victim to progressive parenthood.

Godfrey   But with the book dismembered like that, we
were able to spot the map. It was bound right into the
spine, you can see the stitch marks.

Mahoney (*picking the map up*)   It seems to have been
drawn with East at the top instead of North.

Godfrey   You really need to turn it sideways on . . .

Mahoney   Ireland and Britain are clear enough.

Godfrey   Iceland. Greenland presumably.

Mahoney   It's these blobs over here that are so

titillating.

Godfrey   It's quite clearly a crude rendition of
Newfoundland, the Gulf of St Lawrence, Nova Scotia, all
round that way.

Victoria   Yes. There's really only one thing missing.

Godfrey   What's that?

Victoria   There's no X to mark the spot where the
treasure's buried.

Pause.

Mahoney (*to* **Godfrey**)   Does she do funny voices too?

Victoria   How it got itself bound into your book, Mr
Mahoney, I really can't say. But whoever drew it had a
quaint sense of make-believe. It's actually dated 845 AD
– which is one hundred years older than the oldest
surviving English map. Yet we have no other evidence of
an early Irish cartographic tradition, it's drawn in a style
which doesn't otherwise appear before 1250, it's showing
bits of North America a century and a half before even
the Vikings reached it, and a further five centuries before
it makes an appearance on any other chart.

Mahoney   You mean that's all you've got against it?

Victoria (*taking it from him*)   I see it also comes complete
with a cartoon caption – '*Terra Repromissionis Sanctorum*'.

Godfrey   George says that was the Irish monks' name
for the legendary paradise out in the ocean – The Land
Promised to the Saints.

Victoria (*ironic disbelief*)   Canada?

Mahoney (*gesturing upwards*)   You know Him – full of
little pleasantries.

Victoria   Only by hearsay.

Mahoney   Well, you can take it from me. I used to

work for Him.

Victoria   In what capacity, exactly?

Mahoney   Two years in County Kerry as a Cistercian monk.

Godfrey   Good God, George. You never mentioned that before.

Mahoney   It's like having a prison record. It makes people wonder about you.

Victoria   Is that where you got this book?

Mahoney   It was a valedictory presentation from the Abbot and all the lads, when I was leaving Ardfert.

Godfrey   Ardfert? Isn't that where St Brendan had his monastery?

Mahoney   Nice work, Godfrey. The Cistercians built on his original foundation.

Victoria   So the book actually came from Ardfert?

Mahoney   It came out the monastery library.

Victoria   Well, then. I expect the map was drawn by some former monk. As a comic illustration for the book.

Mahoney   If so, why was it hidden away in the binding? Why is it drawn on vellum instead of paper? Why is this inscription (*Indicating.*) in Old Irish? And why is there a love poem in seventeenth-century Irish (*Turning it over.*) on the back?

Victoria   You mean that's all you've got in its favour?

Godfrey   Victoria has a lovely pair of Bristols.

Mahoney   How's your Old Irish?

Victoria   Rather rusty.

Godfrey   I saw them once.

Mahoney   I've been to the Department of Celtic Studies with it.

Victoria   And?

Mahoney   The prof. there was beside himself.

The **Professor of Celtic Studies** *enters, waving a photocopy of the map. He is a rarefied Irish don.*

Professor   Here we are, here we are, Richard. Richard, is it?

Mahoney   George, actually.

Professor   George. George. Sorry. All these Anglo-Saxon names sound much the same to me. You don't mind if I keep this photocopy?

Mahoney   Help yourself.

Professor   Because the gist I can give you, you see. I can give you the gist. But the Irish in this inscription has got some very archaic locutions, which I should like the time to tinker with.

Mahoney   So what's the gist?

Professor   Maloney's more easily remembered, you see. For somebody like me. I didn't forget Maloney.

Mahoney   It's Mahoney, actually.

Professor   Yes, indeed, this inscription is remarkable. Very archaic syntax. What it roughly says is, (*Reading.*) 'I, Colman of the Voyages, set down this true image of the blessed isles to the West in the year the Northmen put to the flame great Clonmacnoise.'

Mahoney (*turning back to* **Victoria**)   How did you know that was 845?

Victoria   This building *is* actually a major library.

Mahoney (*returning to the* **Professor**)   What about the poem on the back?

Professor   Plain sailing. Colloquialised poetic diction, very typical of the personal lyric in the seventeenth century, no, no difficulties with that.

Mahoney   So how does it go?

Professor   I can't reproduce the metre, of course.

Mahoney   Give me the gist.

Professor   Well, then, it says roughly, (*Reads.*)

'It is well for the sea to shake its white mane
It is well for the wind and it howling
It is well for the young brides at singing
But I am forbidden a tongue to my love and my grief.'

That's verse one.

'Giles Kemp, of the blue-grey eye and strange talking,
You are sloe-blossom and raven-wing,
You are red berries on a bank of snow,
You are an English master of the English hounds.

'Thus is my most beloved my bitterest foe,
Thus is the sweetest name the cruellest curse,
Thus to aver my love is to lose my life,
As the sun sinks, so does my heart.'

Pause.

Mahoney   Giles Kemp?

Professor   My guess would be an English soldier. An officer. It's a poem from a high-born Irish girl in love with an English soldier. Very touching, really.

Mahoney   Not very politic, though.

Professor   No, no, not in the age of Cromwell, no.

Mahoney   Any more than today.

Professor   Because what she might have done, you see, was scribble her poem out on the back of the map parchment secretly. And then hide it away in the book

well out of harm's way. Just using up the blank side of
the vellum, you see. Because the old map, in those days,
was probably considered worthless. Just some monkish
hieroglyphics.

Mahoney   Fascinating.

Professor   It is rather a sensational find, Giles. No, no
– George, Giles is the poem, isn't it.

Mahoney   Thanks for your help, prof.

Professor   Only too glad, I assure you.

Mahoney   Go raibh míle maith agat. Slán agat.

Professor   Ah yes. Go raibh maith agatsa. Go dté tú
slán.

The **Professor** *exits. Pause.*

Godfrey   Funny how you can feel yourself fading away
into anonymity.

Victoria   It's certainly a curiosity of sorts, I'll grant you
that.

Mahoney   You're the expert, Victoria.

Victoria (*rising*)   Perhaps we can solve the riddle of who
dunnit. I'll arrange to have some laboratory tests done. If
you're agreeable.

Mahoney (*following her*)   Will you be needing a sample
of my urine?

Victoria *and* **Mahoney** *exit, leaving* **Godfrey** *standing. He
moves to the hatstand and begins putting on the shoes.*

Godfrey   So let us all raise our glasses to true believers.
I mean, it's all so clear-cut for them. George says I
believe yes. Victoria says I believe no. And nobody even
asks you what you believe, naturally. Since all you would
say is, it depends what you mean by discover, it depends
what you mean by America, it depends what you mean

by believe.

*Enter **Mr Rhys** – small, round and Welsh.*

Rhys What I mean by believe, Dr Dudley, is simply accepting the evidence. You look at the Inca legends of the fair-skinned alien visitors. You look at the stone carvings in Peru. It all points unmistakably towards one thing.

Godfrey What's that, Mr Rhys?

Rhys The Carthaginians.

Godfrey Good God, you don't believe they discovered America on top of everything else?

Rhys It's an historical certainty which I cannot but accept, Dr Dudley.

Godfrey How did they manage to find the time?

Rhys Time is not a dimension that they bothered with particularly.

Godfrey I suppose space was more their line.

Rhys You think I'm just a harmless crank, don't you?

Godfrey Certainly the Carthaginians were a remarkable people, Mr Rhys, on such scanty historical evidence as we possess . . .

Rhys They'll be back soon, I reckon.

Godfrey Will they?

Rhys Conditions are growing propitious for their return.

Godfrey That's nice.

Rhys I could write you a little essay on it, if you like.

Godfrey Although my course is strictly speaking about map projections, you see.

Rhys Oh, they were fully cognisant with all that sort of thing.

Godfrey Well, I think you might find that's not altogether the case . . .

Rhys You read my evidence, Dr Dudley. That's all I ask.

He goes out, then immediately reappears.

They didn't all return to their own planet, you know. Some of them stayed behind to keep watch. I'm afraid that's all I'm permitted to say at the moment.

He exits.

Godfrey But then all beliefs are cuckoo, if you're looking in from the outside. Though some of you here today are very deft in that regard. You can shuffle through the whole pack without dropping a card. I myself have never really acquired the knack somehow. What I find is – the moment somebody else expounds a point of view which I share . . . my belief in it begins to crumble. I've lost any little beliefs I ever had that way. Which of course is what makes you the perennial spare prick at a wedding though that's scarcely apropos in the immediate context . . .

Victoria *walks in, bearing a tray of glasses.*

Victoria How goes it, Godfrey?

Godfrey Oh, you know. Like a bare neck at a beheading.

Victoria That's the spirit. (*She has deposited the tray on the table and now goes out again.*)

Godfrey (*to her departing back*) You're so delectable, Victoria, that's the one belief I haven't lost after seventeen years of devoted lust. You're the *fine cognac* of womanhood. I just wish you wouldn't always offer me sherry, when what I really want is a large gin.

Serena *enters talking. She has close-cropped hair, and is rather like a greyhound in respect of speed, singularity of purpose, hauteur and IQ.*

Serena I don't really see what the problem is. Supposing it *does* prove that the Irish discovered America? Why shouldn't they have? They seem to govern most of it.

Victoria *follows her on, carrying an ice bucket.*

Victoria Lucky for you somebody discovered it.

Serena Not any more.

Victoria Would you like a sherry, Godfrey?

Godfrey What? Well, uh.

Serena Mine's a large gin, please.

Victoria What do you mean, you're always sending people out canoeing in Colorado and wrangling in Wyoming. (*She has gone to the globe, and now opens it and pours a sherry and a gin.*)

Serena That's old hat now, you might as soon offer them a ferry trip to the Isle of Wight. I blame it on television. They all want to mine for topaz in the Australian outback or go alligator-spotting in Peru.

Godfrey Or hunting Carthaginians. (**Victoria** *hands him the sherry.*) Ah. Thank you.

Serena I don't know, I can't keep up with people's fantasy lives any longer.

Victoria Serves you right for offering them adventure holidays. What kind of cretin believes that adventure can be purchased ready-made?

Serena Only half the vulgar populace, dear.

Victoria If you don't initiate it yourself, where on earth's the adventure?

Serena   Oh, Christ, if you're going to start intellectualising . . .

Victoria   I'm going to baste Godfrey's joint for him.

She exits. **Serena** *drinks, looks around, recalls the existence of* **Godfrey**.

Serena   He sounds like a bit of an odd fish, this Mahoney.

Godfrey   He's Scottish.

Serena   Where did you dig him up from?

Godfrey   Funnily enough, it came about as a direct result of his interest in ESP.

Serena   What the hell are you saying, Godfrey, that he got in touch by telepathy?

Godfrey   Well, not that I was aware of. He just wandered into my office one day, a few weeks back, to enquire about enrolling for a course. Psychology 17: Paranormal Phenomena.

Serena   Enough said.

Godfrey   He was out of the usual run of extramural students, you know, retired teachers and raving monomaniacs, he delivers yachts for a living.

Serena   What's so unusual about that?

Godfrey   I mean he actually sails them to wherever the owner lives, across the ocean, that kind of delivery. He's just helped to deliver a trimaran from the Canary Islands for a man who manufactures artificial snow.

Serena   God – I know any number of men who'd pay good money to have a go at that.

Godfrey   I should think there's a special machine does it.

Serena   So where does he live?

Godfrey   What, the artificial snow man?

Serena   Mahoney, for Christ's sake!

Godfrey   No fixed abode, he roams around all the time, you see.

Serena   He must occasionally sleep somewhere.

Godfrey   Well, at the moment, I'm putting him up in the spare room.

Serena   Ha.

Godfrey   Just till he can find a decent short-term let.

Serena   In other words, he's a shiftless bloody layabout.

Enter **Victoria** *with* **Mahoney**.

Victoria   Talking politics again, I hear. This is my sister Serena. (*Gesturing.*) George Mahoney.

Mahoney   How are you?

Serena   Fine, thanks. I hear you're an ex-monk.

Mahoney   Guilty.

Serena   That's pretty off-beat.

Mahoney   Not particularly. It might be different if I was an ex-nun.

Godfrey (*going to the globe*)   Drink, George?

Mahoney   Thanks, Godfrey.

Victoria   What caused you to drop out?

Mahoney   Sex.

Victoria   Just that?

Mahoney   How much more do you need?

Serena   The thing about monks and nuns is, they always seem to have bad skin.

Mahoney It's on account of the habits.

Serena They give me the creeps. It's such a selfish life.

Victoria In what way selfish?

Serena Concerned only with saving their own souls. Contributing nothing to society.

Victoria (*to* **Mahoney**) Serena runs a travel bureau, you see.

Serena We did a monastery tour a few years back, come to think of it.

Mahoney What kind of a tour?

Serena As far as I remember, it was a sort of imitation pilgrimage, you know, Chaucer and all that. Small groups on horseback, staying at the retreat houses. It was mostly France and Spain, but they were all agog about the Coptic monasteries in Ethiopia and Egypt, that was the ultimate in flash.

Mahoney These were religious groups?

Serena Oh, Christ, no, some of them were in advertising. Just the usual lot, as far as I remember, you know – business types, bureaucrats. Bank officials.

Victoria Serena's definition of ordinary people.

Serena Well, what's wrong with that?

Mahoney So long as they're all contributing something to society.

Godfrey They'll be sailing across the Atlantic in a wheelbarrow next. (*The other three look at him.*)

Victoria Did you say something, Godfrey?

Godfrey Sorry. Just a stray thought.

Victoria (*to* **Mahoney**) You've managed to cling on to your faith in St Brendan, at any rate?

Mahoney   You make it sound like a favourite teddy bear.

Victoria   And is it?

Mahoney   Have you ever tried to teach Godfrey a tune?

Victoria   Meaning what?

Mahoney   It's a waste of time. He's tone-deaf.

Pause.

Victoria   I see. So your religious beliefs are incommunicable – the rest of the world being tone-deaf? How convenient.

Mahoney   The English middle class is not actually the rest of the world, flower. It just thinks of itself that way.

Godfrey   It has been re-enacted, of course.

Serena   What the hell has?

Godfrey   St Brendan's voyage. They reconstructed the ancient Irish type of leather boat and managed to sail it from Ireland to Canada.

Serena   So what?

Godfrey   It doesn't prove George right, of course, but they did demonstrate that it was physically feasible.

Mahoney   Physically, yeah. Spiritually, though, it's not quite so feasible, Godfrey.

Godfrey   True enough, George. Yes indeed. (*Pause.*) How do you mean?

Mahoney   Think of it fourteen hundred years ago. Those monks were living on the final precipice. The West coast of Ireland, the absolute edge of the known world. Every day lifting their eyes across a great grey heaving desert of a sea, stretching to the very rim of the earth itself. An unknown cosmic turbulence. Imagine what it meant to cast yourself into that. No map, no compass, in a shell of stretched cowhide. The boat you can maybe reconstruct ... but not the state of being. Not the unconditional surrender to God's will. Not the wild surge of faith. Or the rapture of it, the blind leap into the dark. That class of a voyage is no longer in the sea's gift.

Pause.

Victoria That sounds more like nostalgia for faith than faith itself. Or am I just being tone-deaf?

Mahoney (*to* **Serena**) Your sister's awful clever.

Serena So I'm frequently told.

Mahoney Could I trouble you for another, Godfrey?

Godfrey Certainly. (*He takes the glass.*)

Mahoney I think I'm going to need it.

Serena So off they paddled to discover America?

Mahoney That wasn't exactly their intention, no.

Serena Well, it doesn't sound like a pleasure cruise.

Mahoney They were spiritual vagrants. The real voyage was an interior one. It was a quest for a state of grace, (*To* **Victoria**.) something which actually does still go on, for those of us deficient in righteousness, I mean.

Godfrey I suppose it's space nowadays.

Serena For God's sake, Godfrey, what is?

Godfrey It's our equivalent today, isn't it? Exploring space.

Serena The flaming astronauts are scarcely what you'd call saints, are they?

Mahoney Glorified projectiles, that's what those guys are.

Godfrey Though some of them are quite saved.

Mahoney   Human cannonballs. In the scientific circus.

Victoria   Your loss of faith extends to science as well, then?

Mahoney   I thought science demolished the need for faith.

Victoria   Well, there are always those who simply refuse to accept evidence. Hard facts. What if I were to tell you, for example, that the lab tests done on your map prove it a fake?

Pause. **Mahoney** *shrugs.*

Mahoney (*upwards to God*)   I'll talk to you later.

Godfrey   Oh, hell, that's rotten news. It was so enthralling, the idea of a boatload of Irish monks stealing a march on all those dagos.

Victoria   I did only say 'what if'.

Serena   You told me in the kitchen that the tests proved it was real.

Victoria   No such thing. What I told you was – there is in fact nothing so far traceable in the vellum or the ink which is inconsistent with a ninth-century provenance.

Godfrey   Really?

Victoria   And truly.

Mahoney (*upwards to God again*)   Pax. (*To* **Victoria**.) That must be rather frustrating for you.

Victoria   Not in the least. You see, the only side I'm on is the side of factual evidence. Whichever way it points, I'll follow.

Serena   I know I'm a mere statistic in the great moronic multitude, but if the tests are so positive, what the bloody hell more do you need?

Victoria   I get people coming in every day of the week

with sensational discoveries. Maps under floorboards, maps on pieces of rock. (*To* **Godfrey**.) Your Mr Rhys produced a Carthaginian map. It was a 1920s diagram of the sewage system in Alexandria. So you see they're all guilty until proved innocent. (*To* **Mahoney**.) It's nothing personal.

Mahoney   Sorry to hear that.

Victoria   As far as yours goes, we simply haven't yet tracked down the author. But we will.

Mahoney   Where does the evidence point you at next?

Victoria   I suppose I'd better visit your monastery library.

Mahoney   It's not up to much.

Victoria   I presume that would be allowed?

Mahoney   Why not? I'll go along as security.

Victoria   That won't be necessary.

Mahoney   I didn't mean for you. I meant for the monks.

Victoria   There's absolutely no need for you to come, I assure you.

Mahoney   I'm due a trip anyway. They love getting visits from the fallen.

Serena   I can make the bookings if you like.

Victoria   It's not going to be an adventure holiday.

Serena   That remains to be seen.

Slight pause.

Victoria   We should be able to eat now, Godfrey. (*She picks up the tray.*)

Godfrey   Ah. Splendid.

Serena I suppose you're a vegetarian.

Mahoney Yeah, but only with regards to liquids.

Mahoney *and* **Serena** *exit.*

Victoria (*to* **Godfrey**) Could you bring that? (*Indicating the ice bucket.*)

Godfrey Of course. Yes.

Victoria *exits.* **Godfrey** *goes to the hatstand, reflects for a moment.*

Godfrey Taking the opportunity. Afforded by your presence here today. To make a religious observance . . . quite good that . . . though I'm sure I speak for many of us. In observing that, religion was always considered quite embarrassing in our family, and it was certainly never discussed in the house, all of us being strictly C of E and indeed my father being the local vicar . . . pause for dutiful laughter . . . but then old George had a way of making you wonder, if you weren't perhaps missing something deep down that you didn't even know you'd lost. All that talk of his, holy vagrancy and spiritual landfalls and so on. Not that you always caught his drift exactly. But it was the way he believed in belief itself, the transcendancy of it. That was the thing. That's what was gripping. A sort of virtuosity in a lost art. (*He picks up the ice bucket.*) Which cut no ice with Victoria, of course. She being the most loyal subject of the entire secular realm. The way the pair of them described that monastery visit, it might have been two entirely different trips.

Serena (*off*) Godfrey!

Godfrey (*in reply*) Coming! (*To himself again.*) When you think back, it was true about him being a vegetarian drinker. There was nothing he wouldn't drink except milk and beef tea. (*He exits.*)

Plainsong starts from off. **Victoria** *and* **Mahoney** *enter, wearing overcoats.*

Mahoney I warned you it wasn't up to much.

Victoria It certainly is a motley collection of books.

Mahoney The guests use it more than the brothers.

She moves along the shelves making notes.

Victoria I suppose it was the St Brendan connection which led you to this place?

Mahoney No, it was more the mother connection.

Victoria Mother?

Mahoney My mother came from round this way.

Victoria You mean you're half-Irish?

Mahoney At the very least.

Victoria My word. So many little surprises.

Mahoney Plenty more to come too. My old man, you see, came over here from Britain right after the war.

Victoria To do what?

Mahoney To work on a building site.

Victoria (*sceptical*) Oh yes?

Mahoney That was how he met my mother. With him being a Presbyterian it was impossible for them here. So they eloped together back to Scotland.

Victoria Gretna Green, I suppose.

Mahoney No, no, Greenock. That's where my da's family stay.

Victoria I'm not sure I believe a word of this.

Mahoney It takes faith.

Pause.

Victoria So your father was the impetuous romantic type?

Mahoney Have you ever been to Greenock?

Victoria No, but I think I take the point.

Mahoney My mother and I escaped back here every summer to stay with my Aunt Lily. It was like the Elysian Fields for both of us. What does *your* father do?

Victoria He's a high-court judge.

Mahoney Good steady work.

Two monkish figures, with their hoods up, cross the stage. One is carrying a small, decorated artificial Christmas tree, and the other an unlit cigarette.

Monk 1 It's bloody daylight robbery, man.

Monk 2 I keep telling you, there's a money-back guarantee.

Monk 1 If you trust that, you're fucking simple. (*Seeing* **Mahoney**.) Pardon me, would you be ever having a light?

Mahoney Sure. (*He lights the cigarette.*)

Monk 2 (*to* **Victoria**) It's a grand day for it.

Victoria Quite.

Monk 1 (*cigarette lit*) Cheers.

The monkish figures exit.

Victoria Is the whole community like that?

Mahoney Not very much. Those fellows aren't monks, they're actors.

Victoria Doing what?

Mahoney Making a television commercial.

Victoria For plastic Christmas trees, no doubt?

Mahoney Something of the sort. It's a useful source of income for monasteries and the like.

Victoria How very worldly of them.

Mahoney There speaks the judge's daughter.

Pause.

Victoria (*turning to the shelves again*) I fear what I'm looking for may not be here.

Mahoney That was certainly my experience.

The **Abbot** *enters, an expansive, florid man in his sixties.*

Abbot Is it himself right enough?

Mahoney Father, are you well?

They embrace.

Abbot God bless you, Kieran. I'd hardly know your face with the hair on it. And this is the English lady you wrote about?

Mahoney Victoria Pratt. Father Alberic.

Abbot You've come a fair step.

Victoria How do you do, Abbot.

Abbot Has he married you yet?

Mahoney Alberic . . .

Victoria We have a professional acquaintance only.

Abbot He'll not be long.

Mahoney Contain yourself.

Abbot I just hope you can keep him at home longer than we did.

Victoria As you know, I'm anxious to trace the origins of the book you presented to . . . Mr Mahoney when he left the order.

Mahoney (*producing it*) The *Navigatio*, Father.

Abbot What about this map, have you it with you?

Mahoney   I've made a copy of it for you. (*He produces it and gives it to the* **Abbot**.)

Abbot   Isn't it near enough a miracle?

Mahoney   Victoria's trying to find that out.

Abbot (*still to* **Mahoney**)   Tell us this, have you peace in your soul this weather?

Mahoney   If I had would you need to ask?

Abbot (*to* **Victoria**)   He's a great man for the journey, you see, but he has no stomach for the destination.

Victoria   Yes. I've looked through your index of books, but it doesn't give any details of dates of accession and suchlike.

Abbot   Does it not?

Victoria   You don't have any other library records?

Abbot   I've got two boyos rummaging round the cellar for you. However, we had an unfortunate incident here some years back, you know. (*To* **Mahoney**.) You mind Brother Eugene?

Mahoney   Very well.

Abbot   A library scholar, mark you. And he did a grand job of tidying up all the old ledgers and inventories and records and what have you scattered around the house. But he separated all the stuff that was to be kept from all the stuff that wasn't and then didn't the two piles get confused. The most of it was burned before he cottoned on to the mistake.

Victoria   Could I talk to him?

Mahoney   Nine years dead, I'm afraid.

Abbot   Tell us this, did you ever hear a yarn like it in all your born days?

Victoria   Pardon?

The **Abbot** *has taken the copy of the* Navigatio, *and is untying it and searching through it for a passage.*

Abbot   Sailors' tales are maybe not renowned for their rigorous honesty, but sure who would call into question the doings of a saint? Isn't that right?

Victoria   Possibly, yes.

Abbot   The Island of the Birds, do you mind that, Kieran?

Mahoney   Victoria knows it too, Alberic.

Abbot   Here we are. A tree of enormous girth. Thick with snowy white birds. And one of them tells Brendan, *Nos sumus de illa magna ruina antiqui hostis*, we are some of that great host of fallen angels, who fell from God's grace along with Lucifer. For ever exiled from heaven, you see, but transformed into white songbirds, here on the island, on holy days, to sing God's praise.

Mahoney   A nice enough fall, as falls go.

Abbot   And at that minute the whole flock strikes up together, singing vespers . . . *quasi carmen planctus pro suavitate*, a song sweet and moving as any lament. (*He closes the book.*) Have you ever been there yourself?

Victoria   Where, exactly?

Abbot   America?

Victoria   Yes. Yes.

Abbot   It must be a sight to behold.

Victoria   It has rather gone to seed since Brendan's day.

A monk in early middle age and a somewhat younger man, shabbily dressed in an ancient suit, enter, carrying a box of old documents between them.

Abbot   Now here's Malachy who takes all to do with

our books this weather and used to lend Eugene a hand.

Victoria   Hello.

Abbot   And this here's young Brendan from the village. (*He ruffles the younger man's hair; the younger man gives a peculiar nasal laugh: he's mentally retarded.*)

Victoria (*looking in the box*)   So what have you managed to excavate here? (*She starts flicking through the contents.*)

Abbot (*to* **Mahoney**)   Have you seen the new creamery, Kieran?

Mahoney   Only surrounded by television trucks.

Abbot   Come on and I'll show you it now.

Mahoney (*to* **Victoria**)   I'll just be a few minutes.

Victoria   Fine.

The **Abbot** *and* **Mahoney** *exit.* **Malachy** *and* **Brendan** *stand watching* **Victoria** *silently.*

Victoria   Tell me, Malachy, how much do you know about where all the books here came from?

Malachy   Not much, miss.

Victoria   What about Brother Eugene, did he know much?

Malachy   He did, miss.

Victoria   I don't suppose he used to forge maps in his spare time?

Malachy   No, miss. He was blind, you see.

Pause.

Victoria   When did he go blind?

Malachy   Before he joined the order, it was.

Victoria (*to herself*)   Stone the crows.

Brendan (*mimicking*) Sthone the kwahs . . . sthone de kwahs! (*He laughs.*)

Malachy You mustn't mind Brendan. He has a want.

Victoria *goes back to the box of papers. They continue to survey her silently.*

Malachy Would you be looking out for any particular thing?

Victoria Yes, oddly enough, I am. (*She pauses, leaves the papers, picks up the* Navigatio.) I was foolishly hoping to trace the origins of this.

Brendan *leaps forward with a cry and seizes the book.*

Brendan Meenogahane, Meenogahane!

Victoria Can you get it off him, please, it's rather valuable.

Malachy He'll not harm it, miss. He has a powerful love of the books.

Brendan Loybee, loybee up'n Meenogahane, Malky. Up'n Meenogahane. (*He laughs, turning the pages very carefully, peering at them, murmuring to himself.*)

Victoria What's he saying?

Malachy Meenogahane, miss.

Victoria What's that?

Malachy The big house north of here. His mother used to be the housekeeper there.

Victoria He seems very taken with the book anyway.

Malachy Oh, yes. That's where it'll be from, you see. He remembers it.

Victoria Why on earth would it be from there?

Malachy Now, it may be it would have come from there when the last of the O'Rourkes died, but I couldn't say for sure.

Victoria Yes?

Malachy There was a time when the brothers lived at Meenogahane, you know.

Victoria Recently?

Malachy In the days of the Penal Laws, it was.

Victoria I see. The family sheltered the monks when Catholicism was outlawed?

Malachy The old Abbey was burned down by the English king in those days. Terrible times.

Victoria And you say the O'Rourkes of Meenogahane have all died out?

Malachy It was an English lawyer bought the house and lands when the old lady went.

Victoria Well, perhaps I shall pay a visit to Meenogahane.

Malachy It was set on fire and burned to the ground last year, miss.

Victoria Oh, wonderful.

Brendan (*mimicking*) Aw waundafah! (*He laughs.*)

Enter **Mahoney**.

Mahoney Any luck?

Victoria Not a lot. The area seems to abound in pyromaniacs.

Malachy (*to* **Brendan**) Time to go, Brendan. (*He takes the book away gently and returns it to* **Victoria**.) God be with the work, miss.

Victoria Thank you.

Exit **Malachy** *and* **Brendan**.

Victoria   I'm damned if I know what to believe in this place.

Mahoney   You don't often hear that said in a monastery.

Victoria   Frankly, it smells utterly bogus, from that old windbag of an abbot on down.

Mahoney   Ten minutes of eternal life, and you'd be saying the same thing about heaven. You're certainly conforming to type, Victoria. Holiness confounds you.

Victoria   I think I know a stage-Irishman when I see one.

Mahoney   How about a condescending Englishwoman?

Victoria   I came here looking for straight answers to simple questions, and nothing more. Colourful anecdotes and blethering holiness I can live without.

Mahoney   How the hell do you think they spend their days here, love? Discussing scientific method? You think they hold seminars on bibliography and carbon dating? 'Any records of provenance here, Malachy?' 'Oh, definitely, Diarmuid, it was hand-printed in the Low Countries on demy-octavo toilet tissue.'

Victoria   Look, so far I'm contending with records destroyed by a blind dead librarian and with the word of a village idiot that the book comes from a local stately home recently firebombed into oblivion.

Mahoney   What, Meenogahane?

Victoria   Don't you start, for God's sake!

Mahoney   It wouldn't maybe have crossed your mind that the map could mean something different to them than it does to you . . . ?

Victoria   No, it wouldn't. A map is a map.

Mahoney   . . . a manifestation of God, even? An icon?

A relic? An object of veneration?

Victoria   How on earth could they venerate something which is very likely a fake?

Mahoney   Possibly because the land promised to the saints already exists for them.

Victoria   That's just further mindless blarney. A map is a spatial diagram. It is not an icon. It is a functional tool for people wanting to get from A to B. And if St Brendan's lot were anything like their present counterparts, I would doubt their ability to discover a route from here to the outside toilet.

Mahoney   You're on the worst possible grounds, my friend, for sarcasm on that score. Your own people are not exactly famous for their powers of discovery round here. You'd think after all these years they would have managed to discover Ireland at least, but then the English genius was always more for expropriation, wasn't it, you could always rely on the continentals to actually find the countries, whereupon you could move in to dispossess them, that's the way you badged the map of the world with red while you kept yourselves sweet and wholesome at home, you exorcised the idea of hell from the English shires by exporting it to the rest of us. Well, this island you're on now is where it started and this is where it's drawing to a close, this is where you've always come to unleash your most damnable nightmares and devils, but once you're out of here, flower, there'll be nowhere left for the dark to go, the English hell will finally come home to roost, it's already happening. So what price then your complacency, your self-righteousness, your sanctimony, your contempt for any other world than your own dwindling patch of barrenness?

Pause.

Victoria   Extraordinary. I never in my life expected to be taken for *Queen* Victoria. I suppose everybody with an

Irish granny learns a speech like that by heart?

Mahoney I read once about an instruction in an old mapmaker's handbook: 'Where you know nothing, place terrors.' Just don't be so certain sure of your ground all the time. You never know when you might find yourself on terra incognita. (*He kisses her lightly on the lips.*) Pax.

Victoria What on earth do you think you're doing?

Mahoney There's a way to check up on the book, incidentally. Assuming you're still interested.

Victoria Ah, yes, the book. I knew there was some dim reason for being in this godforsaken hole.

Mahoney Scarcely godforsaken.

Victoria Correction. God-infested hole.

Mahoney It was the O'Rourke family of Meenogahane who endowed the Abbey. This used to be their land.

Victoria So?

Mahoney Theirs was one of the few Catholic big houses – one of the very few that survived in the family's ownership from Cromwell's day. Till the IRA got it, that is. So the book could very well have come from their library.

Victoria So what?

Mahoney The O'Rourke papers were bequeathed to the state by the old lady. They're in an archive in the Public Record Office in Cork.

Pause.

Victoria I find that too straightforward to be plausible.

Mahoney (*moving close to her*) I'll leave it up to you, flower. I know how much you like to take the initiative.

He kisses her more decisively. After a moment, she disengages.

Victoria Where did you read that epithet?

Mahoney What?

Victoria 'Where you know nothing, place terrors'?

Mahoney I don't know. Some novel.

Victoria It's rather good.

Mahoney Isn't it.

Victoria I should imagine it would apply to Irish hotels. Perhaps you can advise me.

Mahoney We can stay at my Aunt Lily's.

Victoria Thank you, but I think I would feel more at ease in a hotel.

Mahoney It *is* a hotel.

Victoria Oh.

Mahoney A one and a half star rating. It used to be two stars, but one of them got hit with a shotgun pellet.

Victoria Sounds about my level.

Mahoney Very good. Follow me.

They exit. Music.

Godfrey *enters, looks at the clock, which now reads seven minutes to twelve; removes the tie from the hatstand and starts putting it on.*

Godfrey As a great man once said, 'Time is but the stream I go a-fishing in' . . . meaning God knows what . . . and as we regale ourselves today by its slow-moving waters . . . I can certainly pride myself on having landed a prize catch . . . but there again, there must be a better quotation than that you can dredge up. George would have known one, he was a walking dictionary of them. Though most of them were of his own invention, like his Freudian theory of British history: 'England as the ego, Ireland as the id, America as the asylum'. By which

Victoria was not amused . . . quite good that . . . in fact, she was pretty thin-lipped about that whole Irish escapade. How they got through it together without coming to blows I can't imagine.

Enter **Serena**.

Serena The entire thing is your fault, you realise.

Godfrey It actually wasn't, of course, but I couldn't help enjoying the accusation.

Serena It was you who put him on to her.

Godfrey You have to admit, it's exciting, Serena.

Serena Exciting? It's grotesque. How could she fall for that Glaswegian dingbat?

Godfrey Victoria? For George? Oh, no, there's no likelihood of that, they can't abide one another.

Serena For Christ's sake, Godfrey, they're at each other like dogs in heat! Why don't you do something, you've been mooning round after her for long enough.

Godfrey They've only been together a lot because of today's meeting. Victoria has been working flat out on her report.

Serena Flat out is too bloody right. What meeting?

Godfrey Dr Bridges and his assistant librarians. It's to decide on whether to purchase the map for the library, Victoria could become quite famous, you know.

Serena I don't want her being famous, she's my sister.

Godfrey Think of how you could use it, though, to publicise your business.

Serena That's the same gormless thing Harvey Small said, and he doesn't even have your excuse.

Godfrey Who's Harvey Small?

Serena Nobody. He's taken my old office. He's a private investigator, if you must know.

Godfrey Seriously? A gumshoe, a real sleuth? A private dick?

Serena Well, he certainly hasn't flashed it at me yet.

Godfrey That's great. Is he all trenchcoat and Lucky Strikes and a low fedora?

Serena No, he isn't, he's all plastic mac and a corduroy cap and a packet of Polo mints.

Godfrey What exactly does he do?

Serena He says if this map thing gets in the papers, I ought to cash in on it, but I wouldn't give Mahoney the satisfaction.

Godfrey To tell the truth, I think he'd be inclined to find it rather offensive.

Serena Really? Perhaps I'll reconsider. When does this meeting begin?

Godfrey Any time now. It's all supposed to be terribly hush-hush.

Serena I'll go and ring the *Sunday Times*, in that case.

Godfrey I don't really think you ought to do that, Serena. (*She has gone.*) But she did, of course. And I suppose for the outside world, that was when the story really began.

Victoria *enters, carrying a briefcase, followed by* **Mahoney**. *She sits at the desk and begins glancing over her notes.*

Victoria . . . The mapping of Antarctica, George, is not exactly material just at the moment.

Mahoney All the same, you'd say that when it was finished, after World War Two, the map of the world was essentially completed?

Victoria   What of it?

Mahoney   Even before there was writing, there must
have been jokers scratching directions in the dust. Making
a picture of the known world. And over thousands of
generations, the picture was slowly added to. Fields,
counties. Countries. Continents. Finally, in our own time,
the picture of the world is fully painted at long last. Now
how did this momentous occasion pass by unremarked?

Victoria   Because mapmakers don't indulge in idle
romantic vapourings.

Mahoney   Maybe it fills them with an instinctive dread.

Godfrey   What does, George?

Mahoney   The prospect of a world that's fully known.
No more hidden valleys, no more dark interiors. Just
what's here, what's on the map. The end of adventure.
The death of all the planet's potentialities.

Enter **Dr Bridges**, *a somewhat hapless-looking man in his
sixties, with a very slight middle-European tinge to his accent.*

Bridges   Ah, here you are.

Mahoney   About to embark on a beverage, Dr Bridges.

Bridges   Well, thank you for looking in today. You
certainly have confounded us with this find of yours.

Mahoney   It was all due to Godfrey, he assured me
that nobody could touch Miss Pratt.

Bridges   Quite so.

Victoria   Goodbye, Mr Mahoney. Goodbye, Godfrey.

Mahoney   God be with the work, miss.

Godfrey   Right, then. See you later. Perhaps.

Exit **Godfrey** *and* **Mahoney**.

Bridges   Dear me. You don't suppose there's likely to

be a fuss over this, do you?

Victoria   I devoutly hope so, Dr Bridges.

Bridges   You're still young, Miss Pratt. Accept the
word of an old campaigner that it's best never to believe
with too much seriousness. Comedy, you know, ends in a
wedding but tragedy always on a stage bestrewn with
deeply convinced corpses.

Victoria   In my case, neither outcome has the least
appeal – any more than endless equivocation does.

Bridges   Quite so. Though short-term equivocation has
much to recommend it.

Enter **Proctor** *and* **Gamble**, *heads of department, youngish,
supercilious, mildly louche.*

Proctor   May we intrude ourselves into these
proceedings?

Bridges   Ah, gentlemen. Do come in. Sit down, please.

They sit down on the office chairs.

Bridges   Now, then. As you are aware, the time has
arrived to review our preliminary findings on this map.
Which I suppose we must call the Brendan Map, since
everybody else will.

Gamble   My dears – Brendan Map Sensation!

Proctor   Shamrock Saint First Ashore, Say Experts.

Gamble   Columbus Capsized!

Proctor   Saintly Seadog Showed The Way.

Bridges   Indeed yes. Well, I have interviewed both Mr
Mahoney and Dr Dudley. There seems to be no question
that it was a bona fide discovery. Whether anything else
will be at all clear from this point on, I beg leave to
doubt.

Proctor   We are of course all agreed that it's a

seventeenth-century forgery, I take it?

Gamble   Speak for yourself, dear.

Bridges   I must say I would prefer it to be a seventeenth-century forgery. It would have so much more charm.

Gamble   I'm still convinced it's an April Fool from that spiteful witch at the British Museum.

Proctor   We haven't been paying attention to our wormholes and stitchmarks, have we?

Gamble   I can't think what you mean, nurse.

Victoria (*to* **Proctor**)   On your evidence, Mr Proctor, the stitching and worming in the parchment match that in the book?

Proctor   To a veritable nicety.

Victoria   Good. I've traced the book to its source. It was printed and bound in Limerick in 1649.

Proctor   Limerick?

Gamble   There was a seafarer called Brendan . . .

Victoria   This was in a small printing-house owned by a branch of the O'Rourke family of Kerry.

Gamble   . . . Who engendered dissension unendin' . . .

Victoria   It remained in the library of the family seat at Meenogahane up until twenty-five years ago, when it passed into the care of the Ardfert Cistercians, from where Mr Mahoney acquired it.

Proctor
. . . He'd have spoken more faintly
And acted less saintly
If he knew what he'd started a trend in.

Bridges   Well done, Miss Pratt. Now what about this poem?

Victoria I've heard better limericks, though it's not a form I admire.

Bridges I was thinking more of the love poem on the back of the map parchment.

Victoria Yes, of course.

Bridges Is there a candidate for it?

Victoria There were three daughters of the family at the relevant time. The youngest, Finnoula, appears to have died in 1650, and was buried in unconsecrated ground along with the mutilated body of an English captain of artillery.

Proctor (*whistling*) Spicey.

Gamble Shaping up very nicely for a television deal.

Victoria So far I have no clear lead on the map parchment prior to this date, but one point is worth noting. The O'Rourke family's close relationship to the monastery goes back beyond the Dissolution in 1536 to its foundation in the twelfth century. The map almost certainly originated in Ardfert, only to return there unbeknownst in our own time.

Pause.

Proctor You're not suggesting it's older than the book?

Victoria Why not? The vellum certainly is, by your own account. So apparently is the ink.

Gamble Suddenly I have a sickening feeling that our Miss Pratt has decided to go for bust on this one.

Proctor You don't actually buy it, Vic?

Pause.

Victoria Yes. I believe I do. (*Pause.*) Well, at least I've secured your undivided attention.

Gamble People who threaten to jump from tall

buildings generally do, dear.

Bridges   It does rather entail the rewriting of the history of Western cartography, Miss Pratt.

Victoria   Oh, I should have thought that was the least of it.

Bridges   But on such tenuous evidence . . . ?

Victoria   The provenance is sound enough. The forensic results are at worst neutral. The historical evidence we haven't even touched on yet.

Proctor   An Irish map . . . it's like some terrible joke.

Victoria   The foremost medieval geographer was an Irishman called Dicuil. In the early ninth century – the period in question – he was court geographer to Charlemagne.

Proctor   Yes, but I don't recall him leaving us lightning sketches of the American coastline.

Victoria   In his 'Book of the Earth's Measurement' he describes the midnight sun and refers to colonies of Irish monks in the Faroes and in Iceland. This was three hundred years after the time of Brendan himself, remember – three centuries of continuous seafaring and of academic enquiry in the Irish schools.

Gamble   I'm amazed they hadn't started flights to Boston, aren't you?

Victoria   The 'Martyrology of Donegal' lists twenty-six notables named Colman. One of them has the given name 'Immrama' – meaning 'of the Voyage' – the name that appears on the map.

Proctor   Show us a few more of his maps and I might even begin to believe it.

Victoria   I can certainly show you maps. (*She goes to the bookshelves and slides a section of them back to reveal a screen.*)

Gamble   And to think that people complain about the dearth of live entertainment . . .

Victoria *switches on a concealed projector, which shows on the screen a big, vivid close-up of an early map of Europe's Atlantic seaboard.*

Victoria   This is the Hereford Mappa Mundi of 1275. The Island of Saint Brendan is located just here. (*She indicates.*)

Proctor   Leave off, Vic, this is four centuries further on.

Victoria   All in good time, Mr Proctor. (*She switches to a second slide.*) Here we have the globe of Martin Behaim, constructed immediately prior to 1492. So this is the world as Christopher Columbus perceived it to be before his voyages. Saint Brendan's Island is here. (*She indicates. She now switches to a third slide.*) Another century further on, a chart by Ortelius. By now, of course, the American discoveries are well established. Notwithstanding, St Brendan's Island lingers on, right here. (*Indicates, moves on to a fourth slide.*) As a last example, here it is again in the celebrated Mercator-Hondius Atlas of 1595. (*She indicates, then switches the projector off and slides the bookshelves back over the screen.*)

Gamble   It was certainly very big in its day.

Proctor   A legend, in fact, in its own lifetime.

Gamble   The longest running imaginary island in the history of real estate.

Proctor   Or in this case, unreal estate.

Victoria   It's a tradition which survives on countless other charts well into the seventeenth century. The question is – where did it originate?

Proctor (*picking up the* Navigatio)   Right here, darling, in Uncle Brendan's Bedtime Book of Topping Tales, high on the fiction list for a good half-millennium.

Victoria   That's what has always been assumed. But supposing St Brendan's Island was an actual cartographic tradition? Supposing Mercator and Ortelius and Behaim and all the others, stretching back into obscurity, were preserving the authoritative evidence of an early Irish map such as this one? It's inconceivable that the Irish monks of the ninth century, the learned heirs of a long seafaring tradition, lacked the capacity to draw maps. So why have no others been discovered yet? It's very simple. In the succeeding two hundred years, the Vikings picked Ireland clean. (*Lifts the Brendan Map.*) I, Colman Immrama, set down this true image of the blessed isles to the West, in the year the Northmen first put to the flames great Clonmacnoise.' In my view this map is an astonishing, unique and authentic survival from that lost era. (*She sits down. Pause.*)

Bridges   So. Miss Pratt believes in the map.

Victoria   I think it's imperative that we acquire it.

Bridges   And Mr Proctor?

Proctor   Oh, me of little faith! Sorry, love, but I'm for saying we're just looking, thanks.

Bridges   And Mr Gamble?

Gamble   I simply loathe being sold a pup, and God knows plenty have been.

Bridges   Indeed, yes. There must be the unhappy memory of the Vinland Map in all our thoughts.

Gamble   Even before that there was those Italian fakes the Brazilians bought for a packet.

Bridges   I think the consensus seems to be for a further period of work on the map, before we decide for or against purchase.

Pause.

Victoria   Fine. (*The others prepare to leave.*) One question,

though. What if Mr Mahoney decides to offer the map
elsewhere?

Bridges I shouldn't think there's any likelihood. He
knows we're acting in good faith.

Victoria He *has* had an invitation from Harvard.

Pause.

Proctor Harvard?

Gamble How the bloody hell did they get on to it?

Victoria I suppose he made photocopies.

Proctor Oh, well.

Bridges Dear me.

Gamble Isn't it marvellous?

Proctor It puts the flaming fat in the fire all right.

Gamble We bloody well can't let the Yanks get it, I
mean, they never miss a trick, do they? Smarmy buggers.

Bridges It does put a slightly different complexion on
the matter.

Proctor I'll say.

Pause.

Gamble What have they offered him?

Victoria I've no idea.

Proctor We'd better look sharp, though, knowing those
ponces. They'd have the pants off your grannie. (*To*
Gamble.) How much could we afford?

Gamble How much would he swallow?

Bridges If the map were ninth-century, it would of
course be beyond price. As a seventeenth-century fake it
would be a vastly more modest acquisition.

Victoria   I don't see how we can get away with less than fifteen thousand.

Gamble   Oh, leave off, five would be plenty to gamble at this stage.

Victoria   My understanding is that Mr Mahoney intends donating the entire sum to the monastery.

Proctor   Oh, well, let's make it five.

Victoria   Harvard, of course, as we all know, is loaded.

Pause.

Bridges   Perhaps we had better stretch to ten.

Gamble   We're going to look like prize chumps if it turns out a dud.

Bridges   On the other hand, if it has value, we won't be accused in retrospect of swindling a community of monks. Agreed?

Victoria   Certainly.

Proctor   Fine.

Gamble   If you all say so, but it's going to leave an ugly great gaping hole in the budget.

Bridges   I fear that trouble of this calibre never comes cheap. You'd better make the arrangements right away, Mr Gamble. Be sure to attach a proviso of confidentiality.

Gamble   Too right. The further at bay the presshounds are kept the better.

Bridges   Thank you all. (*He exits.*)

Proctor   Bravo, Vic.

Gamble   The audacity of the child!

Proctor   We *are* impressed.

Gamble   You'll do a book about it, of course?

Victoria If it's warranted.

Proctor There'll be no talking to her after this.

Gamble My dear, a star is born. (*Exit* **Proctor** *and* **Gamble**.)

Music. **Victoria** *smiles slightly to herself as she collects her papers together.* **Mahoney** *enters, followed by* **Godfrey**.

Mahoney There's a journalist across in the pub wanting to talk to you.

Victoria Yes?

Mahoney He claims it's about an Irish map.

Victoria That's odd. The library's just decided to buy one. For ten thousand.

Pause.

Mahoney You're not serious?

Victoria Oh yes, I am.

She kisses him. They stay kissing, as **Godfrey** *shuffles downstage.*

Godfrey I really disapprove of people behaving like that, in company, I mean. It's a form of emotional advertising, isn't it. The height of bad manners, that's what I call it. Of course people are at their most inconsiderate and selfish when they're in love. You only have to watch them. (*He does.*) OH, FOR GOD'S SAKE PUT A STOPPER IN IT!

Mahoney *disengages from* **Victoria**.

Mahoney They didn't challenge your findings?

Victoria What, in the face of the evidence? (*They start to exit.*) Oh, by the way, if anyone mentions Harvard to you, just confirm that you've had an enquiry, okay?

Mahoney Harvard? (*They exit.*)

Godfrey *goes to the hatstand and puts on the waistcoat during the following.*

Godfrey   Today, of course, is above all an occasion for sharing. The sharing of our happiness with all of you. The sharing of so many things with one another. Memories. Hopes. Ptomaine poisoning, and in Mahoney's case it was Victoria's entire flat after he moved in with her. Still at least it solved his accommodation problem. They got quite domesticated, with her working away on the book, I saw a lot of them that year. I remember the four of us going horse-racing, where was that? It was a steeplechase somewhere. In the big race, there was a horse called Magic Map, which of course George and Victoria backed. I backed one called Bystander. Serena backed Guided Missile which needless to say was the winner. What happened to Magic Map? I can't remember whether it even finished or not.

Serena *(calling from off)*   Godfrey, can you come here please?

Godfrey *(calling)*   Just coming! *(Pause. To himself again.)* As for Bystander, it broke a leg and had to be shot. *(Ruminates; looks at the clock, which now reads five to twelve.)* Oh, my God. *(Exits, hastily.)*

Music.

Act Two

Bondage

The scene is exactly as it was at the end of Act One.

Music. **Godfrey** *re-enters, goes to the hatstand, removes the jacket and puts it on.*

Godfrey There are always those cynics amongst us who will maintain that matrimony is defunct.

Victoria (*from off*) Leaving in five minutes, Godfrey!

Godfrey (*in reply*) Nearly ready! (*To himself again.*) Those who are always ready to cry wolf with regard to wedlock. To whom marriage is a brightly-packaged anachronism, which is quite true of course. People do it more out of inertia than belief these days, still, you can hardly say that, can you? It was lucky, though, that George subscribed to the institutional theory. Clubbability. One person doesn't marry another, they both just get wedded to the institution of marriage itself, which seems reasonable enough to me, actually, that's why you tell people 'I'm getting married' instead of saying who to. But I suppose having fought his way out of one institution, George wasn't about to sign himself into another. At least, neither he nor Victoria showed any such tendency, much to your secret relief. She just beavered away at the book, and he just, come to think of it, what *did* he do during those eighteen months? He was a barman for a while, I remember, and then he was a taxi-driver. But he spent more time in the bar as a taxi-driver than he had as a barman. Which accounted for those two jobs. Then he was a hospital porter. Actually he spent a lot of time in the bar irrespective of jobs, and you, Godfrey, were generally with him on these occasions.

Enter **Mahoney**, *in dressing-gown, very morning-after. He* *carries a pile of Sunday newspapers under one arm, which he dumps on the table, and an old canvas kitbag full of rumpled clothing over the other shoulder, which he dumps on the bench.*

Mahoney (*groaning*) Mercy, mercy, mercy.

Godfrey No wonder you've trouble remembering most of it.

Mahoney Still alive, Godfrey?

Godfrey How goes it at the hospital, George?

Mahoney Much as when you left it last night, I imagine.

Godfrey I seem to have trouble remembering most of last night.

Mahoney You kissed the entire nursing staff of the maternity wing.

Godfrey Oh no.

Mahoney Most of the mothers and babies too. I had to send you home in an ambulance.

Godfrey Good God, was I injured?

Mahoney You were totally disabled.

Godfrey But that's despicable. What about you?

Mahoney I was sacked.

Godfrey But that's terrible. All because of me?

Mahoney I'm afraid not, Godfrey. It's merely that horseplay and drunken repartee is the exclusive privilege of the student doctors. I have been dissolute above my station.

Godfrey What'll you do now.

Mahoney I suppose we could try ripping up a few more old books.

Pause.

Godfrey   George?

Mahoney   Guilty.

Godfrey   I woke up clutching a single red wellington boot.

Mahoney   It belongs to a radiographer from Troon. You drank a pint of bitter out of it.

Godfrey   I hate beer.

Mahoney   We inferred as much from the speed with which you disgorged it.

Godfrey   Oh, lord. It's so shaming.

Mahoney   Sunday morning weather, Godfrey. A low-lying miasma of guilt and remorse blankets the entire country.

Godfrey   Speaking of Sunday morning. How are the papers today, any reviews?

Mahoney *picks up the top paper from the pile on the table.*

Mahoney (*reading*)   'It is not too often that a work of scholarship reads like a top-flight thriller, but Victoria Pratt is a spell-binder. As to the case which she makes out for the authenticity of this remarkable map, I for one am no more inclined to put it down than I was her enthralling book.'

Godfrey   My word. Are they all like that?

Mahoney   Not entirely. Some of the others are less carping.

Godfrey *picks up a few of the other papers and peruses them.*

Godfrey   It's turning into a real monster success.   —

Mahoney   Or a monster, anyway.

Godfrey   But it's creating a sensation.

Mahoney   Only as a novelty item. They're all so damned predictable. Have you yet read one comment on the impulses behind that map? The hunger to navigate your way into the knowledge of God? So far as this culture goes, it's just another commodity, I should have thrown it in the fire.

Godfrey   That's a bit strong, George.

Mahoney   No, I'm half-inclined to disown it as a fake.

Godfrey   Nobody would believe you, not without proof.

Mahoney   What the hell, Godfrey, it'll be forgotten soon enough, once the next sensation turns up.

Godfrey   Not in the profession, it won't.

Mahoney   Ah, yes. The profession.

Enter **Serena**, *also with newspapers under her arm.*

Serena   Morning.

Godfrey   Hello, Serena.

Serena   I suppose the main attraction is still in bed, with a champagne breakfast?

Mahoney   She was shaving when last seen.

Godfrey   That was quite a coincidence last Sunday, Serena.

Serena   Wasn't it.

Mahoney   What was?

Godfrey   I bumped into Serena on the Glasgow sleeper. (*To* **Serena**.) Harvey Small is certainly a lively sort.

Serena   Isn't he.

Mahoney   Who's Harvey Small?

Serena A business associate.

Godfrey He's Serena's private dick.

Serena For God's sake stop calling him that!

Mahoney What do you need a private dick for?

Serena We happen to have adjacent offices.

Enter **Victoria**, *in dressing-gown, sipping coffee.*

Victoria Who does?

Mahoney Serena and Harvey Small, she was saying that they have adjacent orifices.

Serena Such a hoot.

Mahoney *has been pulling jeans and a sweater from the kitbag and sniffing them: he now starts to put them on.*

Godfrey Good show, Victoria. With the reviews, I mean.

Victoria Thank you, Godfrey.

Serena (*brandishing a colour supplement*) Have you read this interview?

Victoria Oh, that thing.

Serena It's pathetic. (*Reads.*) 'All I can say is, the brunette and brainy Victoria Pratt does for blue stockings what Mae West did for the life-jacket.'

Victoria He was a lecherous old fart, that one.

Serena 'Let's hope, as more women rise to the top in their careers, that Ms Pratt is indeed the shape of things to come.' Why do you stand for such insulting bilge?

Mahoney *is now sniffing his way through assorted socks.*

Victoria George, do you really have to do that?

Mahoney I can hardly go into the Lord's house bollock-naked, flower.

Victoria So we're supposed to watch you sniff your way through your entire wardrobe?

Mahoney A simple test of the freshness of my apparel. Conducted out of concern for my fellow man. By the by, I had a wee sniff round your chemise earlier on, it smells a mite garlicky.

Victoria There *is* a launderette down the road well worth a visit.

Serena Not as long as you're prepared to do it for him.

Mahoney Never shrink, girls, from the properties of the flesh. In our fallen state, spirit and matter are interwoven in the one fabric. The more you lose touch with the physical world, the blinder you grow to the metaphysical one. Until you end up with Anglicanism. There is no paradox in the fact that the most devout section of any society is always the peasants, people who can stick a pig or geld a horse with the greatest of equanimity.

Serena If you're so concerned for your fellow man, you might have the decency to dress in the bedroom.

Mahoney Tell us this, Serena, how does old Harvey manage, with his smalls, I mean?

Serena I'll fetch him round and you can ask him yourself.

Mahoney I was just interested on account of his line of business – you know, washing other people's in public.

Victoria I thought you were on duty today in the hospital, George.

Mahoney Godfrey and I have decided to go on a church-crawl.

Godfrey (*who has been engrossed in the supplement*) Sorry?

Mahoney We intend to return fragrant with the odour of sanctity, isn't that right?

Godfrey Church?

Mahoney In the great *Navigatio* itself, it is written – that those few who returned from the land promised to the saints had a sweet unearthly smell clinging to their garments. This was even before there were launderettes.

Victoria You've been sacked again, haven't you?

Godfrey It may have been largely my fault, I think.

Victoria (*ignoring this*) I thought as much from your fragrant odour arriving home at five this morning.

Mahoney Yes indeed, I was up half the night, adamantly refusing all their entreaties to withdraw my resignation.

Victoria Such strength of character.

Mahoney Don't fuck around, flower. If you've got something to say, say it.

Pause.

Victoria You'd better go, it would never do to keep the Lord waiting.

Serena Damn you, if she won't say it, I will, you're nothing but a shiftless lazy hypocritical bastard!

Victoria Quit it, Serena!

Mahoney Restrain yourself, Godfrey! We shall say a special prayer for the repose of Serena's soul. Come. (*Exit* **Mahoney**.)

Godfrey Right. See you a bit later, then. (*Exit* **Godfrey**.)

Pause.

Serena How you can bear him I'll never . . .

Victoria   Let's just leave it there, shall we.

Serena   No, we shan't. He's an idle dosser and you let him walk all over you.

Victoria   If he's walking all over me, then you can scarcely call him idle, can you?

Serena   Mummy was right, that man is dragging you down to his own level.

Victoria   I expect she was and he is, so why don't you fuck off home, Serena.

Serena   Charming. Now that you're a media personality, I'm not permitted to open my mouth, I suppose.

Victoria   Finally we come to the real point, at least.

Serena   What the hell's come over you? Why are you suddenly turning on *me*?

Victoria   It's the little-sister act in full swing, isn't it?

Serena   I take it this is meant to imply that I'm jealous of your famous book.

Victoria   You're certainly ungenerous to a fault.

Serena   I'm what?

Victoria   Look at these papers. My name is splashed all over them, in the news section, the reviews, even in the ghastly supplements. My book has finally appeared to near-unanimous raves. It doesn't happen that often. I'd like to hear a few bells pealing, I beg permission to indulge in just a glimmer of satisfaction, for Christ's sake. Instead of which I get you stumping in here, glowering at all and sundry, and bitching away about one trashy interview.

Pause.

Serena   Well – it's all Mahoney's fault. The very sight of him drives me into a frenzy.

Victoria You've never forgiven him for discovering the map.

Serena It's nothing to do with that, it's the way he's been sponging off you for a year and a half now. He's taken this place over, he's everywhere, like a mouldering lump of old Stilton. I never see you any more, either you're buried in your work or you're with him.

Victoria I expect it's because we're living together, wouldn't you say?

Serena I just don't know what you see in him, Vic.

Pause.

Victoria I suppose it's his desperation really. It's like one of those Westerns. The schoolmarm who falls for the desperado. People like me always end up falling for an outlaw.

Serena It's the thought of him as an in-law that frightens me.

Victoria That's never how it works out. And least of all in this picture.

Serena He's so awful to you.

Victoria Only because he holds me personally responsible for Cromwell, the Battle of Culloden, the Highland Clearances, the Great Famine and Bloody Sunday.

Pause.

Serena All right, so I've been a shrew, agreed, unspeakable, you're in the right as usual, fair enough?

Victoria You've been having a rotten time, I know that.

Serena I've never really got over losing those

chartered accountants in Borneo.

Victoria   Nobody blamed you for it.

Serena   I was categorically assured that the trip had been cleared with the tribal elders.

Victoria   It was obviously just some misunderstanding.

Serena   How can there be a misunderstanding with headhunters? I mean, it has to be either/or, doesn't it?

Victoria   Supposing they'd died in a plane crash, it would have amounted to the same thing.

Serena   People don't look at it that way, it's become a standing joke in the business. At conferences and what not, they all just fall about – 'Oh, hello, Serena, how are things at Head Office', all that crap.

Victoria   I'd no idea.

Serena   If it hadn't been for Harvey's support, I really think I'd have shut up shop by this time.

Victoria   You and Harvey seem to have grown very close.

Serena   It's not what you think, though. He's a mother's boy, they live together in a bungalow and during the day she sticks pins in my effigy.

Victoria   Not the normal image of a private eye.

Serena   I reckon he does the job to compensate.

Victoria   So you've every reason for feeling got at?

Serena   It's still no excuse for behaving like a berk. The fact is, I'm not a bit jealous of your fame, I'm just insanely green with envy, that's all.

Victoria   You needn't be. It feels like being pitchforked into a freak show. You heard what happened to the book in the States?

Serena No, what?

Victoria The award-winning publisher managed to launch it on the twelfth of October.

Serena So?

Victoria It only happens to be Columbus Day. His offices have been picketed by the Friends of Italy. The Spanish Ambassador has delivered a note of protest to the State Department. And I've got a parcel of hate mail from outraged mafiosi.

Serena You're not serious.

Victoria Listen, that's only the most recent outbreak, you wouldn't credit some of the letters and phone-calls I've been getting.

Serena What, nasties?

Victoria They just keep crawling out of the woodwork. The latest was the editor of a pornographic magazine.

Serena Wht sort of proposal did *he* have in mind?

Enter the **Magazine Editor** *– camel-hair coat and tinted aviator glasses.*

Editor What we have in mind, Miss Pratt, is a tasteful two-page spread. My, what a handsome globe you have.

Victoria I expect you say that to all the girls. What do you foresee being spread, precisely?

Editor That's it right there, you see. Witty repartee. Fantastic. Received wisdom would have it that a woman of intelligence and wit is not a sexy woman, but I assure you, the opposite view is held by the kind of man who reads *Gonad*.

Victoria I see. It's a sort of *Map Collectors' Weekly* of the hard-core magazine trade?

Editor   Eroticism provides the main thrust, I don't deny. Notwithstanding, we are constantly upheld for the redeeming social content of our features and short fiction.

Victoria   Supposing I write you a paper on 'Women in the Cartographic Professions'?

Editor   I appreciate the thought, Miss Pratt, but we are I'm afraid in a competitive position subject to the constraints of the leisure market. No, what I envisage is a short disquisition on your life and work, quite jocular in tone, accompanied by a pictorial study of yourself, in similar lighthearted vein.

Victoria   You're going straight for the jocular vein, in short.

Editor   What a fantastic caption that would make. 'I like to go straight for the jocular vein,' says Victoria.

Victoria   Thirty-four, M.Sc., F.R.G.S.

Editor   As to the photograph itself, perhaps we could persuade you to sit astride a globe rather like your own here. One of those illuminated ones would be amusing. You could be perusing your book.

Victoria   What would you suggest I wear?

Editor   Just a mortarboard, perhaps? Blow me, I haven't even mentioned our terms yet.

Victoria   Well, goodbye.

Editor   I'm happy to say we can pay contributors the very highest rates.

Victoria   Out.

Editor   Yes, you'll want to have a little think. Do bear in mind, though, it is a wasting asset. (*He exits.*)

Victoria   I'd almost do it – just to see how it would be received in the conference hall.

Serena   With an onslaught of heavy breathing, I should think. What conference hall?

Victoria   The International Society of Cartographers. They're laying on a special Brendan Map Conference. It's to give all the leading authorities a chance to have a show-down with me. All the ageing gunfighters, they'll be riding into town, it should be quite a shoot-out.

Serena   You're the desperado in this house. Why should they have it in for you, anyway?

Victoria   I'm jeopardising their accepted theories and their definitive studies. Meaning they'll go to any lengths to discredit the map and the book both. Still. All this press support is very encouraging. I think I can take them.

Serena   The poor buggers don't know what they're in for.

Victoria   Guess what I have in the fridge.

Serena   Shrunken heads.

Victoria   That's for later.

Serena   So long as they don't belong to my chartered accountants.

Victoria   It's a magnum of Bollinger.

Serena   I suppose you expect me to drink it with you.

Victoria   Well, you must have quite a thirst from eating all that humble pie.

Serena   Bitch. (*They exit.*)

Music. **Godfrey** *enters, folding a handkerchief. He stands by the hatstand, tucking the hanky into his breast pocket.*

Godfrey   It has been said that those who can, do, and those who can't, teach. As to those who can't teach, there's always administration – you being the case in point – or, of course, attending conferences. It was like a bad day at the United Nations, that conference.

Enter **Dr Juan Cortez**, *a Spanish academic in his sixties.*

Cortez   When we speak of the birthplace and growth of our cartography, we speak of Genoa, Pisa, Milan, Castile, Lisbon, we do not speak of Northern primitives.

Godfrey   He was quite beside himself, that old Spanish gent. Him and the Norwegian became a sort of double act.

Enter **Professor Thorvald Eriksson**

Eriksson   The Viking discovery of America, around the year 1000, solidly documented, is in no way challenged by Miss Pratt's wild hypotheses. In his re-discovery of the continent in 1492, Columbus was of course massively indebted to his Norse predecessors.

Cortez   Piffle.

Eriksson   Excuse me?

Cortez   I challenge Professor Eriksson to name any map or document from the whole of southern Europe during the entire Middle Ages which makes the least mention of a Norse landfall in America.

Eriksson   Dr Cortez knows of course that I cannot.

Cortez   Thank you.

Eriksson   However.

Cortez   The reason being, the Norse landfall was an isolated insignificant incident. Discovery is opening a country up, establishing it in the network of world communications. Let nobody pretend that America was discovered by anybody other than Christopher Columbus.

Godfrey   Although it wasn't really. (*Pause. The two academics stare at him.*) Well, not in the way you're

defining it. In that sense, Columbus was in the same
boat as the Vikings and the Irish, none of them was
aware of the existence of a large independent continent.
An actual new world was surmised first by Vespucci,
and established first by Vasco Núñez de Balboa. (*Pause.*)
That shut them up all right. Or it would have done, if
you'd said it. Still, the others were all behind the map,
especially that young American.

Enter **Shaun Kilroy**.

Kilroy   Gentlemen, from henceforth we're into a brand
new ballgame.

Godfrey   Mind you, with a name like Shaun
Kilroy . . .

Kilroy   Furthermore, Victoria has covered every base
superbly, from the lab analyses on through.

Cortez   Such tests prove nothing.

Kilroy   That's crazy, Juan.

Cortez   Example. There is a certain Italian
palaeographer – known personally to me – whose
pastime is to forge medieval scripts on authentic
parchment. The ink? No problem, he makes his own
from medieval recipes.

Godfrey   We were all quite keen to meet this man.

Cortez   It's all just private fun and games, you
understand.

Eriksson   Also, there has been much talk of
wormholes. Listen, nothing is easier to forge than
wormholes. Poking, with a little piece of hot wire, that's
all.

Cortez   If it comes to that, I have heard from reliable
sources of an English antiquarian who keeps a stable of
live worms. (*He exits.*)

Godfrey   They all had this obsession with worms.

Kilroy   I tell you, the worming is a red herring. Take a look at those holes under a microscope, Thorvald. What have you got? Serrations around the edge of each perimeter. Teeth marks. A piece of hot wire, Thorvald, cannot chew. Furthermore, compare the holes in the map with those in the endpapers. The worms' teeth patterns are identical.

Eriksson   Very well, so maybe we have worms. How do we date these worms? They are ninth-century? Nineteenth-century? Who can tell? (*He exits.*)

Kilroy   What the worming indicates is – the map has been inside that book at least since 1649, because there's no way the map could have been implanted in the book and the worming artificially induced without violation of the binding and the binding in which the book is still bound is the original binding! (*He exits.*)

Godfrey   They went on like that for three days. Though why leading scholars are expected to be more rational then the rest of mankind, I can't imagine, considering their missionary zeal. Any rate Victoria certainly came out of it with the world at her feet. At which point of course she kicked for touch and withdrew. I did think it odd at the time.

Enter **Victoria**.

Victoria   Hello, Godfrey.

Godfrey   Never really suspecting.

Victoria   All on your own?

Godfrey   Not for long round this way. It's all go.

Victoria   It'll be all gone soon enough. (*She sits down.*)

Godfrey   Happy birthday, by the way.

Victoria   Thank you. You remembered the turnips?

Godfrey In the kitchen.

Victoria Well done. I haven't made jack o'lanterns since I was in knee-socks. How are you?

Godfrey (*taken aback*) Me, you mean?

Victoria How's your extramural department?

Godfrey Going strong. You know what they're like, extramural people. Kinky for knowledge. No matter how much red tape you tie them down with, they still somehow wriggle through to the classroom.

Victoria You're an impostor, Godfrey.

Godfrey Am I?

Victoria Aren't we all?

Godfrey Are we?

Victoria All this self-deprecation, it's a sham. You privately care a great deal about your work, but you're too much of a stuffy English academic to admit it. Even to yourself.

Godfrey I do quite enjoy not having to teach any more, I must admit.

Victoria You think, deep down, that you're doing an important job rather well.

Godfrey The thing about teaching was, nobody ever seemed able to listen to what I was saying. I suppose, in a way, because it was all quite bone-achingly pedestrian. Still, it is fairly dispiriting, nobody listening to you like that. There you are, day after day, talking away at this bank of faces . . . with all the heavy eyelids slowly drooping. The diligent ones are all trying hard to swallow a yawn, with horrible facial contortions, while the soppy ones are all glassy-eyed and miles away, simpering foolishly into the middle-distance, it's like a ward in a lunatic asylum. After watching them for a while, you get mesmerised by the sound of your own voice. I was forever nodding off in the middle of my lectures, I woke up from a dream once shouting Cut the rope! None of the students seemed to notice. I'm not boring you, am I?

Victoria Fake.

Godfrey I do seem to be a bit better at administration, I think.

Victoria A sudden burst of candour.

Godfrey Well, nobody expects to have to listen to administrators. They even talk to each other in an impenetrable gibberish. I find all this a little bit unsettling, Victoria.

Victoria All this what?

Godfrey All this way we're having a sort of conversation.

Victoria We used to have conversations.

Godfrey We had a few during our student days.

Victoria Is this how you saw your life turning out back then?

Godfrey (*thinks*) I'm afraid it is.

Victoria Those were the sort of conversations we always used to have.

Godfrey What does the future hold in store.

Victoria Everything in the book except marriage, that was the only constant thing that the whole gang agreed on. Remember that? And look at them all now, a couple of brats apiece and mortgaged up to the rafters. We're the only two left with unblemished integrity, Godfrey.

Godfrey You're not by any chance contemplating

marriage, are you?

Victoria Why, are you?

Godfrey Well, you know. (*Pause.*) Is this how you foresaw *your* life turning out back then?

Victoria I'm afraid it is. Up to a point. Which is now lost.

Enter **Serena**.

Serena Feeling our age, are we, I hope?

Godfrey It's her birthday today.

Serena That *is* what I meant, Godfrey.

Godfrey Ah.

Serena (*giving* **Victoria** *a small box*) I got you a cat.

Victoria Charmed, I'm sure.

Serena You can certainly tell she was a Hallowe'en baby – a born witch.

Godfrey Of course – it's Hallowe'en.

Serena You're getting faster all the time, Godfrey. (*To* **Victoria**, *who has taken a brooch from the box and is putting it on.*) I got a black one. Just to bring you that change of luck you're so much in need of.

Victoria I always used to like having a birthday at Hallowe'en, it made it more special.

Godfrey What's your birthday, Serena?

Serena I was a little Leap Year baby. February bloody 29th.

Victoria Don't get her started.

Serena Where's this booze-up I was promised?

Victoria Help yourself, I have to see to the victuals. Godfrey's going to make us jack o'lanterns.

Serena   The onset of infantile regression, I suppose.

Exit **Victoria** *and* **Godfrey**.

Serena   Can I use the phone?

Victoria (*off*)   Go ahead.

Serena *goes to the phone, dials.*

Serena (*on phone*)   Harvey? Hello, it's me . . . I'm all
right, did you have any luck with your vanishing
choirmaster? . . . not the organist's wife . . . did you?
Well, how much were you able to find out? . . . oh, my
God . . .

Mahoney *has entered quietly behind her, unseen, wearing a
large joke nail through his head. She turns round, sees him, shrieks.*

Serena   . . . aaagh!

Mahoney   Don't mind me.

Serena   Have you been eavesdropping?

Mahoney   No. I was born like this.

Serena (*picking up phone again*)   Hello, Harvey? . . . no,
I'm fine, look, I'm in Vic's flat at the moment, I'll see
you later, all right? Bye.

Mahoney *has gone to the globe to pour himself a drink.*

Mahoney   How *is* Harvey, by the by?

Serena   Busy.

Mahoney   Be sure and give him my regards.

Serena   I'll have a gin and tonic, thank you.

Mahoney   And how's your tourist trade, Serena?

Serena   A very large one, please.

Mahoney   As bad as that, eh?

Serena   I don't suppose you're delivering a yacht to

some distant place soon, George? Like the Bermuda
Triangle?

Mahoney   That's the place some of your tours go,
isn't it?

Serena   You haven't delivered any yachts at all in the
time we've been privileged to know you.

Mahoney   Rich men's toys, Serena. I've put the life of
the sybarite behind me. (*He gives her the drink which she
knocks back.*)

Serena   That's too bad.

Mahoney   I've been spending my days conning
wisdom from Victoria's bookshelves.

Serena   The self-taught working-class intellectual.
Though Harvey says he met someone who claims she
read Geography with you. At Glasgow University, I
think it was.

Pause.

Mahoney (*moving close to her*)   Tell us this, Serena – did
you ever hear tell of Eratosthenes?

Serena   Not for ages.

Mahoney   Eratosthenes, what a man. A scholar of the
Ancient Greek persuasion. Third century BC. Although
they didn't know then it was BC of course. Any more
than they knew what size the world was. So
Eratosthenes set out to measure it.

Serena   Is this going to go on all night?

Mahoney   Was the question he was himself asked,
rather cretinously, since he was at the time observing
shadows cast by a vertical pole at noon on midsummer's
day. Though at a place called Syene, there was no
shadow cast at all, so he deduced that it must lie on the
summer tropic. But north of it, at Alexandria, there was

a shadow cast which was measurable as the fiftieth part of a circle. So he concluded that the distance between the two places, multiplied by fifty, would yield the true circumference of the earth.

Serena   Clever old him.

Mahoney   Except, he was wrong about Syene being on the tropic, wrong about it being due south of Alexandria, wrong about the distance between them, and he wasn't to know that the earth isn't a perfect sphere anyway. A comedy of errors indeed, but the gods favoured Eratosthenes. His mistakes magically cancelled one another out. He proclaimed the earth's circumference to be 24,600-odd miles. Which was within fifty miles of the exact figure.

Serena   Well, I never. Loud applause.

Mahoney   Alas, more was to befall.

Serena   You can pour me another drink, in that case.

Mahoney   (*taking her glass and refilling it*)   A couple of hundred years later, a meddlesome fellow called Posidonius decided to put matters right. He took new bearings from the stars, and denounced Eratosthenes as a messer, whose sums he'd been clever enough to straighten out. The trouble was, though, Posidonius's new figure for the earth's circumference was only 18,000 miles, which you and I and Eratosthenes know to be twenty-five per cent too small. (*He gives her the drink.*)

Serena   Thank you, I certainly needed this. (*She drinks it.*)

Mahoney   This gross miscalculation went unchallenged for the next sixteen hundred years. All that time, the world was believed to be a quarter smaller than it really was. That's why Columbus went to his grave still convinced that he'd reached Asia the back way. All on account of a wee Greek get from 90 BC.

Serena   I presume there's a point to all this.

Mahoney   Oh, I believe there is, Serena. Here's to the spirit of Eratosthenes. And boils on the bum for the descendants of Posidonius. (*He drains his glass. They survey one another.*)

Serena   In our case, George, I've got your number and no mistake. Exact to the nearest decimal point.

Mahoney   Try not to bet on it, flower. You could be making yet another gross miscalculation.

Victoria *enters, carrying a clock radio, with* **Dr Bridges** *in tow.*

Victoria   Dr Bridges has called in.

Bridges   I'm interrupting your party . . .

Victoria   I don't believe you've met my sister Serena.

Bridges   How do you do?

Serena   Oops, it's meet-the-boss time.

Victoria   George you already know, of course.

Bridges   Yes, hello once again.

Mahoney (*at the globe for a refill*)   What's your tipple, Dr Bridges?

Bridges   Thank you, but no, I don't indulge. I wouldn't impose on you in this way if it weren't for an unforeseen calamity, but you see my wireless has gone completely dead.

Mahoney   Oh God, don't tell us. You'd only started checking your coupon and you already had two draws.

Bridges   Sorry?

Victoria   Dr Bridges has recorded a talk which is being broadcast this evening.

Bridges   Just a little talk in the interval of a concert.

It's coming on quite soon, you see. I couldn't think of anyone else, I'm so sorry to barge in.

Victoria   You're very welcome, please sit down. I'll set this thing to switch itself on at a quarter past, and that way we'll be sure not to miss it. (*She does so and sets the radio on the table.*) There.

Bridges   My wireless is quite ancient, you know, it's one of the big wooden cabinets full of coloured lights.

Serena   People collect those nowadays.

Bridges   Quite so.

Pause.

Mahoney   We've been having a good old natter about Eratosthenes.

Bridges   Ah yes.

Mahoney   Not forgetting that prize chump Posidonius.

Serena   What is your talk about, Dr Bridges?

Bridges   Oh, nothing very much, I assure you.

Victoria   Semantics, isn't it?

Bridges   With a little etymology – it's just a brief reflection on the various meanings of a cognate group of words. 'Band, bind and bond'.

Mahoney   Sounds like a winner to me.

Bridges   My favourite work is on dictionaries, you see.

Serena   What's so special about 'bind' and 'bond'?

Bridges   Oh well, a little word like 'bond', you know, is almost paradoxical in its various usages. A bond between us is a uniting tie, a bond I place upon you is an instrument of restraint.

Mahoney   And a Bond with a blonde is a spy?

Bridges Yes, yes, I mention that too. James Bond is a clever name for a secret agent, you know.

Mahoney It certainly sounds better than Harvey Small.

Bridges It has the ring of strength and dependability. An Englishman's word is his bond.

Serena As opposed to a Scot's or an Irishman's.

Bridges Hardly that. The word is Teutonic, of course, via Old English.

Mahoney Curious, isn't it, the Anglo-Saxon infatuation with bondage.

Victoria (*to* **Bridges**) You're giving all of your talk away before we have a chance to hear it.

Bridges That's true, it is only five minutes long.

Victoria I'm overdue for a drink, George.

Mahoney Allow me, dear.

Serena While you're at it. (*Holding up her empty glass.*)

Mahoney (*taking the glass*) This craving for alcohol is a sorry sight, Dr Bridges.

Bridges Well, they do say it kills off the brain cells.

Mahoney Although Serena has no cause for concern on that score. (*He dispenses the drinks during the following.*)

Bridges I meant to mention, by the way, I had a phone call from Dublin this afternoon, from the Director of the National Library there. He spoke very warmly of your work. He says that all of Ireland is behind you.

Serena I should keep a close eye on your rear-view mirror in that case.

Bridges It seems, however, there is a campaign growing to have the Brendan Map repatriated there.

Victoria   That's all I need at this stage.

Bridges   Perhaps it could be shared, on a rotating basis. I don't suppose this would persuade you to withdraw your resignation?

Victoria   Just the opposite.

Pause.

Serena   Resignation? What does he mean?

Enter **Harvey Small**, *in a plastic mac and corduroy cap, and his mother, a dumpy woman in a shiny leopardskin coat and a peaked cap with ear-flaps.*

Harvey (*going to* **Mahoney**)   All right, Mr Mahoney, the game's up. (*To the company at large.*) I've been waiting for years for a chance to say that.

Serena   Harvey, how did *you* get here?

Harvey (*to* **Serena**)   Was he tampering with you on the telephone? Mother heard it too, on the extension, didn't you, dear?

Mrs Small   Pierced right through my skull, that scream of hers.

Mahoney (*adjusting the joke nail*)   Count yourself lucky it was only a scream.

Harvey (*removing the joke nail*)   I'll take that, if you don't mind, Mr Mahoney. Or should I say Murray?

Mrs Small   Watch him, Harvey.

Harvey   I wouldn't advise anyone to get any ideas.

Mrs Small (*indicating* **Dr Bridges**)   He looks the type.

Harvey   Both Mother and I are well practised in the martial arts.

Serena   Harvey, please go home.

Mahoney   Not till he's finished his party piece. Come

on, Harve, we're all hooked.

Victoria I presume in the course of time you'll all explain yourselves.

Harvey Easily done, Miss Pratt. (*He takes out a new tube of Polo mints and, during the following, picks open the silver paper and pops a mint into his mouth.*) Hearing of my need to pursue enquiries in a case in Scotland, Serena requested that I look into our friend Mahoney's credentials. Not a pretty sight, I may say.

Serena We'll talk about this later, Harvey. Please!

Mrs Small That's the thanks you get from her.

Harvey Once apprised of his real surname, Murray – Mahoney having been the maiden name of his Irish grandmother – I uncovered other revealing facts about this man.

Mahoney (*to* **Bridges**) In the course of this, Dr Bridges, you may be able to assist us with a problem in semantics which arises *inter alia*.

Bridges Really?

Harvey Such as his dismissal from the Ordnance Survey in Edinburgh, and subsequently from the United States Navy Hydrographic Office.

Mahoney It has to do with the hopeless inadequacy of yet another group of cognate words. Hoax. Fake. Forgery. Swindle. Con.

Serena Stop it, both of you!

Harvey Then there was the matter of his diploma in Palaeography and his training in the restoration of old documents.

Mahoney (*still to* **Bridges**) Let's say a man sets out on a spiritual adventure. None of your punting up the Limpopo crap, but a real dangerous gambit in uncharted waters. A calculated transgression of the moral law.

Bridges You mean a crime?

Harvey I think you'll find that is the *mot juste*, in fact.

Mahoney Let's say that it starts as a satirical deception but it gathers a momentum which he hadn't foreseen.

Victoria Or let's just say that the Brendan Map is a fraud, shall we?

Deafening applause and cheering – the radio has switched itself on at the end of a Proms concert. **Victoria** *switches it off.*

Mahoney (*to* **Bridges**)   Sorry. I left out fraud.

Pause.

Bridges (*to* **Mahoney**)   You mean you personally forged it?

Serena (*to* **Victoria**)   You mean you already knew?

Victoria Since the day after the conference ended. Resignation day.

Serena He told you?

Victoria He'd been making it obvious enough, hadn't he. But I wasn't listening, was I. I was too busy believing. It wasn't till the first day home from the trenches that at last I was able to see just what I'd fallen for.

Serena I never wanted this, Vic.

Victoria The poem was authentic enough, mind you. Remember the poem?

'Thus is my most beloved my bitterest foe,
Thus is the sweetest name the cruellest curse,
Thus to aver my love is to lose my life,
As the sun sinks, so does my heart.'

That was the real McCoy, quaintly enough.

The lights go out. **Godfrey** *enters carrying a lighted jack o'lantern and wearing a luminous-skull Hallowe'en mask.*

Godfrey (*singing*)
  Happy birthday to you,
  Happy birthday to you . . .

Victoria *turns on her heel to leave, loses her balance, and falls.*

Serena   FOR CHRIST'S SAKE PUT THE LIGHTS ON, GODFREY!

He does. **Victoria** *is trying to get up. Some of the others move forward to help her.*

Victoria   NO! (*She picks herself up, and stumbles out.*)

Godfrey   I didn't mean to actually frighten anyone.

Serena   Why don't you all just go away? (*She throws herself into an armchair and starts to cry quietly.*)

Harvey (*to* **Mahoney**)   You and I and Mother had best pop on down to the police station, Mr Murray.

Godfrey   Have I missed something? Why are you and Harvey going to the police, George?

Mahoney *moves to the exit and then turns.*

Mahoney
  'What's the good of Mercator's North Poles and
      Equators,
  Tropics, Zones and Meridian Lines?
  So the Bellman would cry: and the crew would reply
  They are merely conventional signs!'

Harvey   Very droll.

Mahoney
  'Other maps are such shapes, with their islands and
      capes!
  But we've got our brave captain to thank

(So the crew would protest) that he's brought us the
best –
A perfect and absolute blank!'

Exit **Mahoney**, *closely followed by* **Harvey Small**.

Mrs Small   If you ask me, they're all involved. (*She exits.*)

Pause.

Godfrey   Lewis Carroll wrote that.

Bridges   I think I had better go also.

Godfrey   Must you? It's still so early.

Bridges   I think I should. Goodbye, Dr Dudley.

Godfrey   Bye-bye, Dr Bridges.

Exit **Bridges**. **Serena** *is curled up in the chair.*

Godfrey   Lewis Carroll. 'The Hunting of the Snark'. I
only happen to know because it's on one of our courses.
English 47. Literature of the Absurd, Ridiculous and
Grotesque.

Serena   Godfrey.

Godfrey   Yes?

Serena   Come here.

He moves to beside the chair.

Godfrey   Yes, Serena?

She stands up slowly and leans against him.

Serena   Hug me.

*He places his arms round her with an expression compounded of
embarrassment, bafflement and alarm.*

Godfrey   The whole point of the thing being, that
they never actually catch a snark. They think they've got
one, but it turns out to be a boojum.

Serena I'd better go and see how Vic is doing. (*She exits.*)

Godfrey I suppose the idea being that we all start out pursuing great ends, but they generally materialise as boojums. Or in George's case, a few months in prison. Even after I'd been to see him you still couldn't credit it ... because I'd been right there when the map was discovered, I can still picture Ragnar Nilsson's horrible toddler with the ripped-up book in his podgy fists. Never dreaming then, of course, it was all a plant, some woman in America had torn it up months before in a jealous rage, that's how the parchment with the poem on it came to light, genuinely enough. Or so he claims. Though the literary people accept the poem, but then they would, wouldn't they. Still, a poem isn't like a map. It can be true without being genuine. The truest poetry is the most feigning. As a great man once said.

Serena (*re-entering*) She's all right, she just wants to be left on her own. Poor love.

Godfrey I suppose George had the same idea when he turned the parchment over and started to draw.

Serena I could use a lift home, Godfrey.

Godfrey Sorry?

Serena I'll just put my face back on. See you in the car. (*She exits.*)

Godfrey So let us all raise our glasses to absent friends, or not, as the case may be, and in this case very emphatically is. I still say Victoria could have weathered it professionally, it wouldn't have been her, though, would it. Self-renunciation was called for. Immured in some rickety little commercial firm.

Victoria *enters upstage with a sheaf of proofs, and seats herself at the desk.*

Godfrey When you think of her spending her days on

tourist brochures and school atlases ... not that it isn't useful work in its way. I mean, it'd probably be all right if I was doing it, I suppose.

Serena (*off*) I'm ready, Godfrey!

Godfrey I wouldn't be surprised if that's what *he* said to her too. (*He exits.*)

Lights full up on **Victoria** *at the desk. The door is knocked from off.*

Victoria Come in!

Mahoney *enters. Pause.*

Mahoney Not guilty, Victoria.

Victoria That's a laugh.

Mahoney No, I really didn't know it was you. Not till they told me at the desk.

Victoria It didn't stop you coming on in.

Mahoney I need a job. (*Holding up completed application form.*) The firm did advertise. (*He offers her the form.*) I didn't mention the prison record. It's like having been in a monastery, it makes people wonder about you. (*She takes the form, scrutinises it.*) Of course it's always possible I'm lying. All those letters you returned unopened were costing me a fortune in postage. Although, there again, that's a good reason for needing a job.

Victoria Same old reptilian charm, I see.

Mahoney By the by, about that wee matter of the map.

Victoria Save the explanations, George. I know what all your reasons were.

Mahoney My point exactly – you see, I'm absolutely relying on you to explain them all to me.

Pause. She looks up at him.

Victoria You've got what you wanted. Amusement value, academic pratfalls, showing up the vanity of experts, whose horizons were so much less visionary than your own. Near enough to the perfect crime, in fact – except for the customary one thing that hadn't been allowed for. In this case, a map-curator with nice tits.

Mahoney Great to see you again, Victoria.

Victoria There was also, of course, your promotional work on behalf of spiritual vagrancy and dear old St Brendan. But that was rather less of a winner. Given that he's now forever linked in the public mind with fraudulence and moonshine.

Mahoney I never thought your tits were all that great. But I somehow fell in love regardless.

Victoria Which was why you were prepared to sit back for two years and watch me make an international laughing-stock of myself?

Mahoney How could I tell you? I would have lost you. Anyway, you covered yourself in glory, nobody's reproaching your work. How many early maps do you think there are, proudly displayed round the world, that would stand up to the kind of scrutiny which that map survived?

Victoria I wouldn't dream of belittling your genius, George, believe me. It was a forgery absolutely of the first rank. As a matter of fact, there's a lecturer in Wisconsin who's currently claiming that the map is really genuine after all. He's convinced you lied about the hoax in a bid for notoriety.

Pause.

Mahoney Suppose he's right?

Victoria Who cares? It's not my field any more. It's not even a field that I'm playing any more.

Mahoney How's Serena? Terminally ill, I trust?

Victoria Never happier.

Mahoney If she hadn't sicked her pet bloodhound on to me, nothing would have changed.

Victoria Wrong again. The map might have soldiered on, but we certainly wouldn't. Besides, why should you worry? The public has taken you to its heart. Folk hero of the month.

Mahoney You haven't quite got it yet, flower. I need you. I'm asking for another chance.

Pause.

Victoria What have you brought along this time, George? A signed photograph of the Loch Ness monster?

Mahoney What are you doing in this dump, Victoria? You haven't got the figure for sackcloth and ashes.

Victoria I do realise you were in the right, of course. Beliefs govern the world, not facts. Facts are as neutral as bullets, and as plentiful. But some of them are small and fairly harmless, and that's my area of competence. It's very pleasant here, George. Let me show you out. (*She stands up.*)

Mahoney What about the job?

Victoria I'm afraid the firm considers you an unsuitable applicant. You have a truly appalling set of references. (*She exits. He follows.*)

Music. **Godfrey** *enters, goes to the table, takes the carnation and puts it in his buttonhole. Music ends.*

Godfrey Let me not conclude these heartfelt remarks . . . as they are indeed now nearly at an end . . . without some final few words, by way of drawing to a close, not forgetting in the final analysis what though last but not

least is the parting shot with which I wish to Christ I
knew how to sum up and sign off . . . (*Looking at the clock
which now reads one minute to twelve.*) . . . oh, my God.
Count myself fortunate. Happiest man alive. It only
remains, though you never know, he might just turn up,
walk in unannounced, like that very first time in my
office, the man from God knows where. Well, Glasgow I
suppose. Originally. I doubt it, though. I'm afraid we've
seen the last of him now, old George Mahoney.
(**Mahoney** *enters quietly, goes to the globe, pours himself a
drink, props himself against the desk.*) The truth is, I miss him
quite disgracefully. Whisper it not in Gath. Especially
just at the moment. Think of the speech he would have
made. Think of the speech I'm going to make. Terrible
thing he did, of course. But there was more than a
touch of the poet about George. For all the joy it
brought him.

Victoria *enters, wearing a large wedding hat and carrying a
bouquet.*

Victoria   Well, this is it, Godfrey.

Godfrey   I suppose it is it, yes.

She hugs him.

Victoria   After all these years.

Godfrey   Seventeen, I think you'll find.

Victoria   You're not feeling qualms?

Godfrey   It seems as though I'm lost for words.

She kisses him.

Victoria   Words don't count now.

Godfrey   We can count ourselves fortunate, then.

Victoria   I couldn't be happier.

Godfrey   Happiest man alive, I am.

Victoria   It's just so right. For both of you.

Enter **Serena**, *in bridal gear.*

Serena   God, I feel like a prune in this get-up.

Victoria   Don't be silly, you look like a peach.

Serena   I hope you've got everything, Godfrey. Look at the time, for God's sake, we should have already pushed off!

Victoria   You get your bouquet, I'll get the car.

Victoria *and* **Serena** *exit.* **Godfrey** *stands irresolute.*

Godfrey   Ahm.

Victoria *and* **Serena** (*off*)   Godfrey!

Godfrey *turns towards* **Mahoney**, *who raises his glass in salute, drinks and shrugs.* **Godfrey** *turns out front again. The clock strikes twelve. The lights slowly fade.*